普通高等教育"十三五"规划教材

高等学校教学质量工程建设项目精品教材

美国经典歌曲欣赏

韦建华　龚　雯　莫云春　贾再俊　主编

中国石化出版社

图书在版编目（CIP）数据

美国经典歌曲欣赏／韦建华等主编．—北京：中国石化出版社，2019.6(2025.7 重印)
ISBN 978-7-5114-5364-8

Ⅰ．①美… Ⅱ．①韦… Ⅲ．①英语-口语-高等学校-教材②歌曲-音乐欣赏-美国 Ⅳ．①H319.32

中国版本图书馆 CIP 数据核字（2019）第 107640 号

中国石化出版社出版发行
地址：北京市东城区安定门外大街 58 号
邮编：100011　电话：(010)57512500
发行部电话：(010)57512575
http://www.sinopec-press.com
E-mail：press@sinopec.com
北京捷迅佳彩印刷有限公司印刷
全国各地新华书店经销
*
787×1092 毫米 16 开本 17.75 印张 424 千字
2019 年 7 月第 1 版　2025年7月第3次印刷
定价：46.00 元

前言

《美国经典歌曲欣赏》的编写，以《国家中长期教育改革和发展规划纲要》《高等学校本科英语专业规范》《本科专业类教学质量国家标准》为重要依据。教育部高等教育司司长吴岩在2019年召开的第四届全国高等学校外语教育改革与发展高端论坛的现场报告《识变应变求变——新使命大格局新文科大外语》中指出："外语教育不是小众的事，甚至不仅仅是大众的事，是普及化的事。"他特别强调：高等外语教育的责任重大，因为它是国家对外开放的"桥梁"和"纽带"，关系到高等教育人才的培养质量，关系到中国同世界各国交流互鉴，更关系到我国参与全球治理体系改革建设。如何加强高等外语教育改革，提高高等外语教育质量，已是摆在我们面前的一项十分艰巨的任务。

语言是文化的载体，同时也是文化的组成部分。高校学生要想学习和掌握英语这一重要交流工具，除了学习、交流先进的科学技术或专业信息之外，还要了解国外的社会与文化，增进对不同文化的理解、对中外文化异同的意识，培养跨文化交际能力。而人文性的核心是以人为本，弘扬人的价值，注重人的综合素质培养和全面发展。所以，我们学习英语，不仅要掌握它的工具性，更要掌握好它的人文性，即只有同时学习好、掌握好英语的工具性和人文性这两个特征，才能更好地让它为本国大众服务，以实现在全民中普及英语，促进不同语言、不同文化之间更好地交流互通的最终目标。

众所周知，要学好一门语言，兴趣教学非常重要。本教材的编写，正是为了配合高校开展新时代大学生综合素质教育课程建设的需要，试图通过丰富多彩的有效教学形式，在提高高校不同专业学生英语学习兴趣的同时，以最终培养他们的英语语言能力、人文素养和正确的审美情怀为主要培养目标。在本教材中，我们精选了较为流行、最为广大青年学生所熟悉的45首美国经典歌曲。每一首曲目均包含本歌曲的简谱、英文歌词、参考译文、语言点解析、注释与欣赏等五个部分，集英语语言基础能力培养与课堂欣赏、演唱娱乐、视唱技能、歌曲背景知识的学习为一体。其主要目的，是为了让广大在校大学生通过对公共选修课程《美国经典歌曲欣赏与演唱》《经典英文歌曲欣赏》或英语专业(特别是师范方向)《英语歌曲教唱》等专业领域课程的学习，在课堂上愉快欣赏、快乐演唱经典英文歌曲之际，不知不觉中调整发音器官功能，自主改善英语语音面貌，进一步激发起对英语学习的浓厚兴趣。与此同时，期盼青年学生在初步掌握简单的乐谱识别要领和视唱技巧之后，能够以自娱自乐的学习方式，一方面逐渐提高英语口语的表达能力，一方面通过潜移默化的课堂效应，吸收和消化经典歌曲所蕴涵的有益文化元素，逐步树立起正确的爱情观、价值观、人生观和世界观，在一定程度上建立起基于产出导向(OBE)的英语语言基础能力自信和跨文化交际能力自信，进而循序渐进地提高个人综合素质。

在所选曲目的排序问题上，本教材采用先短后长、先易后难的原则，即歌词内容较简单、曲谱较短的先排，内容较多、曲谱较长或较难的后排，以便于学生能够逐步消化吸收。由于歌词具有诗歌的属性，书中单列出来的“英文歌词”部分统一按照诗歌的文体编排；但为了保证语言的连贯性和可读性，简谱中的歌词则一律采用非诗歌文体，去除掉了原诗行中抬头首字母大写的惯例，以便于学生在视唱时更好地识别语法结构，正确理解和记忆英文语句。建议任课教师在课堂教学的初期，首先教给学生一些简单适用的歌谱识别方法和发声技巧，让他们具备一定的识谱基础和视唱能力，然后在教师带领下由浅入深地选学所需曲目。在教唱每一首歌曲前，建议安排学生阅读简谱、尝试拼唱，以培养学生的识谱能力。对于那些有吉它弹唱基础或一定即兴伴奏技巧的教师，建议带上安装有拾音器的民谣吉它或其它便携式电声乐器到课堂上与功放机连接，运用多媒体混响功放设备及伴奏辅助功能，由教师进行必要的范唱和教唱。教师亦可事先准备好PPT课件，课中点击MP3歌曲链接，让学生一起反复听唱和练唱。在教学过程中，教师可穿插对英文歌词的讲解和歌曲背景信息的介绍，以增强学生对歌曲内涵的了解和兴趣，强化学习效果。

本教材由广东石油化工学院韦建华担任第一主编，负责全书材料的搜集整理、编写与最后审校工作；岭南师范学院龚雯担任第二主编，主要负责部分文本材料的整理、编辑与校对工作；广东石油化工学院莫云春担任第三主编，负责全书文字录入和相关文字编辑工作；中山大学新华学院贾再俊任第四主编，负责部分文本材料的整理、编辑与校对工作。

本书得到广东石油化工学院2017年度“教学质量工程”建设项目“精品教材”课题立项资助。在编写过程中，得到广东石油化工学院各级领导、诸多同事和友人的关心和帮助，特别是得到中国石化出版社的大力支持，在此一并表示衷心感谢！

由于编者水平有限，书中肯定存在不足和错误，欢迎广大读者批评指正！

2019年7月　于广东·茂名

目录

1. Five Hundred Miles
(五百里路)

1=G 4/4

Words & Music by Hedy West

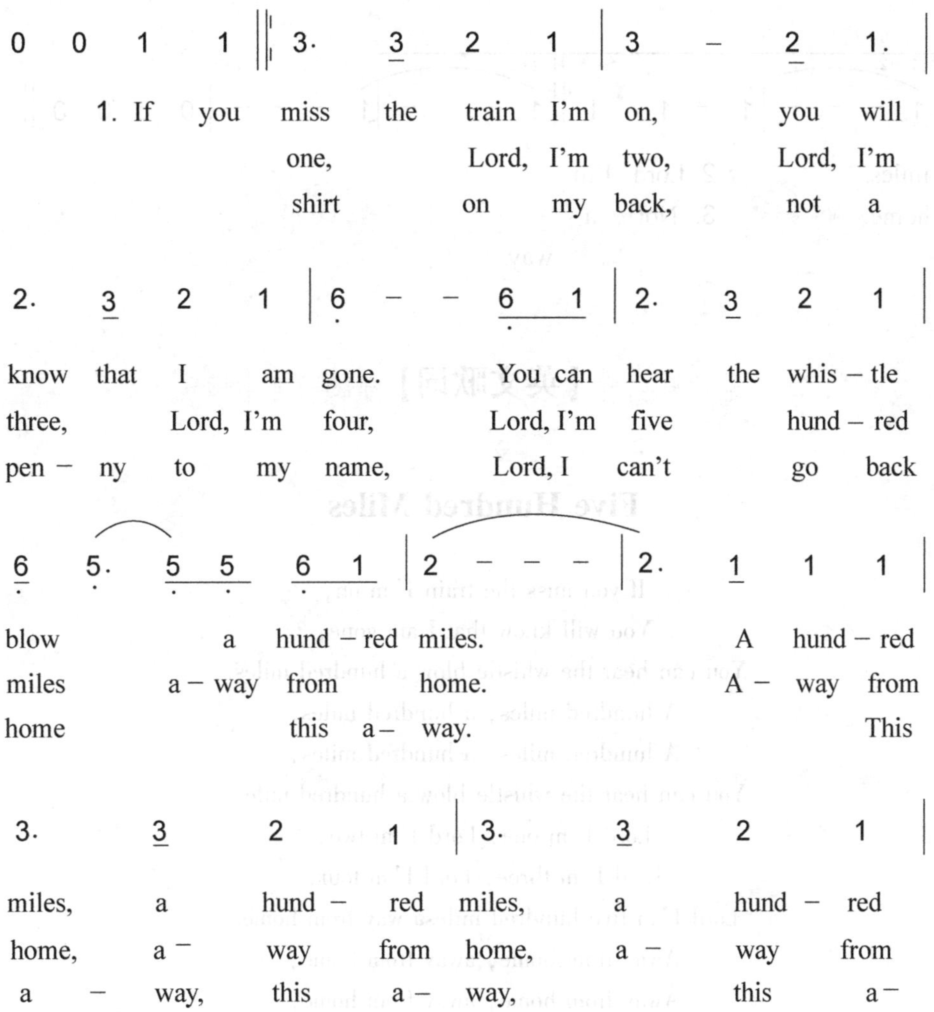

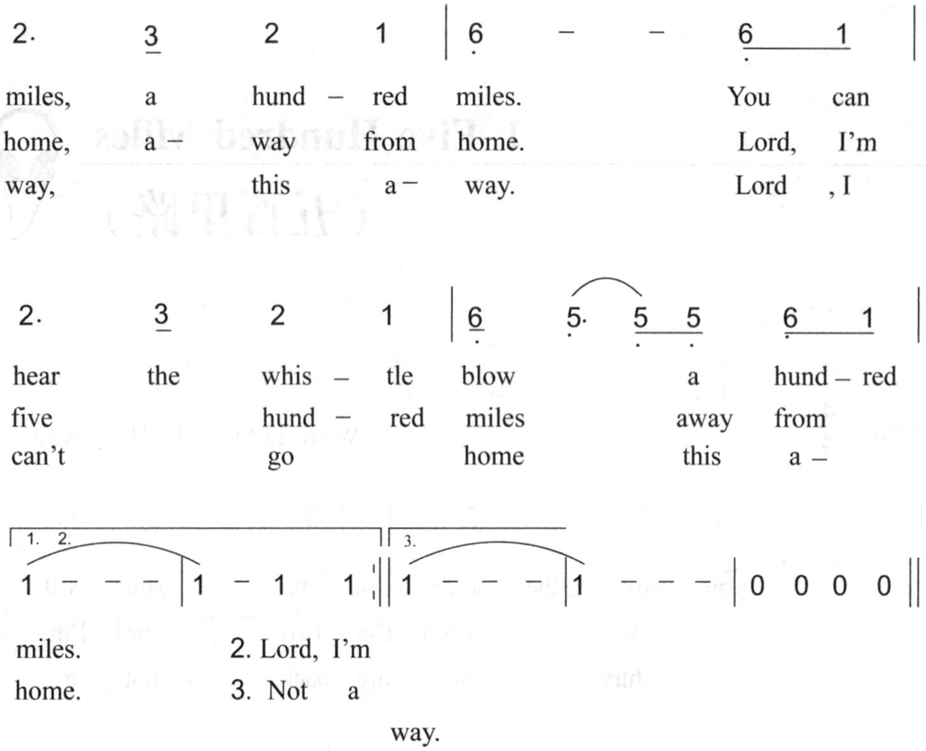

【英文歌词】

Five Hundred Miles

If you miss the train I' m on,
You will know that I am gone,
You can hear the whistle blow a hundred miles.
A hundred miles, a hundred miles,
A hundred miles, a hundred miles,
You can hear the whistle blow a hundred miles.
Lord I' m one, Lord I' m two,
Lord I' m three, Lord I' m four,
Lord I' m five hundred milesa way from home.
Away from home, away from home,
Away from home, away from home,
Lord I' m five hundred miles away from home.

Not a shirt on my back.
Not a penny to my name.
Lord I can't go back home this away.
This away, this away,
This away, this away.
Lord, I can't go back home this away.

【参考译文】

五百里路

如果你错过我坐的火车,
你会知道我已离开,
你可以听见一百里以外汽笛在响。
一百里,一百里,
一百里,一百里,
你可以听见一百里以外的汽笛在响。
天啊,一百里,二百里,
天啊,三百里,四百里,
天啊,我已离家五百里。
离开了家,离开了家,
离开了家,离开了家,
天啊,我已离家五百里。

无衬衫穿在身,
身上也无分文,
天啊,我不能这个样回家园。
这个样,这个样。
这个样,这个样,
天啊,我不能这个样回家园。

语言点解析

(1) If you miss the train I'm on, you will know that I am gone. = If you fail to catch the train that I take, you will know that I have left.

miss *vt.*: fail to catch a train (bus, ship, etc.); fail to see a film (play, performance, etc.)

例如：

She always *misses* the bus. 他总是错过公共汽车。

to be gone：have（has，had）left

例如：

All her friends ***are gone***. 她的朋友们都走了。

His happy days ***are gone***. 他幸福的日子过完了。

（2）You can hear the whistle blow a hundred miles. =You can hear the train whistle blow at a place a hundred miles away.

注：实际上，一百英里以外的火车笛声是听不见的，只有用“心”而不用“耳”才能听到。此处用的是夸张手法。

（3）**Lord**：天啊，主啊。

（4）I'm five hundred miles away from home. 我离家有五百英里远。

“离……有……远”，一般不可删去**away**。

例如：

My hometown is five hundred kilometers ***away*** from Beijing. 我的家乡离北京有500公里远。

（5）Not a shirt on my back. = I have not a shirt on my back.

have not a shirt on one's back：穷得衣不蔽体

get sb.'s shirt off（out）：惹怒某人

keep one's shirt on：（美俚）耐着性子；保持镇静

（6）Not a penny to my name. = I have not a penny to my name. 一文不名。

注意：此处介词要用**to**。

例如：

He has not a penny ***to*** his name. He lives on help from friends. 他现在一文不名，靠朋友接济而生活。

注释与赏析

这首歌曲原由四兄弟采用多声部重唱进行演唱。

《五百里路》频繁使用数次和重复手段，表达了人生路途之艰辛。主人公乘火车走了。“如果你错过我坐的火车，你会知道我已离开你可以听见一百里以外的汽笛在响。”在第一段重复了五遍“一百里路”，表达了他恋恋不舍，有此彷徨甚至凄凉之感。为何你要走？要去往何方？火车不停地走，一百里，二百里，三百里，四百里，五百里。此刻，主人公离家已有五百里。在这第二段中，away from home 共出现六次，即重复五次，表达了主人公对家的眷恋。第二段歌词说他身无分文，这个样子，这么遥远，不能回家。This away 共出现了六次，充分表明他的无可奈何，穷困在异地，不能返回家乡。

这五百里路，是人生艰辛路，古今中外，离家挣钱或喜或悲，但结果不同，有的富足而归，衣锦还乡，有的穷困潦倒，处境尴尬，我们猜这首歌所唱的情况与后者相似。离家五百里路，伴有人生酸楚，在家千日好，出门一时难。

2. Love Me Tender

(温柔地爱我)

1=G 4/4　　　　Words & Music by Elvis Presley

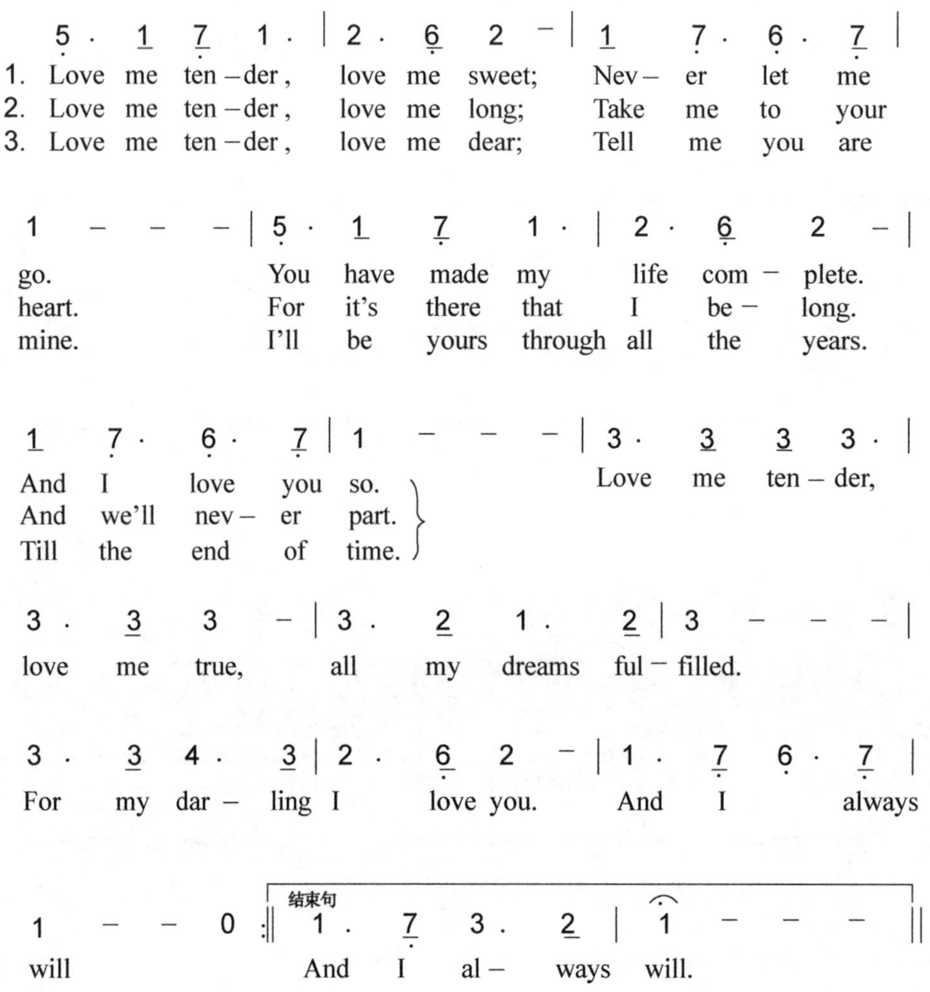

【英文歌词】

Love Me Tender

Love me tender, love me sweet,
Never let me go.
You have made my life complete,
And I love you so.
Love me tender, love me true,
All my dreams fulfilled.
For my darling, I love you,
And I always will.

Love me tender, love me long,
Take me to your heart.
For it's there that I belong,
And we'll never part.
Love me tender, love me true,
All my dreams fulfilled.
For my darling, I love you,
And I always will.

Love me tender, love me dear,
Tell me you are mine.
I'll be yours through all the years,
Till the end of time.
Love me tender, love me true,
All my dreams fulfilled.
For my darling, I love you,
And I always will.

【参考译文】

温柔地爱我

温柔地爱我，甜蜜地爱我，

永不让我走。
你使我的生活美满，
我是如此爱你。
温柔地爱我，真心爱我，
我的梦想都实现。
亲爱的，我爱你，
永远会爱你。

温柔地爱我，永远爱我，
带我到你心中，
因为我属于那里，
我们永不分离。
温柔地爱我，真心爱我，
我的梦想都实现。
因为亲爱的，我爱你。
我会永远爱你。

温柔地爱我，深情地爱我，
告诉我你属于我。
我也永远属于你，
直到世界末日。
温柔地爱我，真心爱我，
我的梦想都实现。
因为亲爱的，我爱你，
我永远爱你。

语言点解析

(1) Love me tender, love me sweet. =Love me tenderly, love me sweetly.
tender 和**sweet** 两个形容词被用作副词。建议初学者不要这样使用。

(2) You have made my life complete. =You have made my life full.
make sth. +形容词：使……怎么样
例如：
Reading *makes life interesting*. 读书使生活有趣。

(3) All my dreams fulfilled. = All my dreams come true. 此句位于"Love me tender"之后，属于独立主格结构。

fulfil *vt.*：履行；实现；使应验

例如：

They did not ***fulfil*** the contract. 他们没有履行合同。

His mistake resulted in a failure to ***fullfill*** his production plan. 他的错误使他没有能完成生产计划。

(4) And I always will. = And I always will love you.

(5) Love me long. = Love me for a long time.

(6) For it's there belong. = For I just belong there (to the heart).

belong to：属于

例如：

This bag ***belongs to*** a teacher. 这个包是我们老师的。

(7) And we'll never part：And we'll always stay together.

part *vi.*：告别；分手；中断联系，断绝关系

例如：

When we ***parted***, you were a little girl. 当初我们分别时，你还是个小姑娘。

She and her boyfriend ***parted*** all because of his mother. 她与男友分手完全是由于他母亲的缘故。

(8) Love me true. = Love me truly.

truly *adv.*：真正地；确切地；真诚地；忠实地

例如：

I'm ***truly*** sorry to have told you about this. 跟你讲这事真是抱歉。

(9) Love me dear. = Love me dearly.

(10) I'll be yours through all the years：I'll belong to you in all my life.

through *prep.*：经历

例如：

The company I work for went ***through*** a rough patch. 我所在的公司经历了一段困难时期。

注释与赏析

一般来说，一首电影插曲，大都是“对号入座”，即归宿于某部特定的影片。但这首《温柔地我》歌曲却是例外，它是1956年美国影片《兄弟情仇》的插曲，并由“猫王”埃尔维斯·普雷斯利根据自己的电影创作并担任主唱的经典金曲。而1970年美国影片《情暖童心》上映时，又采用了这首歌作为该片的主题曲。该歌曲曾经多次被评为奥斯卡金曲。

埃尔维斯·普莱斯利(Elvis Presley)被誉为乐坛上“摇滚乐第一偶像”，是美国迄今为止最有影响的摇滚歌星。他1935年出生在每个一个贫寒的家庭，自幼喜爱音乐。他18岁时到一家录音室，准备花4美元录首歌作为献给母亲的礼物，他的歌唱才华被“太阳”唱片公司的老板发现，从此由一个卡车司机涉入乐坛。1956年他凭着这首歌闯入电影，担任影片《兄弟情仇》的配角并唱了四首歌。他将黑人音乐和南方的乡村音乐融合为一种节奏感很强的摇滚形式，深受青年们的喜爱。“猫王”凭借与生俱来的天赋，从一个默默无闻的乡下歌手奋斗成一个国际摇滚超级巨星，一生中获奖无数。唱片销售总量达十亿张之后，这个纪录恐怕永远也不会被后来者打破。1977年8月16日，被认为是一个美国神话的“猫王”普莱斯利由于心脏病突发而遽然去世，年仅42岁。后人在评价“猫王”时，称他“在张扬欲望，解放生活方式这条路上开出了第一片阳光。”甚至“成为了一代叛逆青年的先驱!”然而唱片公司的老总们可不管这些，他们从不考虑“猫王”这种叛逆方式对青年们的反文化传统有这多么无可替代的影响，也不关心这种叛逆方式对诱导青年们进入“叛逆”之路的举足轻重的催化作用，他们唯独注意的是这种叛逆是多么地大受欢迎以及因此带来的滚滚不尽的财源。唱片公司的怂恿和策划，广大歌迷的疯狂喜爱，促就就“猫王”事业上的辉煌业绩。至1977年他去世时，这位英年早逝世的歌星共有106首歌曲荣登美国流行歌曲排行榜，38张金唱片和80多张销售超百万的唱片，令后人难以望其项背，叹为观止，恐怕从今以后，再也不会出现第二个“猫王”式的人物了。

《温柔地爱我》共四节(段)歌词，其中一段又重复两遍。每节的句法结构基本相同。此歌突出的特点是，每节首行都有两个Love me，四节中的每个第一行的第一个love me后边都是tender，之后这四节每个第一行的后一个love me分别用不同的词来描写这种爱，它们分别是sweet，true，long，dear等。

在这首歌四段歌词六遍演唱中，love me出现12次，love you出现4次，实际上不带这些字眼的歌词部分都表达了这种柔情蜜意。四段歌词概括了爱应有的特征：温柔、甜蜜、真诚、长久、深情。当然，爱还包括其它一些特征，如相互忍让、相互关心、相互理解、相互尊重、相互体谅等等。可以说，《温柔地爱我》给爱下了个定义。

爱常见于日常生活，有时需要誓言，更多的是需要水滴石穿并付诸于行动。

3. When a Child Is Born
(当圣婴降生时)

Words by Fred Jay
Music by Ciro Dammicco

1=D $\frac{4}{4}$

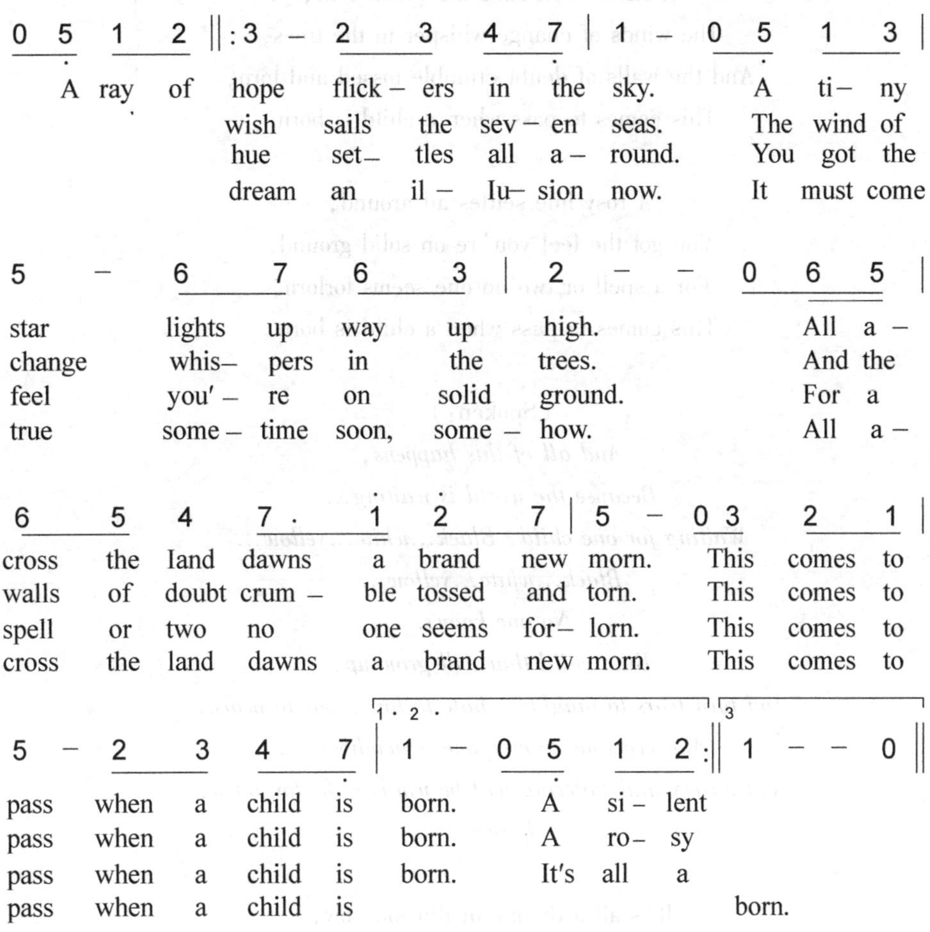

【英文歌词】

When a Child Is Born

Ah…oh…
A ray of hope, flickers in the sky,
A tiny star lights up way up high,
All across the land dawns a brand new morn,
This comes to pass when a child is born.

A silent wish sails the seven seas,
The winds of change whisper in the trees,
And the walls of doubt crumble tossed and torn,
This comes to pass when a child is born.

A rosy hue settles all around,
You got the feel you're on solid ground,
For a spell or two no one seems forlorn,
This comes to pass when a child is born.

(Spoken:)
And all of this happens,
Because the world is waiting…
Waiting for one child, Black…white…yellow…
Black…white…yellow…
No one knows.
Buta child that will grow up,
And turn tears to laughter, hate to love, war to peace,
And everyone to everyone's neighbour…
And misery and suffering will be words to be forgotten,
Forever.

It's all a dream an illusion now,
It must come true sometime soon, somehow.
All across the land dawns a brand new morn,
This comes to pass when a child is born.
Ah…oh…

【参考译文】

当圣婴降生时

啊……啊……

一线希望之光划破天穹，
一颗小星高照指明路程，
世人翘首祈盼崭新曙光，
一个婴孩将降生在世上。

无声的愿望航过七海，
转向的风在树梢呢喃，
猜忌之墙崩塌倾圮，
这全是因为一个婴孩的诞生。

四周一片玫瑰般的艳丽，
你感到脚踏在坚实的大地，
再也不会感到凄凉痛苦，
一个婴孩将降生在世上。

(道白)
所有这一切都要到来，
因为世界正在等待……
等待一个圣婴的诞生，黑肤……白肤……黄肤……
没有人知道。
但是婴孩他会长大成人，
他将变哭为笑，变恨为爱，变战争为和平，
人们和和睦睦彼此相处……
痛苦和不幸将永远被忘却，
永远！

现在这一切是梦幻，是幻影，
但将来这一天一定会实现。
世人翘首祈盼崭新曙光，
一个婴孩将降生在世上。
啊……啊……

语言点解析

(1) A ray of hope flickers in the sky. 一道希望之光划破苍穹。
a ray of hope：一道希望之光
a ray of intelligence：一线智慧的光芒
flicker：(常作及物与不及物动词)意为(火、希望等)摇晃、闪烁、忽隐忽现

(2) A tiny star lights up way up high. =A tiny star, which is high up in the sky, lights up way. 一颗小星高挂天空照亮了路程。
tiny *adj*.：(作形容词) 极小的、很小的、娇小的
light up：点着、点灯、照亮、变快活

(3) All across the land dawns a brand new morn.
此处为倒装句，主语放在了句子最后，正常语序应为：A brand new morning dawns all across the land. =A thoroughly new morning appears throughout the world. 整个世界上一个全新的晨光出现了。
dawn *vi*.：(作不及物动词)破晓，(时代，局面等)开始出现

(4) A silent wish sails the seven seas. 默默祝愿飘过五洲七洋。
sail *vt*.：(作动词用) 航行于、起航、飘过
the seven seas：世界七大洋，全球

(5) The wind of change whispers in the trees. =The wind is changing or moving from a place to another just like whispering among the trees. 风在林中飘动变化，仿佛在林中轻轻絮语。

(6) And the walls of doubt crumble tossed and torn: The doubt like high walls will fall down into pieces when the child is born. 当圣婴降生后，如高墙般的相互猜疑便会土崩瓦解。
这句话的含义明显带有圣经文化的色彩和宗教意义。当圣婴降生后，整个大地和人民将会得到和平，无战争，无疾病，人们将生活在安详和睦的大地上。
crumble *vi*.：(作动词) 弄碎、崩溃，破碎
例如：
The walls were ***crumbing***. 那几座墙坍塌了。

(7) For a spell or two no one seems forlorn. =For a period of time or two no one seems forlorn. 没有人看来会再遭受不幸。
for a spell or two：指时间的一段或延长，此处指很长时间

forlorn(作形容词用，永远受苦：lorn ，unhappy，forsaken)：不幸的，孤苦的，被遗弃的
seem：看上去、仿佛(常常做系动词用，而又具有实义动词的意义)

(8) But a child that will grow and turn tears to laughter, hate to love, war to peace = But a child who will grow up and be powerful enough to change tears into laughter, change hate into love, change war into peace. 但孩子长大后，他能由哭为笑，变恨为爱，变战争为和平。
turn sth. to = change sth. into 把某事(某物)变成为……
例如：
Turn defeat into victory. 转败为胜。
Turn grief into strength. 化悲痛为力量。
Change francs into Renminbi. 把法郎兑换成人民币。

(9) And everyone to everyone's neighbour. = And everyone gets along with each other well. 人们和睦相处。

注释与赏析

歌手约翰尼·马蒂斯(Johnny Mathis)素有“乡村歌王”的美称，最擅长演唱具有典型民族地方特色的优秀歌曲。他的歌曲悠扬动听，嗓音圆润宏大，显示出一种乡村旷野的无垠和空旷，易于触动人们的心弦。因而，无论老人、孩子或年青人都喜欢听他演唱的歌曲。

《当圣婴降生时》是美国电影《人狼之恋》中的主题插曲，也是一首圣诞歌曲。这首歌带有明显的宗教色彩和西方基督文化气息。

这种以基督思想作底蕴的传统文化渗透了西方社会的各个方面，这种文化背景，对于理解西方人，特别是美国人有着特定的深刻意义。歌曲演唱的静谧与圣洁更加增添了这种文化的氛围和风格的浓重。演唱该曲时，合唱队伴以集体和声，接着引出独唱，在洁亮静谧，严肃安详中讲述这一位婴儿的诞生，是那么的圣神和传奇。整个世界都在祈祷孩子，该曲自始至终以一种略呈上行的曲式安排，几个段落的反反复复，速度安排近似那首《平安夜》，平缓稳健，慢而稳实，升而严谨。但在节奏的安排与音程的处理上明显不似《平安夜》那么祥和、稳实。因而，在时常出现的上升与跳跃的旋律上形成了激动与放射，喜悦与祈盼。最后一句又回趋平缓稳定，表现了在坚定、希望、激动后定会实现愿望所产生的安定和圆满。整首歌曲以圣婴诞生喻出新生命的伟大和希望，将为世界带来福音。

4. Moon River
(月亮河)

1=C 3/4

Words & Music by
Johnny Mercer

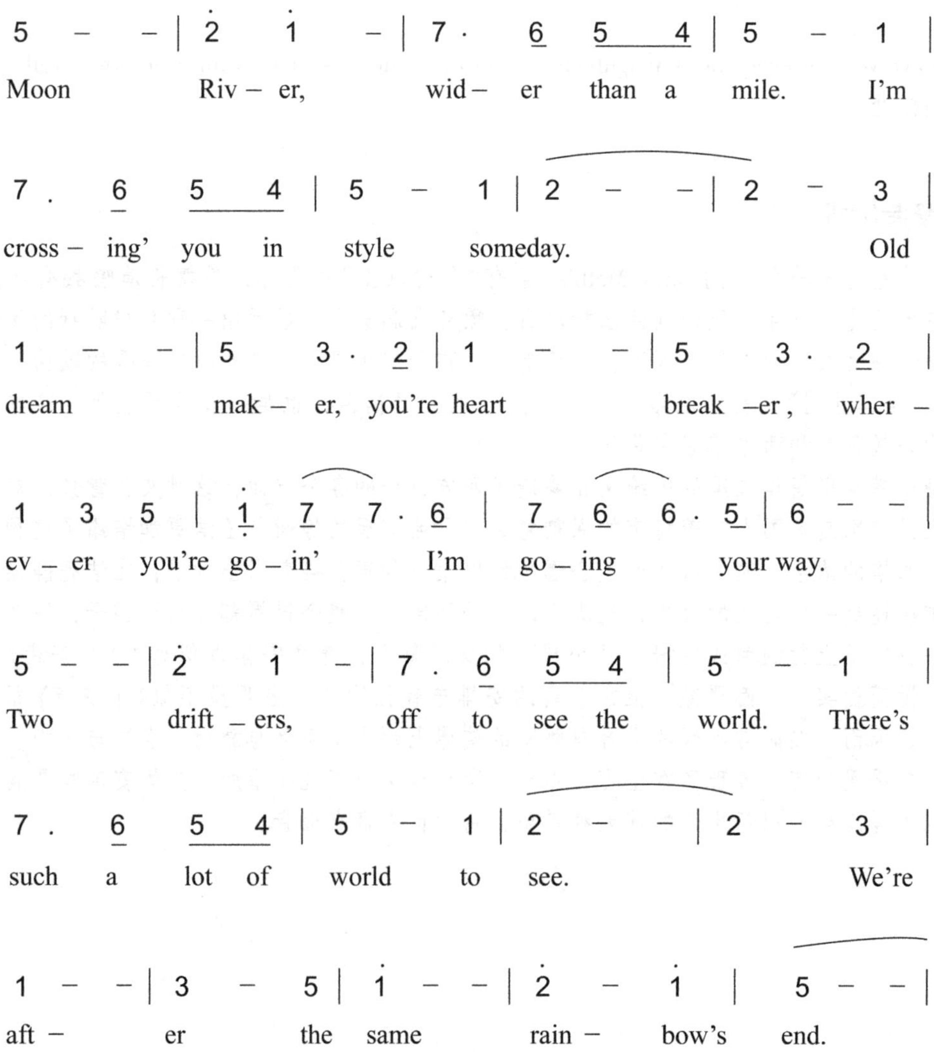

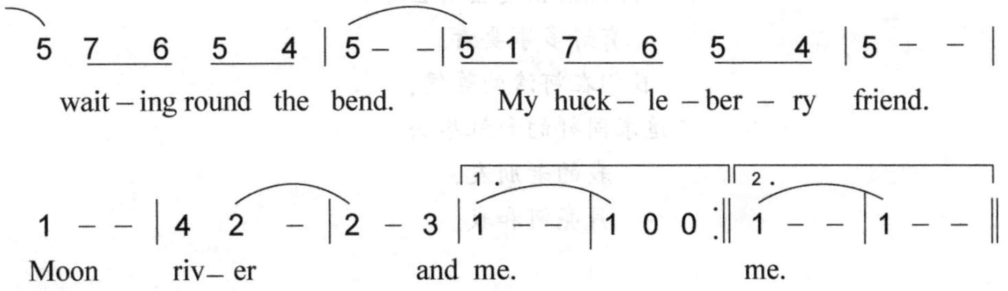

【英文歌词】

Moon River

Moon river, wider than a mile,
I'm crossing you in style some day.
Oh, dream maker, you're heart breaker.
Wherever you're goin',
I'm goin' your way.

Two drifters, off to see the world.
There's such a lot of world to see.
We're after the same rainbow's end,
Waitin' round the bend.
My huckleberry friend,
Moon River, and me.

【参考译文】

月亮河

月亮河，一英里宽，
总有一天我会把你横渡，潇洒又体面。
哦，激起梦想的河，令人心碎的河，
无论你流向何方，
我将跟你前往。

两个漂流者出发去看世界。
有好多事要看。
我们在河湾处等候，
追求同样的彩虹尽头。
我的老朋友，
月亮河和我。

语言点解析

(1) Moon River, wider than a mile: Moon River, you are wider than a mile.

(2) I'm crossing you in style some day: 我总有一天会把你体面地横渡。此处的 you 指 Moon River.
some day：将来总有一天
one day：一天，多用于表达过去的某一天
in style：有气派的(地)；阔气的(地)；时尚的(地)
例如：
Some day I will also be dressed ***in style***. 将来总有一天我也会穿得很体面。
穿过一条街道或横过一条河要用 cross。
例如：
cross a street：穿过街道
cross a river：横渡一条河

(3) Oh, dream maker, you heart breaker: Oh, you are a dream maker and a heart breaker.
歌词作者在说：Oh, Moon River, you make my dreams and also break my heart. 意思是说：你使我产生梦想，因为你美丽，你使我心碎，因为我梦不成真。《北京人在纽约》的开始曲把纽约比作天堂，也比作地狱："New York is a heaven and a hell"与"Oh, Dream maker, you heart breaker"有异曲同工之妙。

(4) Wherever you're going: 无论你去哪里。

(5) **疑问词+ever**：表示强调，"无论……""不论……"
例如：
Wherever he went, there was trouble. 无论他去哪儿，那里就有麻烦。
Whoever you are, you must abide by the law. 不管你是谁，都要守法。

(6) I'm going your way. 我要跟你去。**way** 表示方向。

例如：

Come this *way*. 往这边走。

(7) two drifters：两个漂流者。

在马克·吐温的小说《哈克贝利·费恩历险记》里，Huckleberry 逃出家，被有钱人收养，又受不了文明社会的拘束，便逃走。与黑人吉姆共乘一筏，在河上漂流，沿途见到许多各种各样的事，包括诸多丑恶现象。在共同漂泊的日子里，他们结下深厚的友谊。其实，电影《餐桌上的早餐》中的青年作家和霍利也是两个出来闯世界的 drifters。德莱赛笔下的嘉莉妹妹也是一个类似的人物，都是 drifters。

(8) There's such a lot of world to see. 世界丰富多彩，足够看的。

(9) We're after the same rainbow's end：我们都在追求同样的彩虹尽头。

be after：追求。

例如：

He *is* always *after* fame. 他总是追求名声。

The rainbow's end：彩虹的尽头：指欢乐

(10) Waiting round the bend：Waiting around the bend.

bend *n.*：指河湾

(11) My Huckleberry friend：引用马克·吐温小说中人物名，表示非常亲近的朋友。这里译作"老朋友"见第 7 条解析。

huckleberry：一种深色水果(有别于蓝果蓝莓)

注释与赏析

《在蒂凡尼处早餐》("Breakfast at Tiffany's")是根据德鲁门·凯波特(Truman Capote)同名畅销小说改编，由布莱克·爱德华兹(Blake Edwards)执导的爱情电影。奥黛丽·赫本(Audrey Hepburn)出任本片主角，并凭此片第四度获得奥斯卡最佳女主角的提名。

影片讲述一个爱慕虚荣的农村女孩到纽约去寻找自己"理想的归宿"，结果因谋生艰难，最后沦落为高级交际花。此时的她过着自由无羁的生活，整天在格林尼治村闲逛渡日，一心想找个有钱的金龟婿。她时常在清晨徘徊在知名的珠宝店外，看着闪闪发亮的首饰，她想忘了自己的过去，但是过去的阴影却不时出现缠绕着她。但在遇到一名作家之后，她才发现人生有真正的爱情。奥黛丽·赫本的角色行为和演出颇为夸张，对白喋喋不休，演出似娼妓又似寻梦少女；乔治·佩帕德(George Peppard)演的人物更妙，是作家也是男孩。《纽约时报》的影评说：霍利·戈莱特利是一个"野东西"，扮演霍利的海普伯恩小姐是个天生具有魅力的小精灵，谁看了都会相信她，称赞她。

这首《月亮河》是电影《在蒂凡尼处早餐》中的插曲，由亨利·曼西尼(Henry Mancini)作曲，安迪·威廉斯(Andy Williams)演唱，并获得奥斯卡最佳电影歌曲。歌曲婉转低回的旋律回肠荡气，引人深思。月亮河，一条多么美丽的河啊！而在影片中，奥黛丽·赫本坐在窗前拿着吉它的原唱，细腻地倾诉她的梦想，更成为一个令人难忘的经典场景！歌唱者把“Moon River”拟人化，向她倾诉心肠。月亮河很宽，但是歌唱者表示将来总有一天要把她体面地渡过，有征服困难的决心。正是这条令人向往的河又使人肝肠寸断。但不管怎样，歌者还是愿意随她前往任何她流经的地方，表达了一种知难而进的决心。接着歌者自比为两个漂泊者出来看世界，坚持不懈地追求彩虹的尽头，即欢乐的境界，月亮河和歌者仍是亲密无间的好朋友。最后四行重复前面的内容，再次表达了歌者追求美好生活的愿望。

5. Oh, Carol!
（哦，卡罗尔！）

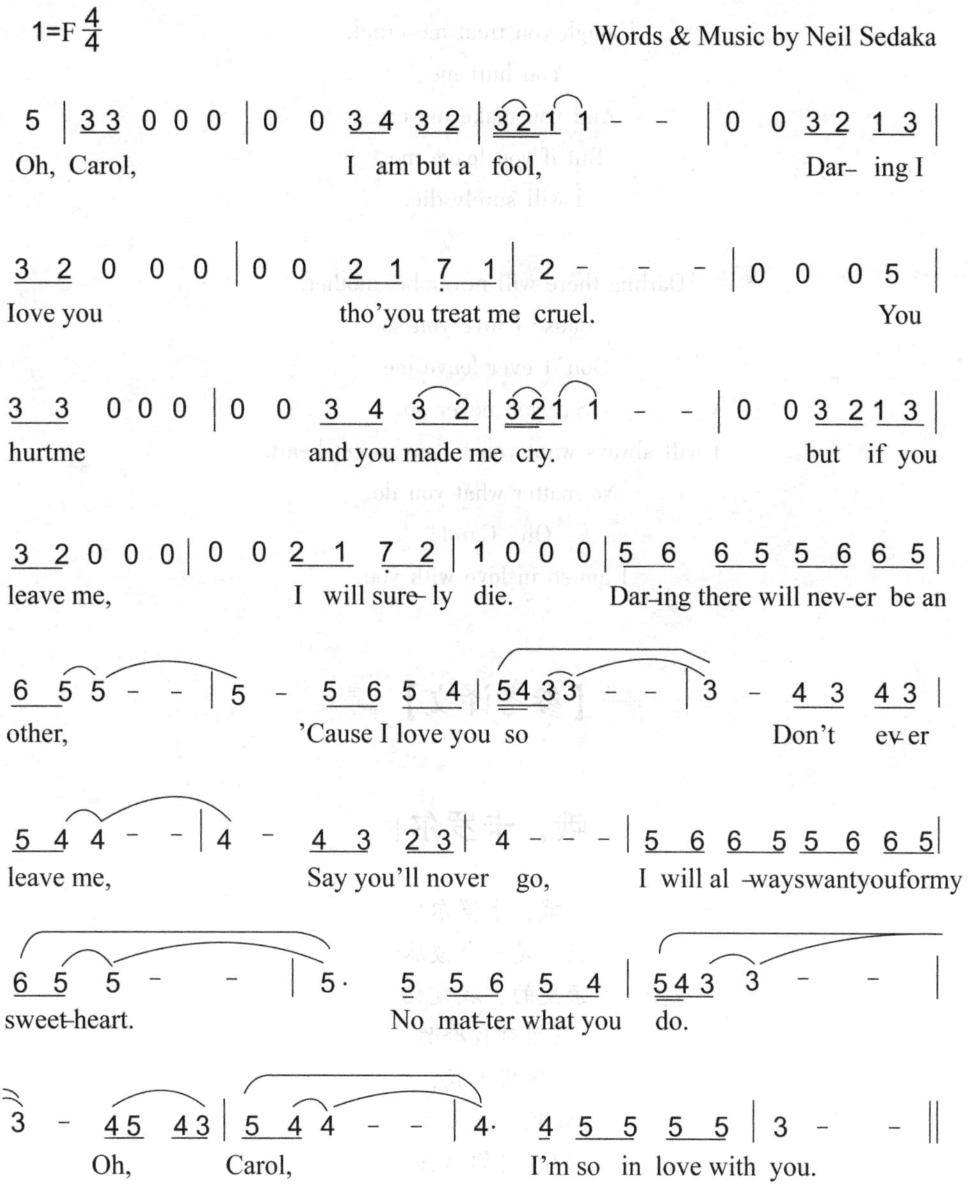

【英文歌词】

Oh, Carol!

Oh, Carol!
I am but a fool.
Darling I love you.
Though you treat me cruel.
You hurt me,
And you make me cry.
But if you leave me,
I will surely die.

Darling there will never be another.
'Cause I love you so.
Don't ever leave me.
Say you never go.
I will always want you for my sweet heart.
No matter what you do.
Oh, Carol!
I am so in love with you.

【参考译文】

哦，卡罗尔！

哦，卡罗尔！
我只是一个傻瓜。
亲爱的，我爱你，
虽然对我冷酷。
你伤害我，
让我为你哭泣。
但只要你离去。
我必死无疑。

亲爱的，没人比我爱你更深。
我爱你胜于一切
请不要离开我
说你绝不会走，
我要你做我永远的爱人，
不管你怎样对我。
哦，卡罗尔！
我深深地爱你。

语言点解析

(1) I am but a fool. =I am only a fool. 我只不过是个傻瓜。
but *adv*.：只不过；仅仅
例如：
He is ***but*** a child. Don't except too much of him. 他只是个孩子，别对他期望太大。

(2) though you treat me cruel. =though you treat me cruelly. 尽管对我太残酷。

(3) There will never be another=There will be no other who loves you more than I do. 没人比我更爱你。

(4) 'cause=because.

(5) don't ever =never.

(6) Whatever you do=no matter what you do=no matter how you treat me. 不管你怎样待我。

注释与赏析

这是一首在我国流传很广的外国歌曲。我国许多著名歌手都曾在演唱会上演唱过这首歌。歌词富有节奏感，曲调优美动听。歌曲表达了一种至死不渝的爱。爱并不为了索取，并不为了占有，因为爱并不把眼前的或长远的利益作为前提。爱一个人就爱得彻底，爱得干脆，爱得伤心，爱得海枯石烂，爱得死去活来。匈牙利伟大的爱国诗人裴多菲·山托尔说得好："生命诚可贵，爱情价更高"。

可见，在有些人的眼里爱情是位于生命之上的。难怪有些人会因为爱而以泪洗面，因为爱而心中淌血，因为爱而去殉情。听了这首歌，我们不禁会脱口说出"哦，卡罗尔。你真是太幸运了！"据说，这是美国钢琴家、作曲家奈尔·希达克(Neil Sedaka)向女歌手卡罗·金(Carol King)的求爱歌。可惜最后 Carol King 还是投入了别人的怀抱。

6. Edelweiss
(雪绒花)

Words by Oscar Hammerstein II
Music by Richard Rogers

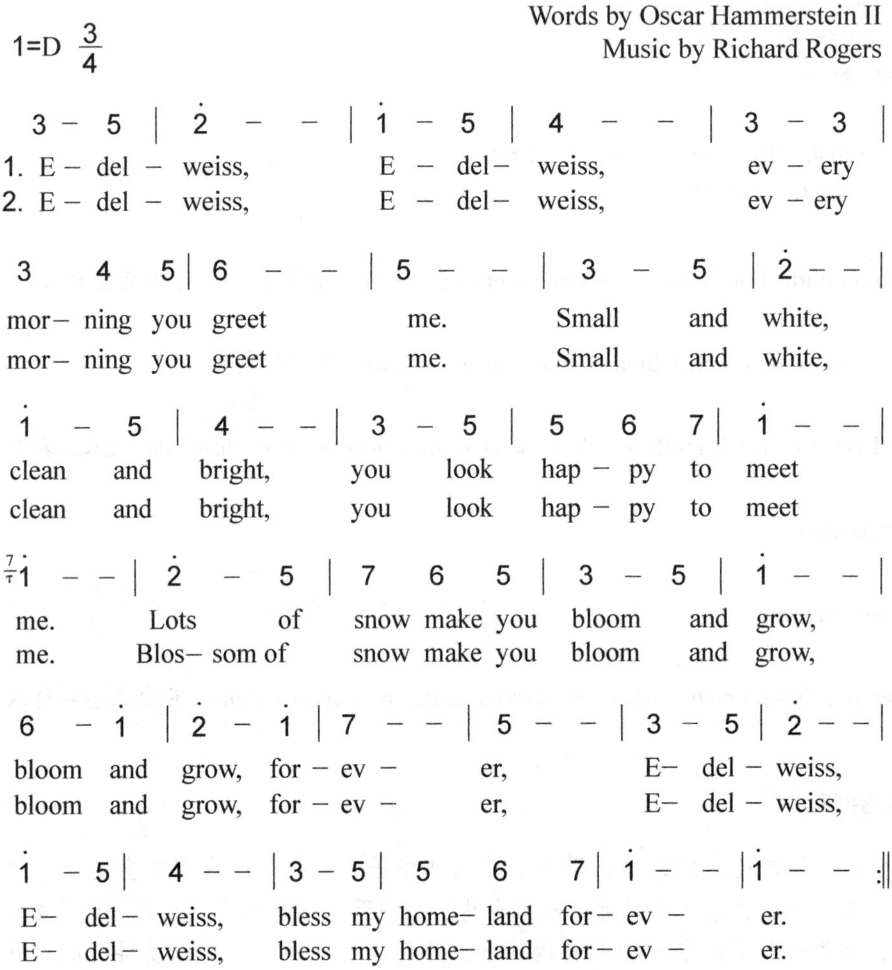

【英文歌词】

Edelweiss

Edelweiss, edelweiss,
Every morning you greet me.
Small and white, clean and bright,
You look happy to meet me.
Blossom of snow,
May you bloom and grow,
Bloom and grow forever.
Edelweiss, edelweiss,
Bless my homeland forever.

Edelweiss, edelweiss,
Every morning you greet me.
Small and white, clean and bright,
You look happy to meet me.
Blossom of snow,
May you bloom and grow,
Bloom and grow forever.
Edelweiss, edelweiss,
Bless my homeland forever.

【参考译文】

雪绒花

雪绒花，雪绒花，
每天清晨你问候我。
小而白，洁又亮，
见到我你面露喜色。
雪白的花朵，
你开放成长，

永远开放、成长。
雪绒花，雪绒花，
要永远保佑我的国家。

雪绒花，雪绒花，
每天清晨你问候我。
小而白，洁又亮，
见到我你面露喜色。
雪白的花朵，
你开放成长，
永远开放、成长。
雪绒花，雪绒花，
要永远保佑我的国家。

语言点解析

(1) edelweiss：读作[ˈeɪdlvaɪs]，是个德语词，a type of plant with flowers；growing in the Alps 火绒草，薄雪草之一种。Edelweiss 一词在中国有多种译发，主要有薄雪花、雪绒花、火绒草、小白花等。

(2) **greet** *vt.*：say hello to 问候，向(跟)……打招呼
例如：
He ***greeted*** his teacher in English. 他用英语跟老师打招呼。

(3) Small and white, clean and bright, you look happy to meet me.
前边的四个形容词作主语的补足语，说明主语的状况。这句话可以这样理解：You are small and white, clean and bright. You look happy to meet me.

(4) **look happy**：看起来高兴。“系动词+形容词”是一个常用的**系表结构**，说明主语的情况。
例如：
He ***looks*** very old. 他长得很老相。
The story ***sounds*** interesting. 这个故事听起来有趣。
The food ***tastes*** sour. 这食物品尝起来有酸味。

(5) blossom of snow：blossom 指盛开的花。blossom of snow 是 blossom like snow 的意思，指洁白如雪的花朵。

（6）May you bloom and grow：

bloom *vi*.：指花儿开放

May you bloom. =愿你开花。

"may+主语+动词"是一个祝愿性结构。

例如：

May you succeed. 祝你成功。

May our friendship last forever. 愿我们友谊长存。

（7）Bless my homeland forever：要永远保佑我的祖国。

homeland：可以指家乡、祖国、国家

bless：保佑

例如：God ***bless*** you. 上帝保佑你。

注释与赏析

这首歌是故事片《音乐之声》（1965年）的插曲之一。电影《音乐之声》描写的女主角是生性活泼、不安心当修女的姑娘玛丽亚。故事发生在第二次世界大战前的奥地利，实习修女玛丽亚到一个海军上校家里当家庭教师并逐渐获得七个孩子的喜爱。最后，上校也爱上了她并与她结婚。

在影片中的相关内容：上校一家参加为德国军官举行的音乐会，他们决定当夜离开奥地利，前往瑞士。音乐会上，上校弹起吉他，唱起了这首奥地利民歌，之后哽咽地唱不下去了，玛丽亚和孩子们走上去与他一起唱，他们的深情感动了在场的奥地利观众，在上校的示意下奥地利观众都激动地与他们合唱了起来。

歌中edelweiss被拟人化，使它具有人类的感情和高尚的品格，难怪男主人公在开始唱之前对观众说他要唱首情歌。不错，他将自己的感情注入这一生长在高山的植物，更主要的是，也通过这"小而白，洁又亮"的小花儿保佑自己的祖国永远平安，顽强。这首歌歌词不长，却情深意远。主人公赞扬雪绒花的美丽，实际也在希望自己的祖国也不失这些品性。

Edelweiss的歌词是一首优美的小诗，诗行有长有短，三、四行押韵，二、五行押韵，六、七行押韵，一、九行押韵，读起来朗朗上口，唱起来也非常优美动听。

7. Donna Donna

（多呐，多呐）

1=C $\frac{4}{4}$

Words & Music by Sholom Secunda

3 6 7 1 2 | 3 6 7 1 2 |

1. On a wag – on bound for mar – ket,
2. Stop com – plain – ing, said the far – mer,
3. Calves are easi – ly bound and slaughter – ed,

0 3 6 4 3 2 | 1 2 3 – |

there's a calf with a wonder – ful eye.
who told you a calf to be?
ne– ver know – ing the rea – sons why.

3 6 7 1 2 | 3 6 7 1 2 |

High a – bove him there's a swal – low,
Why don't you have wings to fly with,
But who – ev– er trea – sures free – dom

0 3 6 4 3 2 | 1 7 6 – |

wing – ing swift – ly through the sky.
like a swal – low so proud and free.
like the swal – lows, has learnt to fly?

0 5 5 5 4 | 3 2 1 – 0 1 | 2 · 2 5 4 |

How the winds are laugh – ing! They laugh with all their

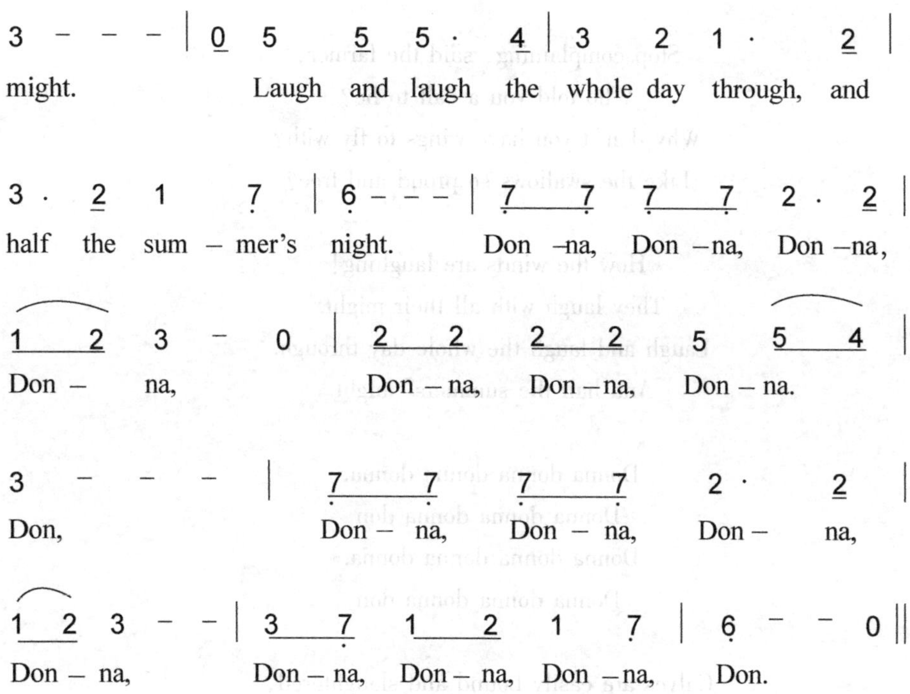

【英文歌词】

Donna Donna

On a wagon bound for market,
There's a calf with a mournful eye.
High above him there's a swallow,
Winging swiftly through the sky.

How the winds are laughing!
They laugh with all their might.
Laugh and laugh the whole day through,
And half the summer's night.

Donna donna donna donna,
Donna donna donna don.
Donna donna donna donna,
Donna donna donna don.

Stop complaining, said the farmer,
Who told you a calf to be?
Why don't you have wings to fly with?
Like the swallows so proud and free?

How the winds are laughing!
They laugh with all their might.
Laugh and laugh the whole day through.
And half the summers' night.

Donna donna donna donna.
Donna donna donna don
Donna donna donna donna.
Donna donna donna don

Calves are easily bound and slaughtered,
Never knowing the reason why.
But whoever treasures freedom
Like the swallow has learned to fly?

How the winds are laughing!
They laugh with all their might.
Laugh an laugh the whole day through
And half the summer's night.

Donna donna donna donna.
Donna donna donna don
Donna donna donna donna.
Donna donna donna don

【参考译文】

多呐，多呐

马车要入市，

车上有小牛，
它满年是忧伤。
在它上方有一只燕子，
在天空轻快地飞翔。

风儿在狂笑！
笑声是那么响亮。
笑啊笑，笑了整天，
又笑半个夏夜。

多呐，多呐，多呐，多呐，
多呐，多呐，多呐，多。
多呐，多呐，多呐，多呐，
多呐，多呐，多呐，多。

“不要抱怨”，农民对牛说。
谁叫你是小牛？
你为什么不长翅膀？
像那小燕子自由飞翔？

风儿在狂笑！
笑声是那么响，
笑啊笑，笑了整天，
又笑半个夏夜。

多呐，多呐，多呐，多呐，
多呐，多呐，多呐，多。
多呐，多呐，多呐，多呐，
多呐，多呐，多呐，多。

小牛容易绑，
又容易被杀，
从来不知道为什么，
但那个珍视自由的人，
已像燕子那样会飞？

风儿在狂笑？
笑声是那么响，

笑啊笑，笑了整天，
又笑半个夏夜。

多呐，多呐，多呐，多呐，
多呐，多呐，多呐，多。
多呐，多呐，多呐，多呐，
多呐，多呐，多呐，多。

语言点解析

(1) **bound for**：朝……去的；准备到……去的；开往……的
例如：
Where ***is*** he ***bound for***？他要去哪儿？
在 bound for 短语中，for 也可用 to 代替。

(2) High above him there's a swallow winging swiftly through the sky：High above (in) the sky.
这天空中自由飞翔小燕子与上绑的小牛形成对比。

(3) How the winds are laughing！风儿正在狂笑！
how *adv.*：(用于感叹句中强调形容词、副词或陈述内容)多么，何等。
例如：
How she must have talked last night！她昨晚一定没停过嘴！
How beautiful this scenery is！这风景多漂亮！

(4) They laugh with all their might：They laugh with their power.
might *n.*：力量；威力；能力
with all one's *might*：竭尽全力；全力以赴
beyond one's *might*：超出自己的能力

(5) Who told you a calf to be？=Who told you to be calf？谁叫你是一头小牛呢？

(6) Why don't you have wings to fly with...=为什么你没有飞翔的翅膀呢？
to fly with 是定语修饰 wings。上半句可以改成：Why don't you have wings with which to fly…？

(7) Calves are easily bound and slaughtered,
calves：calf 的复数。

bound：bind 的过去式和过去分词形式
slaughter *v. t.*：屠杀，宰杀

(8) But whoever treasures freedom like the swallow has learned to fly. 不管是谁，只要是像燕子那样珍爱自由，就已经能够飞翔。这里，“whoever treasures freedom like the swallow”是本句的主语部分。
treasure *v. t.*：珍视，珍爱；储存；铭记
例如：
We should ***treasure*** our friendship. 我们珍惜我们的友谊。

注释与赏析

这是一首传统歌曲，深受犹太人的喜爱，流传甚广。这首歌的词曲作者都是韶勒姆·赛肯达(Sholom Secunda)。

《多呐，多呐》是一个寓言，一个难懂的寓言。我们首先看到的是这样一个画面：要进入城市的马车上绑着一头满脸忧伤的小牛，天空中轻快地飞着一只小燕子。这两个意境形成鲜明对比，中心问题是自由。小牛被绑，失去自由，小燕轻飞，自由自在；一个在地上受苦，一个在空中享受。鸟兽如此两分。风见此状，狂笑不止。小牛容易被绑架，却不知道原因，人是否也有时被宰割而不知为什么？但人鸟也不相同，鸟爱自由并且会飞，人爱自由，可谁能飞？还有那风，面对小牛、小鸟与人，它狂笑不止，这隐藏着什么寓意呢？

风一直在笑，笑个不停，是不是在告诉人们：有些事根本说不清楚，人之命、兽之命、鸟之命均由天定？它在冷眼旁观，还是替谁说话？如果人们根本不与命抗争，终有一天会沦落到类似小牛那样的处境。

8. Que Sera, Sera

(该怎样就怎样)

1=C $\frac{3}{4}$ Words and Music by Doris Day

1	2	3 |	5	–	3 |	5	–	3 |	
1. When	I	was	just		a	lit	–	tle	
2. When	I	grew	up		and	fell		in	
3. Now	I	have	chil	–	dren	of		my	

5	–	– |	3	5	<u>0</u>	<u>3</u> |	6	5	– |
girl,			I	asked		my	mo	– ther,	
love,			I	asked		my	sweet	–heart	
own.			They	ask		their		mother,	

6	5	3 |	4	–	– |	7	1̇	2̇ |
"What	will	I	be?			Will	I	be
"What	lies	a –	head?			Will	we	have
"What	will	I	be?			Will	I	be

7	7	– |	6	7	1̇ |	7	–	– |
pretty?			will	I	be	rich?"		
rainbows			day	af –	ter	day?"		
handsome?			Will	I	be	rich?"		

3	5	6 |	5	–	7̣ |	1	–	– |
Here's	what	she	said		to	me,		
Here's	what	my	sweet	–	heart	said,		
I	tell	them	ten	–	der –	ly,		

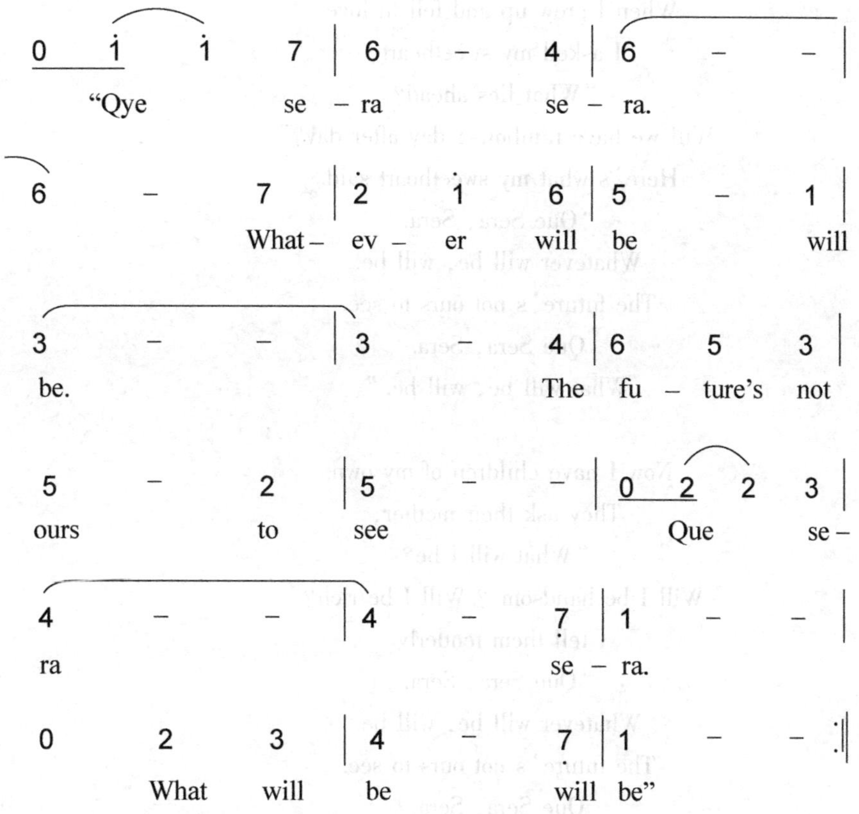

【英文歌词】

Que Sera, Sera

When I was just a little girl,
I asked my mother,
“What will I be?
Will I be pretty? Will I be rich?”
Here's what she said to me.
“Que Sera, Sera,
Whatever will be, will be.
The future's not ours to see.
Que Sera, Sera
What will be, will be.”

When I grew up and fell in love,
I asked my sweetheart,
"What lies ahead?
Will we have rainbows, day after day?"
Here's what my sweetheart said.
"Que Sera, Sera.
Whatever will be, will be.
The future's not ours to see.
Que Sera, Sera.
What will be, will be."

Now I have children of my own.
They ask their mother,
"What will I be?
Will I be handsome? Will I be rich?"
I tell them tenderly.
"Que Sera, Sera.
Whatever will be, will be.
The future's not ours to see.
Que Sera, Sera.
What will be, will be."

【参考译文】

该怎样就怎样

当年我还是个小姑娘，
我问我的妈妈，
"将来会怎样？
我会不会有钱？会不会漂亮？"
她这样对我说：
"该怎样就怎样。
该怎样就怎样。
我们不能预测未来，
该怎样就怎样。
该怎样就怎样。"

后来我长大并恋爱，
我问的爱人：
“前途怎么样？
是否每天都有彩虹挂天上？”
他这样对我说：
“该怎样就怎样。
该怎样就怎样。
我们不能预测未来，
该怎样就怎样。
该怎样就怎样。”

现在我自己也有孩子，
他们会问他们的妈妈：
“将来会怎样？
会不会英俊？会不会富有？”
我温柔地对他们说：
“该怎样就怎样。
该怎样就怎样。
我们不能预测未来，
该怎样就怎样。
该怎样就怎样。
该怎样就怎样。”

语言点解析

(1) Que sera, sera. = Whatever will be, will be. 该怎样就怎样。

(2) Whatever will be, will be. = Anything that will happen will happen. 任何可能发生的事都会发生；该怎样就怎样。
whatever: anything that;
be: happen 或 exist

(3) The future's not ours to see. =We cannot foretell what will happen in the future. 我们不能预测将来会发生什么事。

(4) **grow up**: 长大

例如：

She became beautiful only when she ***grew up***. 她只是长大后才变得漂亮起来。

(5) **fall in love**：坠入爱河、恋爱

fall in love with：爱上……

to be in love with：与……恋爱

fall out of love：失恋

例如：

Mary ***fell in love*** with Tom. 玛丽爱上了汤姆。

Mary is ***in love*** with Tom. 玛丽正和汤姆恋爱。

That film star is ***falling out of love*** again. 那个电影明星又失恋了。

(6) **lie ahead**：位于前方

(7) children of my own：my own children 我自己的孩子

of one's own：属于……自己的

例如：

He does not have a house ***of his own***. 他没有自己的房子。

(8) **handsome**：英俊(多形容男性)

beautiful：漂亮(多形容女子)

(9) **tenderly**：温柔地

例如：

He always talks ***tenderly***. 他说话时总是柔声细气。

注释与赏析

《该怎样就怎样》是美国影片《知情人》("The Man Who Knew Too Much")中的插曲。这首插曲于1956年荣获第29届奥斯卡最佳歌曲金像奖。

这部电影是根据同名小说改编的，讲述的是一家美国人在摩洛哥旅行时的遭遇。一对美国医生夫妇及他们的儿子正在摩洛哥的阿拉伯居民观光区，突然，一个法国人在他们的面前遭到谋杀。这个法国人在死前将情报断断续续地告诉了这位医生，这样一来，这位医生(麦昆医生)就成了知情者。英国间谍组织绑架了他们的儿子作人质，要求他们保持沉默。医生夫妇投入这场揭露间谍的搏斗，他们也被囚禁。母亲唱了这首歌，用歌声给儿子发信号。

这首歌共分为三段，讲述了女主人公不同时期对同一问题的思考。先是当自己是个小女孩时，她问妈妈将来会怎样。妈妈告诉她：该怎样就怎样。反过来也可以理解，不该怎样就别怎样。后来她长大恋爱，就问心上人将来会怎样，是否每日有彩虹高照。心上人对她说：

该怎样就怎样。最后，她自己有了孩子。孩子们问她他们的将来会怎样。她便告诉自己的孩子：该怎样就怎样。有些事不可强求，也不必强求。

这首歌似乎在告诉人们：要安于现状，发生了什么事，就接受什么事，不要为争一日之长短而苛求自己。或者可以讲：淡泊即是真，真即淡泊。

是的，在有些事情上，我们劝世人接受这一忠告：该怎样就怎样。但在自己的理想上，在工作中，还是要有进取心，不能随波逐流；要奋发，创造业绩，让本不怎么样的事也变样。

9. You Raise Me Up
（你鼓舞了我）

1=♭E 4/4

Words by Brendan Graham
Music by Rolf Lovland

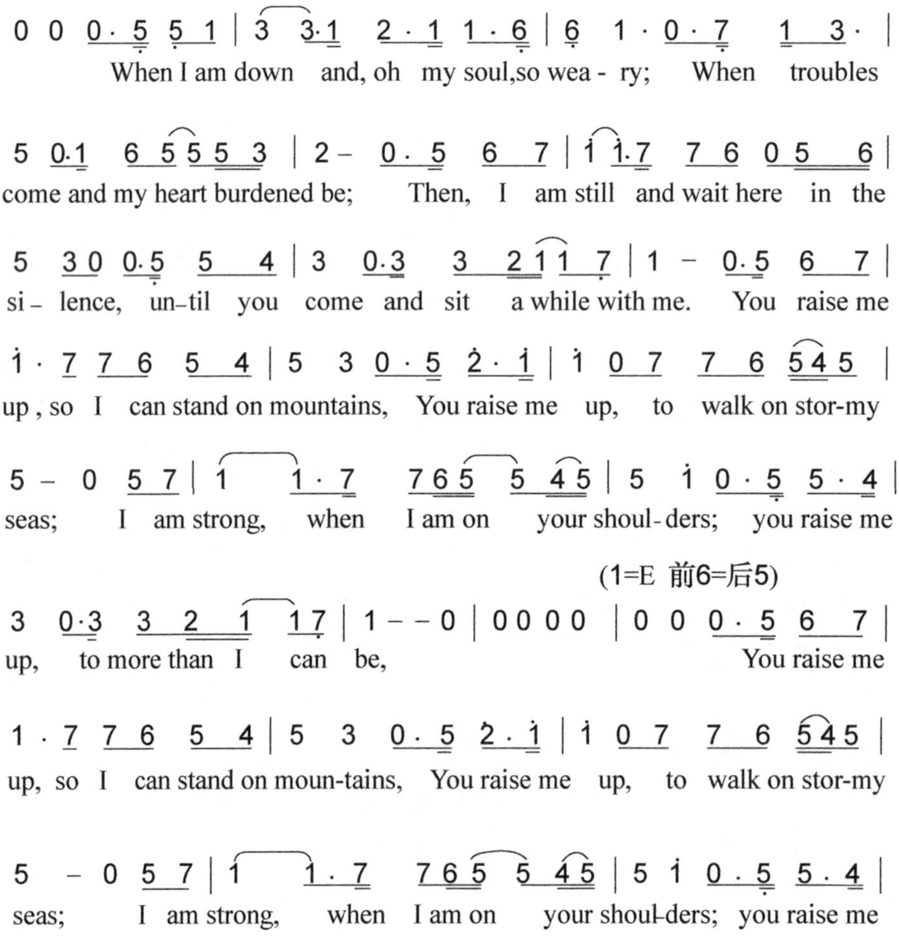

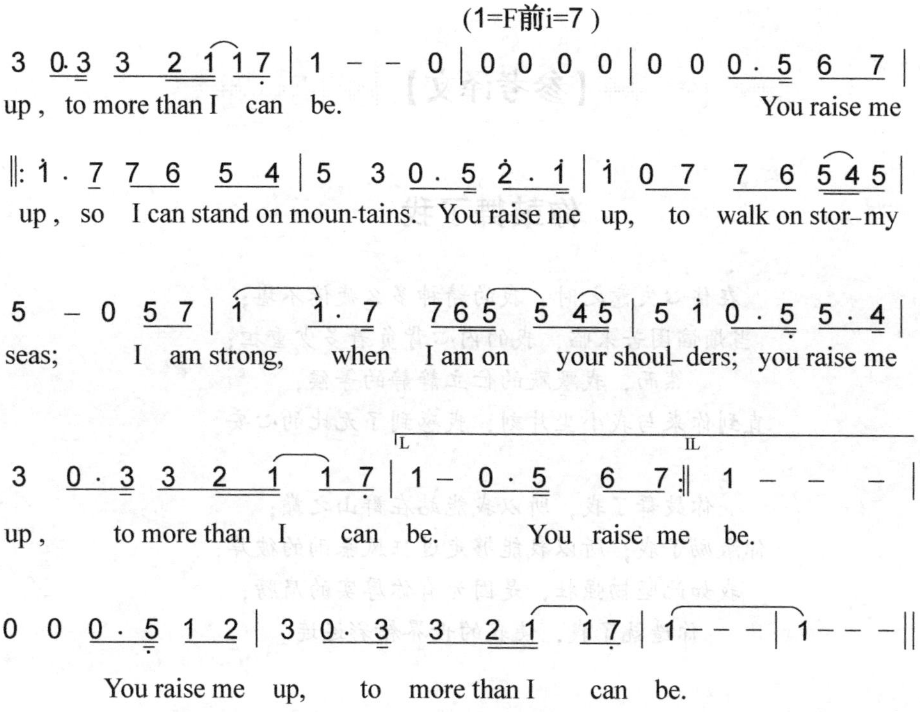

【英文歌词】

You Raise Me Up

When I am down and, oh my soul, so weary;
When troubles come and my heart burdened be;
Then, I am still and wait here in the silence,
Until you come and sit awhile with me.

You raise me up, so I can stand on mountains;
You raise me up, to walk on stormy seas;
I am strong, when I am on your shoulders;
You raise me up, To more than I can be.

【参考译文】

你鼓舞了我

在伤心失意之时，我的精神多么疲倦不堪；
当烦恼困苦来临，我的内心背负着多少重担；
然而，我默默的伫立静静的等候，
直到你来与我小坐片刻，我感到了无比的心安。

你鼓舞了我，所以我能站在群山之巅；
你激励了我，所以我能够走过狂风暴雨的彼岸；
我如此坚韧强壮，是因为有你厚实的肩膀；
你造就了我，使我的世界精彩连连。

语言点解析

(1) When I am down …当我失落的时候。

down *adj.*：沮丧的；闷闷不乐的；情绪低落的

例如：

I have been ***down*** since the injury happened. 自从受了伤以来我一直很沮丧。

Try to support each other when one of you is feeling ***down***. 当有人觉得情绪低落时，要努力相互打气。

The old man sounded really ***down***. 老人听上去情绪十分低落。

(2) …oh my soul, so weary = …oh my soul is so weary.

(3) When troubles come and my heart burdened be…此处的"my heart burdened be"系为了尾韵的需要而倒装，相当于"my heart (should) be burdened"。注意两处使用"when"引导的内容可被视为从句部分，与后面的"then"相关联的内容(主句)，共同构成一个较长的复合句。

(4) **awhile** *adv.* 片刻，一会儿

例如：

He worked ***awhile*** as a pharmacist in Cincinnati. 他有一段时间在辛辛那提当药剂师。

They rested ***awhile*** at the inn and then went out to eat. 大家在旅馆休息一会，便出去聚餐。

Tom struggled ***awhile*** and then retired , utterly defeated. 他结结巴巴要往下背诵，可过了一会，便好像只斗败的公鸡一样溜下场去。

(5) to walk on stormy seas：似乎是从圣经里的一个典故而来——耶稣走在海面上。可理解为勇敢顽强的人们对于战胜惊涛骇浪和一切困难的意志和决心。

(6) You raise me up to more than I can be. =你鼓舞了我(将我高高举起)，让我超越了自己。此句的真正含义是，由于有了你的帮助、你的鼓励，我能做到了自己原本不可能做到的事，到达了原本不可能达到的高度。

注释与赏析

“You Raise Me Up”的创作者为 Secret Garden(神秘园)，属于典型 Secret Garden 的风格。那浑厚的男声能让你的听觉彻底崩溃，间奏的风笛更是让人深陷音乐深海之中无法自拔。作为少有的励志和感恩音乐，最后的合唱气势磅礴，坚定有力。

根据爱尔兰传统民歌，Danny Boy 获得了创作灵感。这首歌最初题为《无声的故事》(Silent Story)，由 Secret Garden 成员 Rolf Lovland 作曲，成为世界上最适合被钢琴和小提琴演奏的经典曲目。Rolf Lovland 在读了爱尔兰小说家和歌曲作家 Brendan Graham(布伦丹·格雷厄姆)的小说后，请他为该歌填词。

“You Raise Me Up”于神秘园 2002 年的专辑《红月》(Once in a Red Moon)中首次发布，由爱尔兰歌手 Brian Kennedy(布赖恩·肯尼迪)(全名 Brian Edward Patrick Kennedy)演唱，并在爱尔兰和挪威销量较佳，当即占据各大排行榜冠军的位置长达十几周。基督教团体 Selah 演绎的版本也于 Billboard 的基督教音乐榜单上位列第一。

此歌曾在纽约市纪念“911”(2011 年)的仪式上为彰显消防员英勇救人的事迹而唱响，其时，这个专辑尚未在美国发行。随后，美国各家电台、电视台不断播放此歌长达一年之久，仅 2004 年，“You Raise Me Up”就在美国的电台共计播放了至少 500000 多次；2005 年年底，仅在美国这首歌就有 80 余个版本，并获得福音音乐奖(Gospel Music Awards)包括“年度最佳歌曲”奖项在内的四个提名。2002 年，神秘园到亚洲巡回演出，布莱恩因病未能同行，由挪威歌手坚·沃纳(Jan Werner Danielsen)演唱此歌，但录音从未发行。亚洲之行让神秘园的成员们大为惊讶是：这首歌其实已经传遍了中国大江南北。

这首经典的歌曲，几乎唱响了全球，却很少人知道这首歌究竟唱的是什么。有人说这首歌事实上是歌颂上帝，因为其中有一句 You raise me up，to walk on stormy seas，似乎是从圣经里的一个典故而来——耶稣走在海面上，但我们也可理解为勇敢顽强的人们对于战胜惊涛骇浪和一切困难的意志和决心。

10. Scarborough Fair

(斯卡布罗集市)

1=G $\frac{3}{4}$

Words & Music by
Paul Simon & Art Garfunkel

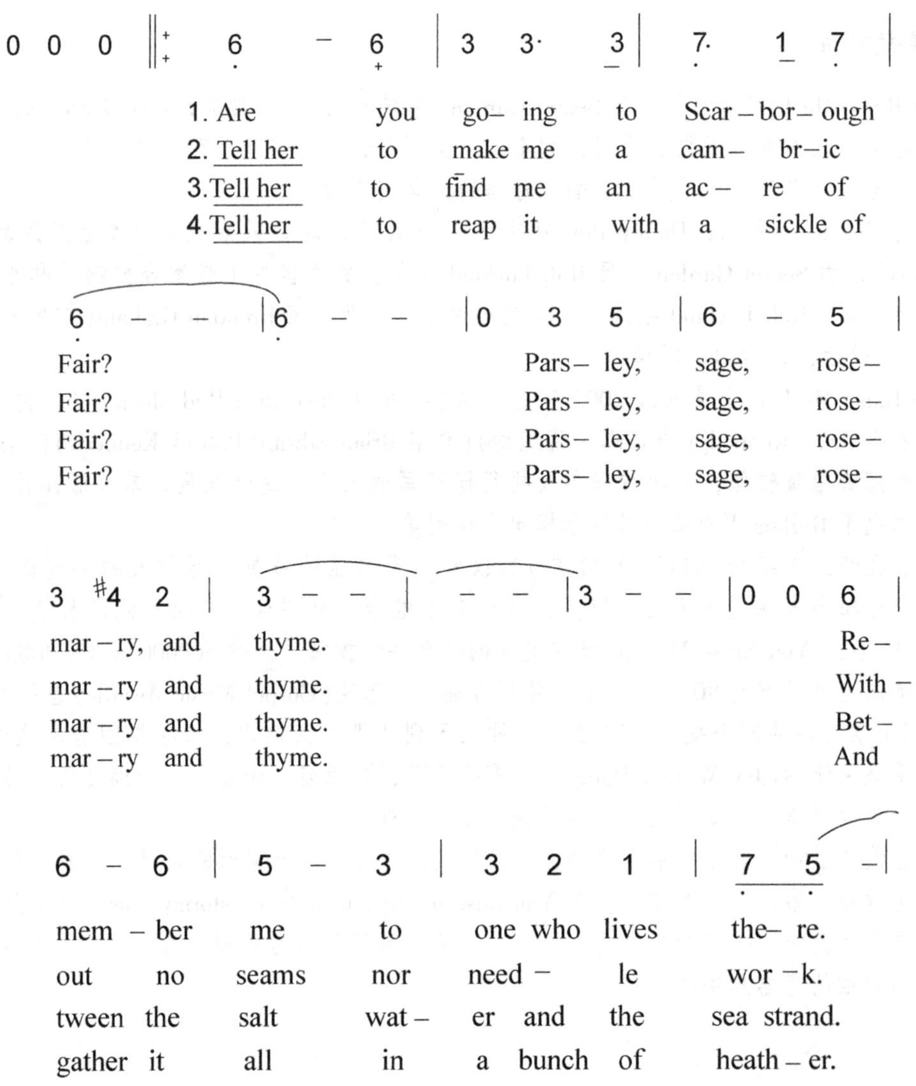

5 0 0 | 6 - 3 | 2 - 1 | 7 6 5 | 6 - -

She once was a true love of mine.

Then she'll be a true love of mine.

Then she'll be a true love of mine.

Then she'll be a true love of mine.

| 6 - 0 | 0 0 0 | 0 0 0 :‖ 6 - -

mine

【英文歌词】

Scarborough Fair

Are you going to Scarborough Fair?
Parsley, sage, rosemary, and thyme.
Remember me to one who lives there.
She once was a true love of mine.

Tell her to make me a cambric shirt,
Parsley, sage, rosemary and thyme,
Without no seams nor needle work.
Then she' ll be a true love of mine.

Tell her to find me an acre of land,
Parsley, sage, rosemary, and thyme,
Between the salt water and the sea strand.
Then she' ll be a true love of mine.

Tell her to reap it with a sickle of leather,
Parsley, sage, rosemary and thyme.
And gather it all in a bunch of heather.
Then she' ll be a true love of mine

Are you going to Scarborough Fair?

Parsley, sage, rosemary, and thyme.
Remember me to one who lives there.
She once was a true love of mine.

【参考译文】

斯卡布罗集市

你要去斯卡布罗集市吗？
那里有欧芹、鼠尾草、迷迭草和百里香，
代我问候那儿的一位姑娘，
她曾是我心上的人。

告诉她为我缝一件衬衫，
那里有欧芹、鼠尾草、迷迭草和百里香，
所有的接口都要用手工缝制，
那她就会成为我的心上人。

告诉她为我选一块地，
那里有欧芹、鼠尾草、迷迭草和百里香，
就在海水和海滩之间，
那她就会成为我的心上人。

告诉她用镰刀去收割，
那里有欧芹、鼠尾草、迷迭草和百里香，
然后用一束石南把庄家扎好，
那她就会成为我心上人。

你要去斯卡布罗集市吗？
那里有欧芹、鼠尾草、迷迭草和百里香，
代我问候那儿的一位姑娘，
她曾是我心上的人。

语言点解析

(1) Scarborough Fair：斯卡布罗集市

Scarborough：译为斯卡布罗，也有根据读音或词义译为其他名字的。Borough 在英国意指享有特权的自治城市，在美国为自治村镇。

fair *n.*：有时写作 fairground，指集市场所

(2) Parsley, sage, rosemary, and thyme.

欧芹，即西芹、洋芫荽，可供食用；鼠尾草(灰绿色蒿属植物)；迷迭香(也称作艾菊)和百里草(也称麝香草)。这几种植物在每段歌词的第二句出现，在歌中呈和声颂唱(canticle)形式，起到一种谐音的作用。利用几种植物即感物怀人，又增加了歌曲本身的无穷韵味。

(3) Remember me to one who lives there：请代我向住在那儿的她问候。

Remember sb. to sb.：代……致意，代……问好

One：这里指一位不便说出名字或身份的人。歌中第四句歌词点明了她的身份。

(4) She once was a true-love of mine. 她曾经是我的心上人。

True-love：(忠实的)恋人，爱人

例如：

a true-love knot：(象征忠贞爱情的)同心结

(5) without no seams nor needle-work. 所有的接口都要用手工缝制。

句中采用否定之否定，意为"所有的接缝"。**Needle-work**：指用机器缝制。所以，原句可译为 You should seam up the shirt without using sewing-machine. 你不要用机器去缝制这件衬衣。

(6) Between the salt water and the sea strands. 在海水和海滩之间。

salt water：sea water 海水

sea strand：海滨，海滩

(7) And gather it all in a bunch of heather. 用一束石楠把庄稼全捆好。

gather *vt.*：聚集，使……聚拢；搜集

例如：

I suggest we ***gather*** enough firewood to last the night. 我建议大家捡足够多的木柴来撑过这一晚。

This would help the prosecutor ***gather*** evidence against him which could be used in court. 这将

有利于控方律师搜集对他不利的证据以在法庭上指控他。

注释与赏析

《斯卡布罗集市》这首歌是保罗·西蒙(Paul Simon)和阿特·加蓬凯尔(Art Garfunkel)创作并演唱的。西蒙以其严肃的创作主题，对流行音乐的不断探索和追求，多次获得美国的葛莱美音乐大奖。他们二人于1989年获得了美国乐坛最高荣誉“摇滚殿堂名人”奖。

这首歌在英国民谣中非常流行。保罗曾于1964~1965年期间在英国度假，并经常出没于英国民谣圈演唱，这首歌实际上是回忆当时的演唱并重新谱写的。歌曲《斯卡布罗集市》表现的是一位在前线作战的士兵对恋人的思恋，士兵请求去斯卡布罗集市镇的人带去给姑娘的问候。在每一段歌词的第一句后，插入了一句看似毫不相关的唱词：“那里有欧芹、鼠尾草、迷迭草和百里香”。正是这句歌词反复出现，使歌曲的怀旧气氛被浓墨重彩，使人对斯镇自然纯朴的美丽风光充满了无限的向往。在歌曲中出现的和声颂唱(Canticle)使得这首抒情歌曲韵味无穷。

这首歌作为60年代最受美国大学生欢迎的电影《毕业生》的插曲，曾被那一代人特别是那一代青年学生视为至爱。在学生运动风起云涌和嬉皮士运动的叛逆潮流中，这首歌为什么会引得那一代人对它情有独钟？或许，一方面是对青春时代的清纯和爱情的缅怀，另一方面是在用梦幻般的曲调和轻吟低诉的唱词，在编织着有关战争的童话。西蒙与加蓬凯尔用他们民歌式的朴素的歌词和动人心扉的吉他，再配以天衣无缝的和声，使这首充满情感梦幻般的歌曲触动着每个人的心弦。

11. El Condor Pasa
(老鹰之歌)

1=G 4/4

Words by Danfiel Alomia Robles & Paul Simon
Music by Daniel Alomia Robles

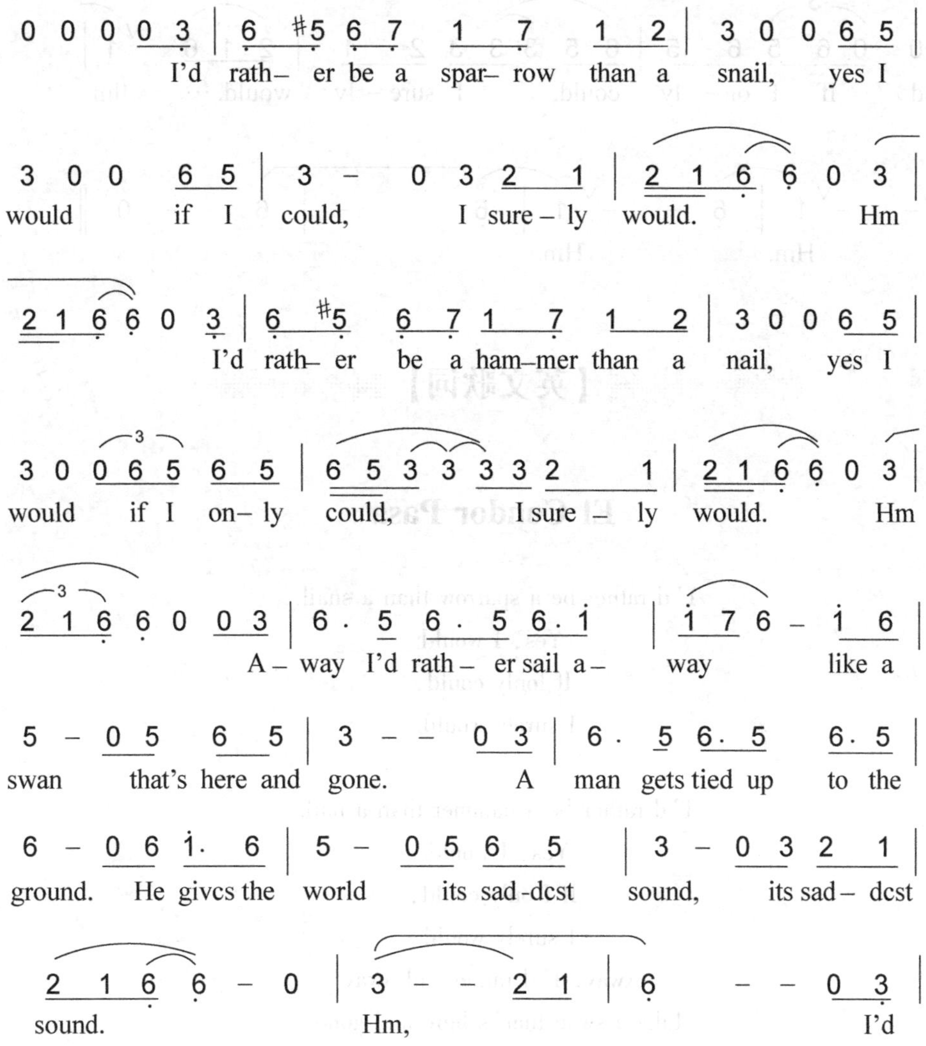

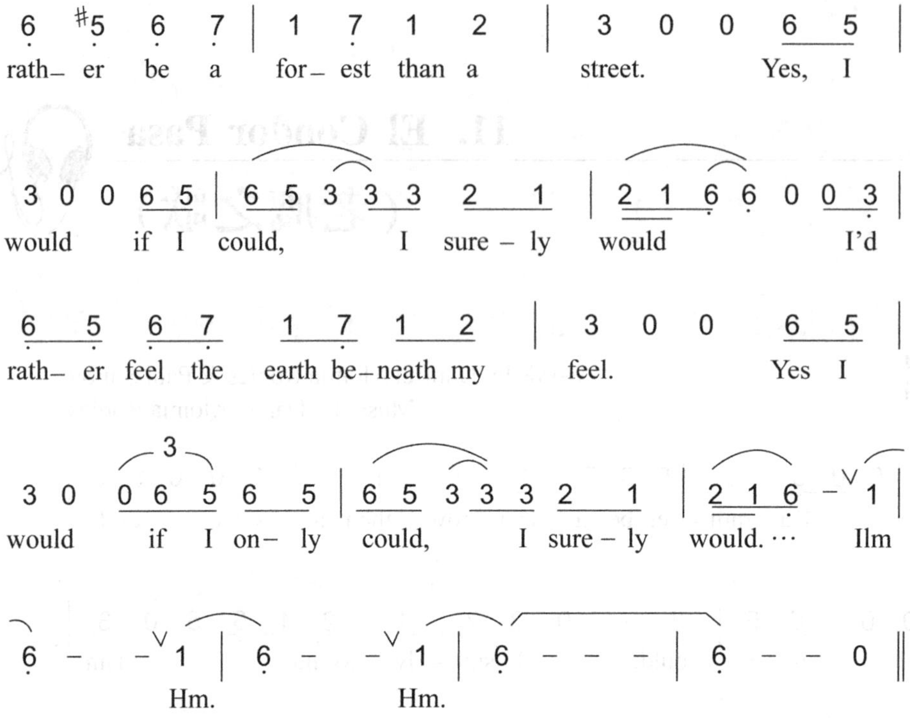

【英文歌词】

El Condor Pasa

I' d rather be a sparrow than a snail.
Yes, I would
If Ionly could,
I surely would.

I' d rather be a hammer than a nail.
Yes, I would.
If I only could,
I surely would.
Away, I' d rather sail away
Like a swan that' s here and gone.
A man gets tied up to the ground.
He gives the world its saddest sound,

Its saddest sound.

I' d rather be a forest than a street.
Yes, I would.
If I could,
I surely would.
I'd rather feel the earth beneath my feet.
Yes, I would.
If I only could,
I surely would.

【参考译文】

老鹰之歌

我宁可当麻雀也不当蜗牛。
我宁愿如此。
如果我能够,
我当然愿意。

我宁可当铁锤也不当铁钉。
我宁愿如此。
如果我能,
我当然愿意。

飞走,我宁可飞走,
像天鹅一样来去自由。
人被地面束缚,
发出的声音最悲,
声音最悲。

我宁可当森林也不当街道。
我宁愿如此。
若我能做到,
我当然愿意。
我宁可感觉脚踏实地。

我宁愿如此。
如果如此，
我肯定愿意。

语言点解析

（1）E1 Condor Pasa：The Condor Flies Away. 秃鹰飞去了。
condor *n.*：大秃鹰

（2）**would rather...than...**：宁愿……而……，宁愿……也不……
例如：
I would ***rather*** be a teacher ***than*** a guide. 我宁愿当老师而不当导游。
I would ***rather*** die ***than*** beg for his help. 我宁可死也不去乞求他的帮助。

（3）**sparrow** *n.*：麻雀；snail：蜗牛

（4）If I could. =If I could be a sparrow.

（5）I surely would. =I surely would be a sparrow.
surely：certainly, of course.

（6）**hammer** *n.*：铁锤

（7）**nail** *n.*：钉子

（8）**sail away**：fly away

（9）Like a swan that's here and gone. 像天鹅一样自由，刚才还在此，现在已飞去。

（10）That's here and gone 是个定语从句，修饰 swan。

（11）**swan**：天鹅，也是高飞于空的自由鸟

（12）A man gets tied up to the ground. 一个人被束缚在土地上。

（13）**get tied up to**：被束缚

例如：He ***gets tied up to*** trivial affairs. 他被一些无关紧要的小事束缚住了。

(14) He gives the world the saddest sound：向世人唱出最悲哀的歌。

the world：指人间

(15) I' d rather be a forest than a street：我宁愿当森林也不当街道。

(16) I' d rather feel the earth beneath my feet：我宁可感觉大地就在我脚下。

注释与赏析

《老鹰之歌》("El Cóndor Pasa")原是秘鲁一带的印地安民歌，歌词以克丘亚语写成。后来作曲家Daniel Alomía Robles于1913年按照安第斯山区民谣风格重新进行了谱写，并用西班牙语填上了歌词，作为同名音乐剧的主题曲。该歌曲具有浓厚的拉丁美洲乡间音乐风格。

《老鹰之歌》真正在世界范围内家喻户晓要归功于美国民谣歌手保罗·西蒙(Paul Simon)。1965年，他和中学同窗好友搭档阿特·加芬克尔(Art Garfunkel)在巴黎一家剧院演出时，遇上了秘鲁的"印加人(Los Incas)"乐队。西蒙被乐队的安第斯音乐风格和阿洛米亚·罗布莱斯的作品深深吸引，于是，他在第二年邀请"印加人"乐队录制了《老鹰之歌》的器乐部分，并为它填上了英语歌词，改名为《老鹰之歌(如果我能够)》，收录在他的著名专辑Old Friends Live On Stage中。由西蒙和加芬克尔合唱的这首歌曲一跃成为世界流行音乐排行榜上的热门金曲。此后，又有许多音乐人将其改编成摇滚、流行、爵士，甚至拉丁舞曲等多种风格演唱，《老鹰之歌》由此传遍世界，成为欧美国家介绍安第斯音乐的标牌乐曲。1980年，它在德国多特蒙德欧洲音乐节上被评为"世界上最美的歌曲"。然而，在南美安第斯国家，人们并不接受保罗·西蒙填词的英语版本。许多当地乐队翻唱的这首歌曲，用的全都是原版歌词的古印加凯楚亚语版或者西班牙语版。他们认为，这才真正代表了《老鹰之歌》的精神。

保罗·西蒙和阿特·加蓬格尔是20世纪60年代世界流行乐坛上的最佳重唱组之一，俩人的演唱配合得天衣无缝，表现手法变化多姿。西蒙的嗓音珠圆自然，加蓬格尔的音乐轻柔高洁，两人和声如诗一般优美，令人如痴如醉。加之保罗·西蒙富于哲理的歌词，具有戏剧色彩的吉他弹奏以及加蓬格尔对声音细腻的完美处理，奠定了二人进入世界级的超级歌星中的地位。60~70年代是西蒙和加蓬格尔音乐生涯中的最佳时期。在这十几年中他们佳作迭出，风靡世界。

歌中先用了三对物体作比较：麻雀与蜗牛、铁锤与铁钉、森林与街道，作者选择了每一对的前者。相比之下，它们享有更大的自由。歌中还有另一对比较物，即天鹅与人。天鹅高飞于空，自由自在；而人被束缚在土地上，唱出悲哀的歌声。但最后一段很有现实感，作者希望能脚踏实地地，所以，作者希望获得的是实实在在，不脱离实际的自由。这样，理想与现实即可达到完美的统一。

12. Sailing

（远航）

1=G $\frac{4}{4}$

Words & Music by
Gavin Sutherland

(5 6 | 3 2 1 4 3 2 1 | 1 — — —) | 0 0 0 5 6 ‖: 1 1 0 3 5 | 6 6 0 6.5 |
I am ①sailing I am sailing home a–
②flying I am flying like a
③hear me? Can you hear me through the

5 4. 0 4.3 | 3 — 0 4 3 | 3 2 2 0 3 2 | 1 1 0 5 6 | 3 2 2 0 2 1 |
gain 'cross the sea. I am sail–ing stormy waters, to be near you to be
bird 'cross the sky. I am fly –ing passing high clouds, to be with you to be
dark night far a– way? I am dy –ing forever crying, to be with you Who can

1 — — 5 6 :‖‖: 1 1 0 3 5 | 6 6 0 6.5 | 5 4. 0 4.3 | 3 — 0 4 3 |
free. I am④sailing, We are sailing home a–gain 'cross the sea. We are
free. Canyou
say? (▲)Theyare

3 2 2 0 3 2 | 1 1 0 5 6 | 3 2 2 0 2 1 | 1 — — — :‖
sail – ing stormy waters to be near you, to be free. D.S

【英文歌词】

Sailing

I am sailing, I am sailing.
Home again 'cross the sea.

I am sailing stormy waters,
To be near you, to be free.

I am flying; I am flying,
Like a bird 'cross the sky.
I am flying passing high clouds,
To be near you, to be free.

Can you hear me? Can you hear me,
Through the dark night far away?
I am dying, forever crying,
To be with you; who can say?

I am sailing; we are sailing
Home again 'cross the sea.
We are sailing stormy waters,
To be near you, to be free.

Oh Lord, to be near you, to be free.
Oh Lord, to be near you, to be free.
Oh Lord, to be near you, to be free.
Oh Lord

【参考译文】

远　　航

我在远航，我在远航，
跨越海洋，回到家乡。
我在远航，迎着风暴，
向你靠近，获得自由。

我在飞翔，我在飞翔，
像只鸟儿，飞越天空，
我在飞翔，与你同行，
穿越白云，获得自由。

远隔万里，茫茫夜空，
你可听到，我的哭声，
我将死去，与你远离，
我在哭泣，为靠近你。

我们远航，我们远航，
跨越海洋，重返家乡，
我在远航，跨越海洋，
向你靠近，获得自由。

向你靠近，获得自由，
想你靠近，获得自由。
向你靠近，获得自由，
今生今世，直到永远。

语言点解析

（1）I'm sailing stormy waters to be near you. =I'm sailing towards you through the rough sea. 我在波涛汹涌的海洋中向着你的身边航行。
stormy waters：波涛汹涌的水域。

（2）flying like a bird：像鸟一样飞翔

（3）'cross the sky=across the sky：飞越天空

（4）passing high clouds：穿越白云

（5）Through the dark night far away. =sailing through the dark night far away. 在遥远的夜空下航行。

（6）**far away**：in a remote place：在遥远的地方
例如：
The airport is ***far away*** from here. 机场离这儿很远。

（7）I'm dying. =I'm going to die. 我很快就要死去

(8) Forever crying to be with you. =Although I'm going to die, I'll long for returning home for all time. 尽管我将死去，我仍将永远把你呼唤，我要把家还。这几行表达了主人公至死不渝、归心似箭的思乡情。

(9) **forever**: always, for all time. 永远
例如:
I'll love you ***forever***. 我将永远爱你。

注释与赏析

这首歌的词曲均由卡文·苏泽兰德(Gavin Sutherland)创作。Sailing 是 Rod Stewart 演唱的一首歌曲，收录于1975年02月14日发行的专辑 Atlantic Crossing 中。这首歌也是《哥伦布传》("1492: Conquest of Paradisc")的主题曲。

歌手洛·史都华(Rod Stewart)，1945年1月10日出生于伦敦，英国的国宝级歌手，豆沙般的嗓音，桀骜不驯的舞台形象，源源不断的创作灵感构成了他的形象。他的这首"Sailing"更成为英文情歌代表作，听得连中国人的耳朵都起了茧子，他的歌声丝丝的、毛毛的，再加上温暖而细腻的和声，如同一只小狗的舌头，将你的手心舔了一遍又一遍。"Sailing"曾获得1975年英国冠军曲。1975年对洛·史都华(Rod Stewart)而言是个崭新的开始：移居美国筹备新专辑的录音，加入新东家华纳唱片，正式离开 Faces 全心拓展个人事业。专辑《跨越大西洋》("Atlantic Crossing")在8月发行，由唱片标题反应出洛苹身来到美国以全新伴奏阵容完成此作；专辑唱片按AB面分为快、慢歌两部分，据说这是他当时的爱人——瑞典女演员 Britt Eland 的建议，结果反应热烈，洛·史都华再展多彩多姿的摇滚巨星风采。专辑中"I Don't Wanna Talk About It"和"Sailing"都是听众非常熟悉且一再传诵的两首抒情佳作。

歌曲表达了作者思乡、怀乡、恋乡的感情，歌中讲述了作者浪迹天涯，远离家乡，跨海远航的经历。面对茫茫夜空，无边的大海，作者无限惆怅。纵然生命之火将熄灭，但叶落归根之情却永恒。为重返家乡，迎着风景，坚定信念，直到永远。这首歌放映出作者无时无刻不在思恋家乡，接近家乡，并获得真正自由的心声。歌曲朴实无华、意境悠远，既有心情的宣泄，又带点淡淡的忧伤，透出一股苍茫，给人以力量。漂洋过海只为与你在一起，有谁会不感动？

13. Green Sleeves
(绿袖子)

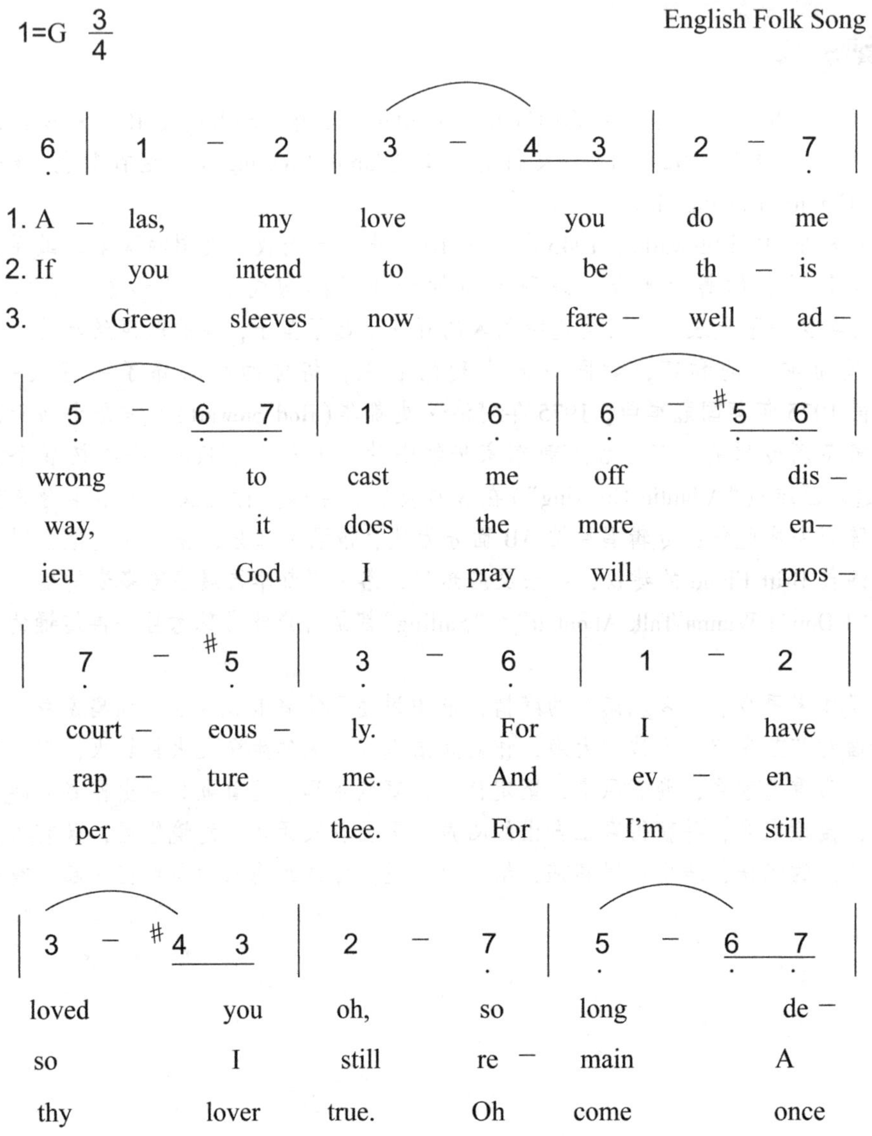

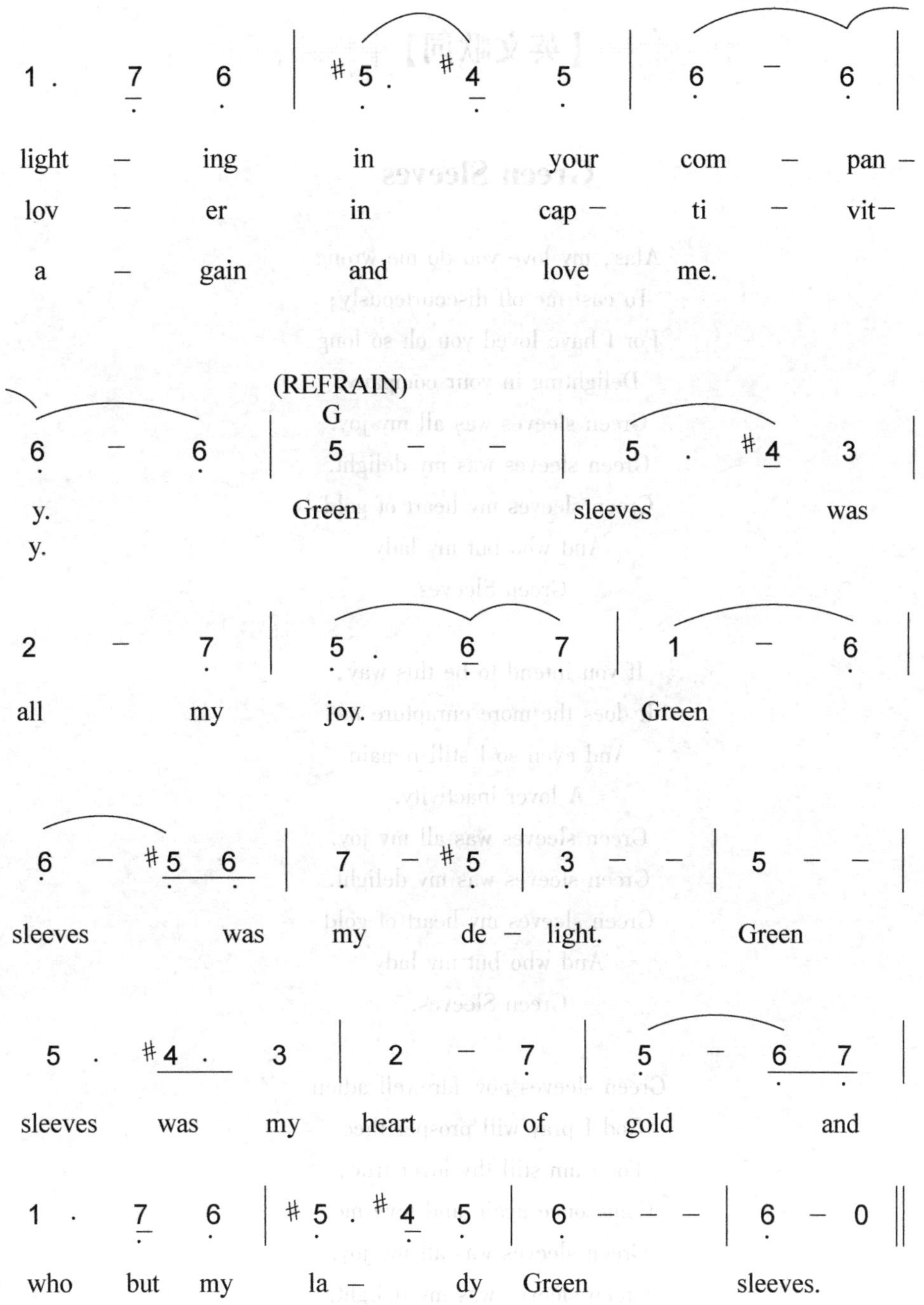
light – ing in your com – pan –
lov – er in cap – ti – vit –
a – gain and love me.
(REFRAIN)
G
y. Green sleeves was
y.
all my joy. Green
sleeves was my de – light. Green
sleeves was my heart of gold and
who but my la – dy Green sleeves.

【英文歌词】

Green Sleeves

Alas, my love you do me wrong
To cast me off discourteously;
For I have loved you oh so long
Delighting in your company.
Green sleeves was all my joy.
Green sleeves was my delight.
Green sleeves my heart of gold
And who but my lady
Green Sleeves.

If you intend to be this way,
It does the more enrapture me.
And even so I still remain
A lover inactivity.
Green sleeves was all my joy.
Green sleeves was my delight.
Green sleeves my heart of gold
And who but my lady
Green Sleeves.

Green sleeves now farewell adieu
God I pray will prosper thee.
For I am still thy lover true,
Come once again and love me.
Green sleeves was all my joy.
Green sleeves was my delight.
Green sleeves my heart of gold
And who but my lady
Green Sleeves.

【参考译文】

绿袖子

啊，我的爱人，你错待了我，
抛弃了我你无义又无情，
我已爱上你，啊，这么久，
有你陪伴多高兴。
绿袖子是我快乐的全部，
绿袖子是我全部的欢乐。
绿袖子是我金子般的心，
只有她才是我的心爱人，
绿袖子。

如若你想要这样，
那会使我更高兴。
即使这样我仍会，
做一个爱情的俘虏。
绿袖子是我快乐的全部，
绿袖子是我全部的欢乐。
绿袖子是我金子般的心，
只有她才是我的心爱人，
绿袖子。

绿袖子，你要告别离去，
我祈祷上帝为你保佑，
但我还是你的恋人，
回来吧，把我爱恋

绿袖子是我快乐的全部，
绿袖子是我全部的快乐。
绿袖子是我金子般的心，
只有她才是我的心爱人，
绿袖子。

语言点解析

(1) Alas, my love, you do me wrong：啊，亲爱的，你错待了我。

Alas [əˈlæs] *interj.*：（表示痛苦、悲伤或害怕、遗憾、不安的叫声）意为：啊啊；哎呀

例如：

Alas，she is gone. 啊啊！她走掉了。

(2) To cast me off discourteously. =To throw me off discourteously. ……抛弃了我，你无义无情。

cast off 意为：抛弃，摆脱，释放

discourteously 是由形容词 courteous 加前后缀构成的。Dis-是个前缀，表示“不”的意思。如：dishonest。

(3) Delighting in your company =Very glad and happy in your company. 有你在身边多高兴。

company（集合名词）意为：伙伴，朋友，同行的人

(4) If you intend to be this way. 如若你一定要这样。

intend to（do）：intend doing 打算

例如：

I don't ***intend*** to be a meal-ticket for anyone. 我无意供养任何人。

They ***intend*** to get their way, by hook or by crook. 为达到目的，他们不择手段。

(5) It does the more enrapture me：It makes me much happier than anything else. 那的确使我更疯狂。

the more：越发，更

enrapture [inˈræptʃə(r)] *vt.*：使狂喜

(6) And even so I still remain a lover in captivity. 即使这样我也是一个爱情的俘虏。

remain *vi.* 留下，逗留，依然

例如：

They went, but I remained. 他们走了，但我留了下来。

captive *n*. 俘虏；adj. 被捕的，被禁的

captivity *n.*（派生的名词）意为：监禁

(7) Green sleeves now farewell adieu. 绿袖子现在要告别说再见。

adieu [əˈdjuː] *int.* 告别

例如：

bid sb. adieu：向某人告别

make（或 take）one's *adieu*：辞行

(8) God I pray will prosper thee: God I pray will bless you. 我祈祷上帝保佑你。

prosper *vt.* & *vi.*：繁荣、成功

例如：

It is not an empty talk to promote world peace, ***prosper*** globe economy! 促进人类和平，振兴全球经济才不可能成为一句空话！

Our country is ***prospering***. 我们的国家正在欣欣向荣。

Thee：you (宾格)你

在古语、诗歌和歌词中常出现这种形式，下面是第二人称单数的宾格的对应形式，这些形式应熟记，以提高阅读速度和理解能力。

Thou→you (主格) thy→your(所有格) thee→you (宾格)

注释与赏析

《绿袖子》是一首英国民谣，在伊丽莎白女王时代就已经已广为流传，具体作者不详，相传是英王亨利八世所作，他是位长笛演奏家。传说这首曲子描述的是国王亨利八世的爱情。

这个在传说中相当暴戾的男人，却真心爱上一个民间女子，那女子穿一身绿衣裳。某天的郊外，阳光灿烂。他骑在马上，英俊威武。她披着金色长发，太阳光洒在她飘飘的绿袖上，美丽动人。只一个偶然照面，他们眼里，就烙下了对方的影子。但她是知道他的，深宫大院，隔着蓬山几万重，她如何能够超越？唯有选择逃离。而他，阅尽美女无数，从没有一个女子，能像她一样，绿袖长舞，在一瞬间，住进他的心房。从此他念念不忘。但斯人如梦，再也寻不到。思念迢迢复迢迢，日思夜想不得，他只得命令宫廷里的所有人都穿上绿衣裳，好解他的相思。他寂寞地低吟："唉，我的爱，你心何忍？将我无情地抛去。而我一直在深爱你，在你身边我心欢喜。绿袖子就是我的欢乐，绿袖子就是我的欣喜，绿袖子就是我金子的心，我的绿袖女郎孰能比？"曲调缠绵低沉。终其一生，他不曾得到她，一瞬的相遇，从此成了永恒。

这首民谣的旋律非常古典、优雅，略带一丝凄美之感，是一首描写对爱情感到忧伤的歌曲，但它受到世人喜爱的层面却不仅仅局限在爱情的领域，有人将它换了歌词演唱，也有人将它作为圣诞歌曲，而它被改编为器乐演奏的版本也是多不胜数。从广义上讲，音乐可分为流行音乐和严肃音乐。严肃音乐包括交响乐、室内乐、歌剧、颂歌和大合唱。流行音乐则分为古典通俗音乐、社交与民间舞曲、传统民歌和现代流行音乐。《绿袖子》这首歌明显属于传统民歌形式，具有典型的地方特色和风格趣味，反应出一个民族对待爱情的体现和态度。

《绿袖子》这首歌曲就像我国一些民歌，如《渔光曲》和《四季歌》那样旋律优美柔绵、曲调清婉隽永，表现出地方民族的生活情趣及爱憎喜恶，同时也有着《花儿为什么这样红》那样火热炽烈的少数民族的热情。歌中的情感别有天地：虽然心上人错待了我，而我仍然无怨无悔，一心一意地爱下去，哪怕永远被抛弃，心中爱的感情也要永葆金色，并为之祈祷。或许，绿袖子只是心爱人的代表和象征，也许是心上人的衣着，也许是心上人对颜色的偏好，这不仅是我快乐的全部，也是我金子般心灵的美好体现。这种对心上人不存在任何虚伪、杂质的爱才是世界上最纯洁、最高尚的真爱。

14. Devoted to You

(全心爱着你)

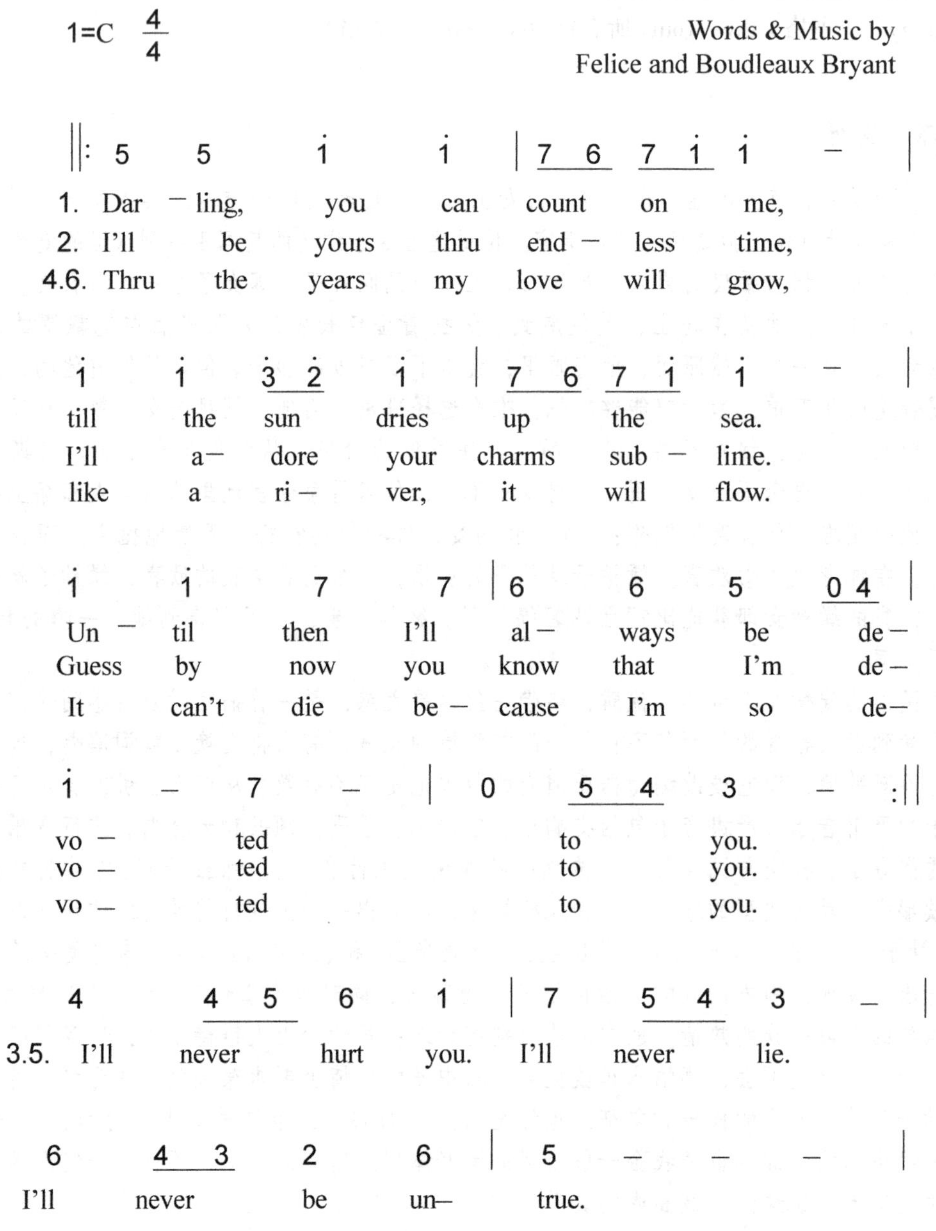

4 4 5 6 1̇ | 7 5 3 6 – |
I'll never give you rea – son to cry.

6 6 6 6 7 1̇ | 7 6 5 4 ||
I'll be un– happy if you were blue.

【英文歌词】

Devoted to You

Darling you can count on me,
Till the sun dries up the sea.
Until then I'll always be
Devoted to you.

I'll be yours till endless time.
I'll adore your charms sublime.
Guess you know by now that I'm
Devoted to you.

I'll never hurt you.
I'll never lie.
I'll never be untrue.
I'll never give you reason to cry.
I'll be unhappy,
If you were blue.

Through the years our love will grow.
Like a river it will flow.
It can't die because I'm so
Devoted to you.

I'll never hurt you.
I'll never lie.
I'll never be untrue.

I'll never give you reason to cry
I'd be unhappy,
If you were blue.

Through the years our love will grow.
Like a river it will flow
It can't die because I'm so
Devoted to you.

【参考译文】

全心爱着你

你可期望依靠我，
哪怕太阳使大海枯干。
到那时我仍爱你，深深地爱你。
我永远都属于你。
你的魅力让我着迷。
现在你该猜到我深深地爱你。

永不伤害你，
不欺骗你，
你面对的是真诚，
永不会让你伤心流泪。
你心情不快，
我也会悲伤。

岁月流逝，爱也会加深，
就像河水永不停息。
爱会永存，
因为我深深地爱你。

永不伤害，
不欺骗你，
你面对的是真诚，
永不会让你伤心流泪。

你心情不快，
我也会悲伤。

岁月流逝，爱也会加深，
就像河水永不停息。
爱会永存，因为我深深地爱你。

语言点解析

(1) **count on (upon)**：指望，期望，依靠
例如：
count on self-reliance：依靠自力更生
You'd better not ***count on*** a raise. 你最好不要指望提高工资。

(2) until then. =until the time when the sun dries up the sea. 直到太阳使大海枯干。

(3) **to be devoted to sb**. (sth.)：献身于……；专心于……
例如：
to ***be devoted to*** the people：全心全意为人民

(4) endless time =forever. 永无止境。

(5) **adore**：崇拜，敬慕，很喜欢
例如：
We all ***adore*** your charms：我们都为你的魅力而着迷。

(6) **sublime**：令人赞叹的；异常的，极端的。该词用来修饰前面的 charms。

(7) Guess by now. = You should guess by now. 现在你该猜到。

(8) If you were blue. 如果你心情不快。
blue *adj*：指情绪低落，心绪不佳。

(9) thru = through

(10) It can't die：句中 It 指 love.

注释与赏析

《全心爱着你》词曲作者为波尔多·布赖恩特 Boudreaux Bryant 和菲利斯·布赖恩特(Felice Bryant)夫妇。最好的录音版本由“艾佛利兄弟”(The Everly Brother)演唱。

“艾佛利兄弟”由 Don Everly 和 Phil Everly 二人组成。两人成名于摇滚乐新兴的 1957 年，他们融合乡村、摇滚、节奏与蓝调的风格，加上两人和谐的二重唱和声令他们的歌曲不仅在当时游走流行、乡村、节奏蓝调三大榜，而且也成为后人一再重唱世纪不朽的流行歌谣。他们最大的成就不仅在他们所缔造的排行成绩，他们也是第一个以二重唱形态成为巨星的团体，于是这样的组合与演唱方式深深影响了后来的西蒙 & 加芬克尔、披头士、海滩少年……

《全心爱着你》是一首纯真的爱情歌曲。曲调舒缓、轻柔，表达了一个人对爱的真诚，对永恒的爱的追求。爱是有生命的，就像歌曲中唱的“岁月流逝，爱也会加深，就像河水，永不停息。”爱一个人就要善待一个人。当你播撒真诚，有所付出的时候，爱的种子就会给你带来甜蜜、丰硕的收获。由“艾佛利兄弟”演唱的这首歌曲，曾列入美国流行歌曲排行榜第 10 名，澳大利亚流行歌曲排行榜第 25 名，加拿大流行歌曲排行榜第 1 名。此外，该歌曲还获得美国乡村音乐第 7 名、节奏蓝调(R&B)排行榜第 2 名。

15. Jingle Bells
(铃儿响叮当)

1=F 4/4

5 3 2 1 5 0 5 5 | 5 3 2 1 6 0 |

1. Dash−ing thro' the snow, in a one− horse o− pen sleigh (06)
2. A day or two ago, I thought I'd take a ride and
3. Now the ground is white. Go it while you' re young.

6 4 3 2 7 0 | 5 5 4 2 3 1 0 |

O'er the fields we go (0 7) laugh − ing all the way, (05)
Soon Miss Fa − nie Bright was seat− ed by my side. The
Take the girls to− night and sing this sleig− hing song. Just

5 3 2 1 5 0 | 5 3 2 1 6 0 6 |

bells on bob − tail ring, (05) mak − ing spir − its bright. What
horse was lean and lank. Mis − for − tune seemed his lot; he
get a bob − tail bay. Two for − ty for his speed; Then

6 4 3 2 5 5 5 5 | 6 5 4 2 1· 0 |

fun it is to ride and sing a sleigh − ing song to−night.
got in − to a drift− ed bank, and we, we got up−set.
hitch him to an o− pen sleigh, and creak you'll take the lead

3 3 3 3 3 3 | 3 5 1 . 2 3 . 0 |

Jin − gle bells, Jin − gle bells, Jin −gle all the way!

4 4 4 · 4 4 3 3 3 3 | 3 2 2 1 2 5 |

Oh! What fun it is to ride in a One− horse o− pen sleigh!

3 3 3 3 3 3 | 3 5 1 · 2 3 · 0 |
Jin – gle bells, Jin – gle bells, Jin – gle all the way!

4 4 4 · 4 4 3 3 3 3 | 5 5 4 2 1 · 0 ‖
Oh! What fun it is to ride in a One – horse O – pen sleigh!

【英文歌词】

Jingle Bells

Dashing through the snow,
On a one–horse open sleigh,
Over the fields we go,
Laughing all the way,
Bells on bobtail ring,
Making spirits bright.
What fun it is to ride and sing
A sleighing song tonight.

Jingle bells, jingle bells,
Jingle all the way.
Oh what fun it is to ride
In a one–horse open sleigh.
Jinglebells, jingle bells,
Jingle all the way.
Oh what fun it is to ride,
In a one horse open sleigh.

A day or two ago,
I thought I 'd take a ride
And soon Miss Fanny Bright
Was seated by my side
The horse was lean and lank
Misfortune seemed his lot
He got into a drifted bank,

And we, we got upset

Jingle Bells, Jingle Bells
Jingle all the way
Oh! What fun it is to ride,
In a one-horse open sleigh.
Jingle Bells, Jingle Bells,
Jingle all the way.
Oh! What fun it is to ride,
In a one horse open sleigh

Now the ground is white,
Sodo it while you're young.
Take the girls tonight,
And sing this sleighing song.
Just get a Bob Tailed Nag,
Two forty for his speed.
Then hitch him to an open sleigh,
And creak you'll take the lead.

Jingle Bells, Jingle Bells
Jingle all the way
Oh! What fun it is to ride,
In a one-horse open sleigh.
JingleBells, Jingle Bells,
Jingle all the way.
Oh! What fun it is to ride,
In a one horse open sleigh.

【参考译文】

铃儿响叮当

冲破大风雪,
坐在单马雪橇上,
奔驰过田野,

一路笑声多欢畅。
马铃响叮当，
令人精神爽。
坐在橇上唱滑雪歌，
今晚多快活。

叮叮当，叮叮当，
铃儿一路响！
(哦，)坐在单马雪橇上，
精神多爽朗！

叮叮当，叮叮当，
铃儿一路响！
(哦，)坐在单马雪橇上，
精神多爽朗！

一两天前，
我想坐雪橇，
范妮·布莱特小姐很快
坐在我身旁，
那匹马守又长，
命运不怎么样，
掉进了漂流的河塘，
我们黯然神伤。

叮叮当，叮叮当，
铃儿一路响！
(哦，)坐在单马雪橇上，
精神多爽朗！
叮叮当，叮叮当，
铃儿一路响！
(哦，)坐在单马雪橇上，
精神多爽朗！

四周都是白色的。
走起来，趁着你还年轻。
今晚带着女孩，
唱着雪橇歌，

找只短尾褐马，
他速度240。
系在敞蓬雪车上。
然后驾起马，你将带起头。

叮叮当，叮叮当，
铃儿一路响！
(哦,)坐在单马雪橇上，
精神多爽朗！
叮叮当，叮叮当，
铃儿一路响！
(哦,)坐在单马雪橇上，
精神多爽朗！

语言点解析

(1) 前四行的正常语序应是：Dashing through the snow in a one-horse open sleigh，we go over the fields laughing all the way.

dash *vi*.：move quickly 急冲

例如：

His wife ***dashed*** into his office. 他的妻子冲进他的办公室。

a one-horse open sleigh：一个由一匹马拉的无棚的雪橇

one-horse：是一个合成词，指由一匹马拉的

a one-horse 中的 one 前边用 a 而不用 an，是因为**one**：读作[wʌn]，[w]不是元音因素。

…o' er the fields we go：我们在田野上奔驰。

O' er 是 over 的省音形式，用 o' er 是为了省去一个音节。这种现象在诗歌中常见。

laughing all the way：一路上笑个不停

dashing 和 laughing 都是现在分词，作谓语动词 go 的伴随状语。

例如：

They came talking and laughing. 他们边说边笑地走来。

all the way："一路上"的意思

例如：

She came to the capital begging ***all the way*** to look for her husband. 她沿路乞讨到京城，找她的丈夫。

(2) Bells on bobtail ring. =挂在短尾马上的铃儿叮当作响。

bobtail：短尾巴的动物，尤指马和狗。

ring *vi.*：响

例如：

The telephone is ***ringing***. 电话铃在响。

(3) making spirits bright：令精神欢快

making 是个现在分词，作谓语动词 ring 的伴随状语，也可以说表示结果。

spirits：指坐在雪橇上的人们的精神

bright：high

例如：

They are in ***bright spirits***. 他们情绪高昂。

She is in low ***spirits***. 她情绪低落。

(4) What fun it is to ride and sing a sleighing song tonight. 今晚坐在雪橇上唱一支滑雪歌，这多么好玩呀!

what fun：相当于 how interesting(funny)。

例如：

What fun it is to ride on a donkey. 骑驴真好玩!

(5) a day or two ago：一天或两天以前，也可以译成"一两天以前"。

ago 表示从说话时算起；**before** 表示"以前"时，指截止到过去某一时间。

例如：

He came three days ***ago***. 他是三天以前来的(从今天算起往前推)。

He came here yesterday. But he had been here **before**. 他是昨天来这儿的，但他以前曾来过这里(这一句中 before 是昨天以前。)

(6) I thought I'd take a ride：I thought I would take a ride. 我想我要坐雪橇兜一圈。

I would 表示过去将来时。

take a ride：指乘某种交通工具兜一圈

例如：

He ***took a*** bus ***ride*** in the city. 他乘公共汽车在市里兜了一圈儿。

(7) was seated by my side：sat beside me

be seated：表示状态，指已坐好；sit 表示动态。

例如：

Please ***sit*** down. 请坐下。

by my side：beside me

例如：

Come andsit ***by my side*** if you love me. 如果你爱我就过来坐在我身旁。

(8) lean and lank：又瘦又长，也指又瘦又高。

(9) Misfortune seemed his lot. 不幸似乎就是他的命运。
lot："命运"的意思。
draw lots：抽签，抽签决定；拈阄儿；抓阄儿

(10) got into a drifted bank = fell into a drifted bank

(11) We got upset. = We got sad and unhappy.

注释与赏析

这首歌是由约翰·皮尔庞特(1805—1880)年创作的。约翰·皮尔庞特毕业于耶鲁大学，当过教师、律师、推销商。这首歌已成为圣诞节不可缺少的部分。歌中虽没有耶稣、圣诞老人等，但歌中的风雪、雪橇、小马拉车、铃声、歌声令人欢快不已。这首歌原本是作为圣诞礼物送邻居孩子们。

这是一首十分欢快的圣诞歌曲，有不同的版本，所以有不同的唱法。有时不唱中间一段，只唱一、三段(见前边曲谱)，有时演唱者只唱前两段，不唱第三段。歌中所唱(除瘦马掉入泥塘令人伤心外)尽是欢乐情景。在浓浓的圣诞气氛里，年轻人充分领略大自然的美丽及其给人带来的欢乐。他们坐着雪橇，冲破风雪，驰骋田野上，一路上笑声朗朗，好不快活，好不逍遥！与歌声同时飘扬的是系在短尾马上的铃铛发出的叮当声。"叮叮当，叮叮当，令人精神爽"。坐着雪橇，唱着雪橇歌，风声，笑声、铃声，伴着雪橇的滑动声，这一切汇于一起，使得这个晚上非常快活，然后四行迭唱加重了这种欢乐的气氛。

16. The End of the World

(世界末日)

1=D 4/4

Words and Music by Skeeter Davis

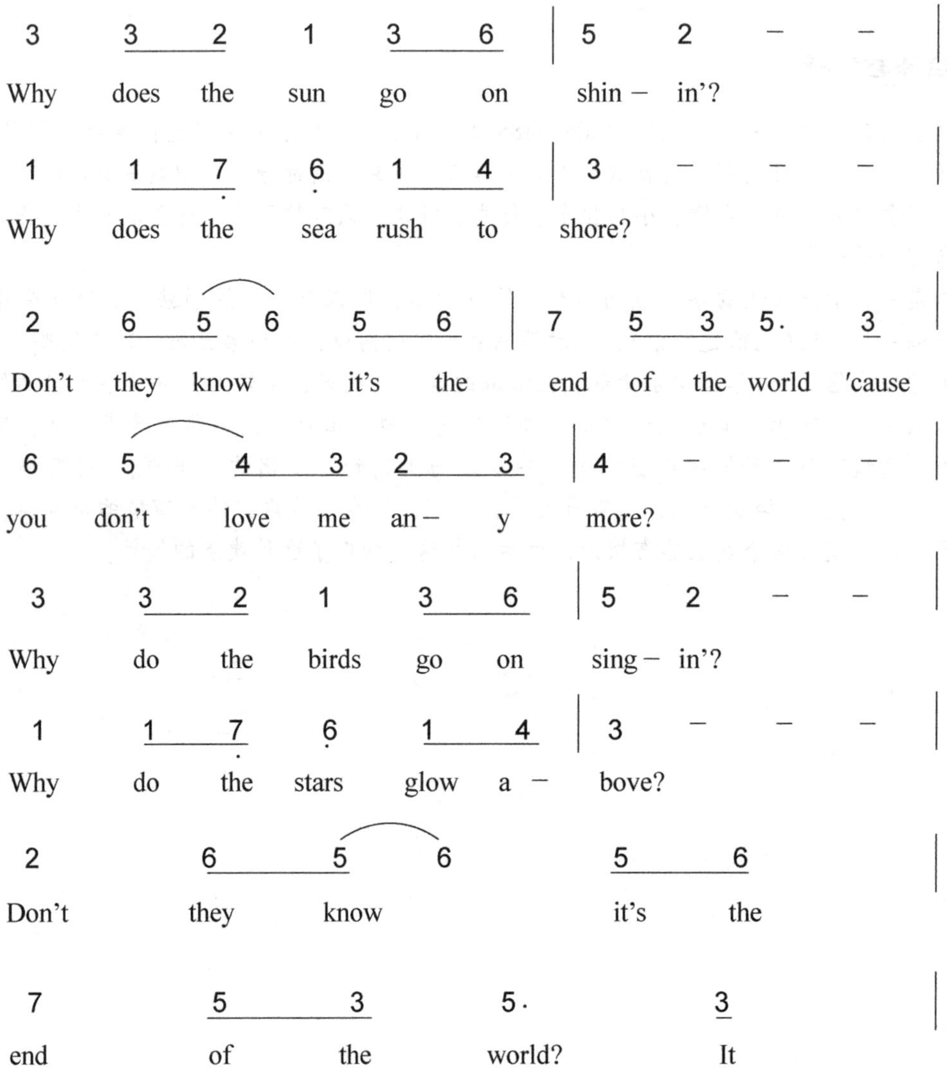

6 4 2 1 7 2 1 – – 1

end – ed when I lost your love. I

6 6 1 1 4 4 6 6 5 3 – 3

wake up in the mornin' and I won – der why

4 3 4 5 4 5 3 – – 5

ev' ry – thing's the same as it was. I

7 5 3 5 3 5

can't un – der – stand. No, I

7 5 3 5. 3

can't un – der – stand. how

6 5 4 3 2 3 4 – – –

life goes on the way it does.

3 3 2 1 3 6 5 2 – –

Why does my heart go on beat – in'?

1 1 2 3 1 4 3 – – –

Why do these eyes of mine cry?

2 6 5 6 5 6

Don't they know it's the

7 5 3 5. 3

end of the world? It

6 4 2 1 7 2

end – ed when you said good–

1. 1 – – – | 2. 1 – – –

bye. bye.

【英文歌词】

The End of the World

Why does the sun go on shining?
Why does the sea rush to shore?
Don't they know it's the end of the world.
'Cause you don't love me any more?

Why do the birds go on singing?
Why do the stars glow above?
Don't they know it's the end of the world?
It ended when I lost your love.

I wake up in the morning and I wonder
Why everything's the same as it was.
I can't understand, no I can't understand.
How life goes on the way it does

Why does my heart go on beating?
Why do these eyes of mine cry?
Don't they know it's the end of the world?
It ended when you said goodbye

Why does my heart go on beating?
Why do these eyes of mine cry?
Don't they know it's the end of the world?
It ended when I lost your love.

I wake up in the morning and I wonder
Why everything's the same as it was.
I can't understand, no I can't understand.
How life goes on the way it does

Why does my heart go on beating?

Why do these eyes of mine cry?
Don't they know it's the end of the world?
It ended when you said goodbye

【参考译文】

世界末日

阳光为何依旧灿烂?
海水为何冲洗沙滩?
难道不知道世界末日已来到,
因为你不再把我爱恋了?

鸟儿为何依旧欢唱?
群星为何仍在闪耀?
难道不知道世界末日已到来?
没有爱世界就不存在。

我清晨醒来发现一起依旧,
什么都没有丝毫改变。
我无法明白,不,我无法明白
生活为何周而复始,去了还回来。

心为何依旧跳动?
眼为何浸满泪水?
难道不知道世界末日已到来?
你与我分手,世界末日便到来。

心为何依旧跳动?
眼为何浸满泪水?
难道不知道世界末日已到来?
你与我分手,世界末日便到来。

语言点解析

(1) **go on doing**：继续做某事

例如：

If you go on smoking, you'll suffer from cancer some day. 如果你继续抽烟，总有一天你会患上癌症。

(2) **rush** *vi*：急去，赶去，使……急去

例如：

He ***rushed*** out of the store. 他从商店里冲出来。

They ***rushed*** the injured boy to the hospital. 他们急忙把负伤的孩子送到医院。

(3) 'cause = because

(4) **glow** *vi*.：发光，发热

例如：

Coloured lights ***glowed*** on the festival night. 节日的夜晚灯火辉煌。

(5) **wonder** *vt*. & *vt*.：不知道，想知道；怀疑

例如：

I ***wondered*** what that noise was. 我纳闷儿那是什么声音。

It makes you ***wonder*** about the effect on men's behaviour. 这让人怀疑其对男性行为的影响。

(6) Why everything's the same as it was：为什么一切都是老样子

the same as：像……一样

例如：

China is no longer **the same** as it was. 中国不再是过去的旧中国了。

(7) How life goes on the way it does? 生活是怎样以它自己的方式过下去。

注释与赏析

"The End of the World"是 Skeeter Davis 作词、作曲并演唱的一首英文歌曲。这首歌曲是作者为怀念亡父所写，体现出了无助和哀愁，让听着感受到对生命的叹息。

这首 1963 年乡村及流行排行榜双料亚军、Cashbox 年终冠军的歌曲，虽是流行曲风，但由 Skeeter Davis 演唱，却赋予其不同的生命，在键盘连绵的三连音中，少女诉说着无助的哀愁，全曲流畅而抒情，声部和音亦来自歌者本人。半个多世纪过去了，当耳畔重又响起她纯

真而略显生涩的歌声，您听到了什么？失恋的故事还是对于生命的叹息？我们应该珍爱此歌，如上所述所言，并不在歌曲的本身，而在于歌者所带来的气息，如同微微风中远去的芬芳……

记得英国诗人乔叟说过："伤心的人应有潦倒的伴侣，愁苦的事应有悲惨的阵容。"爱的种子不一定会结出甜蜜的果实，它也许会结出苦果。如果你失恋了，那你就得自食苦果。那滋味肯定会和感到世界末日来临的滋味差不多，那么，拿生命作为你的伴侣？怎么来布设你的阵容？

古人云：何以解忧，唯有杜康。我们说，借酒消愁愁更愁，何不引吭高歌，宣泄你的情感，换来一个全新的自我？

17. Changing Partners

（交换舞伴）

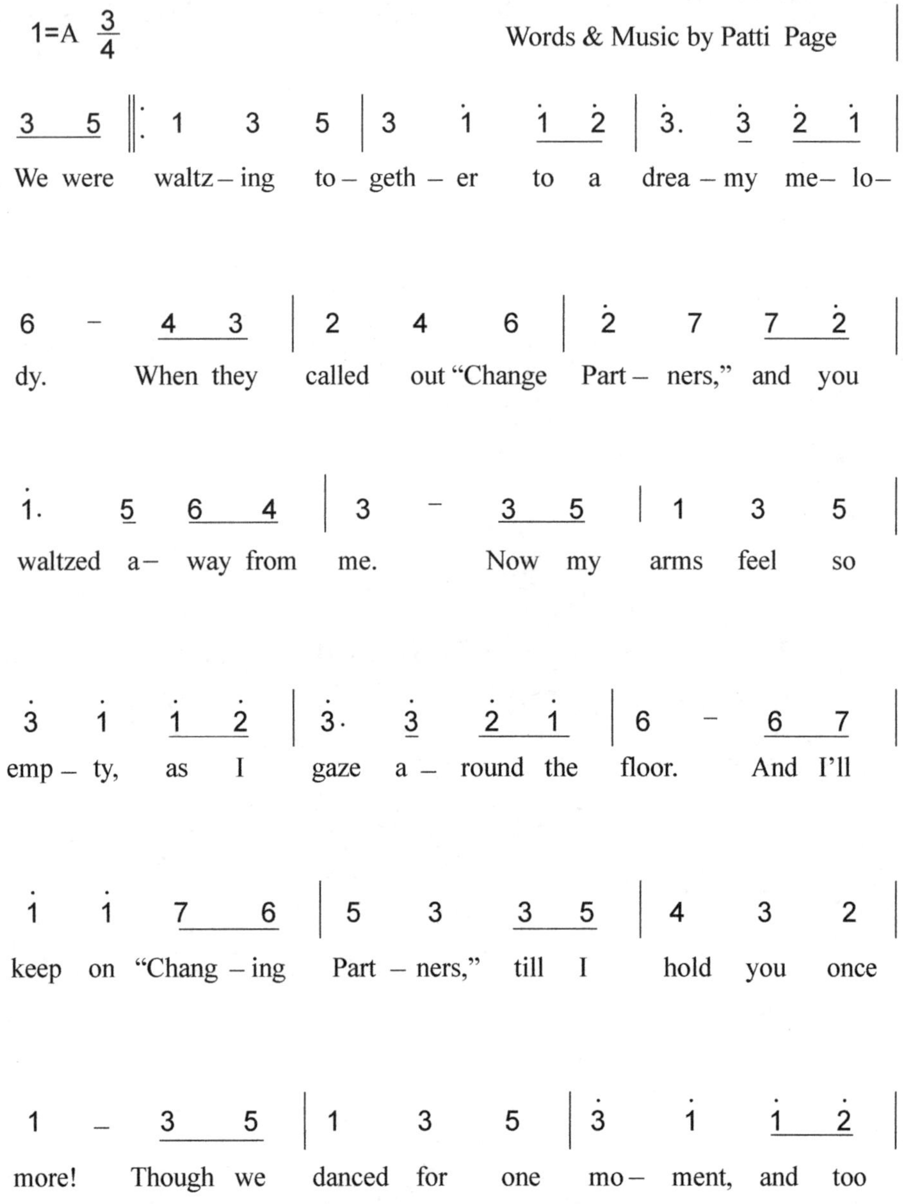

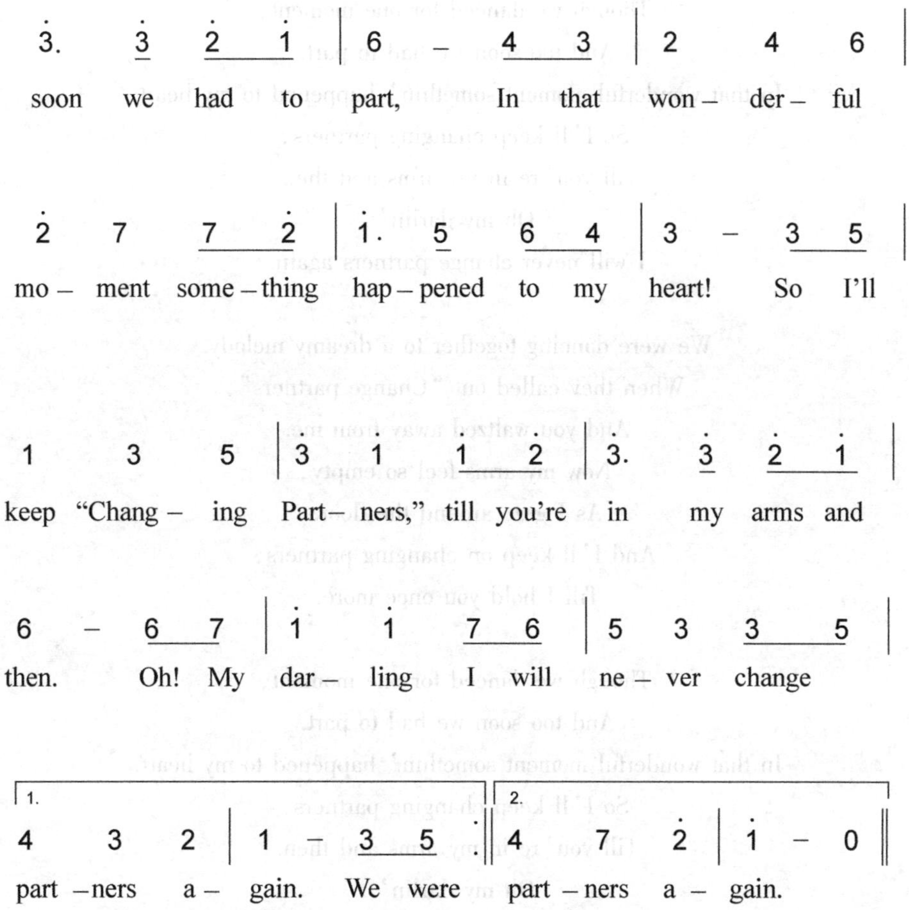

【英文歌词】

Changing Partners

We were waltzing together to a dreamy melody,
When they called out "Change partners",
And you waltzed away from me.
Now my arms feel so empty,
As I gaze around the floor.
And I'll keep on changing partners,
Till I hold you once more

Though we danced for one moment,
And too soon we had to part.
In that wonderful moment somethin' happened to my heart.
So I'll keep changing partners,
Till you're in my arms and then.
Oh my darlin'
I will never change partners again.

We were dancing together to a dreamy melody.
When they called out "Change partners",
And you waltzed away from me.
Now my arms feel so empty,
As I gaze around the floor.
And I'll keep on changing partners,
Till I hold you once more.

Though we danced for one moment,
And too soon we had to part.
In that wonderful moment somethin' happened to my heart.
So I'll keep changing partners,
Till you're in my arms and then.
Oh my darlin'
I will never change partners again.

【参考译文】

交换舞伴

跟随梦一般的旋律，
我们一起跳华尔兹，
当他们喊道："交换舞伴。"
你舞着离开了我。
现在我的双臂空空，
眼睛环顾着舞池，
我要不断地交换舞伴，
直到我再能触拥你。

虽然我们没跳多久，
并且很快就分手。
在那美妙的一刻，
我的心像着了火。
因此我不断换舞伴，
直到你回到我怀抱，
噢，亲爱的，
我将永远不再换舞伴。

跟随梦一般的旋律，
我们一起跳华尔兹，
当他们喊道："交换舞伴。"
你舞着离开了我。
现在我的双臂空空，
眼睛环顾着舞池，
我要不断地交换舞伴，
直到我再能触拥你。

虽然我们没跳多久，
并且很快就分手。
在那美妙的一刻，
我的心像着了火。
因此我不断换舞伴，
直到你回到我怀抱，
噢，亲爱的，
我将永远不再换舞伴。

语言点解析

（1）change partners：exchange partners 交换舞伴
exchange A for B：以 A 换 B
例如：
They ***exchanged*** petroleum ***for*** food. 他们以石油换食品。

（2）We were waltzing together. =We were dancing a waltz together.
waltz：*n.* 华尔兹；*vi.* 跳华尔兹舞

(3) to a dreamy melody = accompanied by fanciful tune

to 是个介词，可译为“伴着”“和着”“配”。

例如：

We sang the song ***to*** a new tune today. 我们今天和着新调子唱了这首歌。

(4) **dreamy**：peaceful 安详的，如梦的

例如：

She has ***dreamy*** eyes. 她长着静如秋水的眼睛。

(5) They are dancing to a soft and dreamy music. 他们正伴着梦幻般轻柔的音乐跳舞。

(6) You waltzed away from me. = You left me while still dancing a waltz.

move away from sb.：从某人处移开

(7) I gaze around the floor. = I fox my eyes on the floor.

(8) keep on changing partners = continue changing partners

keep on：继续；不断

例如：

Prices ***keep on*** increasing while my salary remains stable. 我的工资保持稳定，物价却持续上涨。

keep on at：不停地说或反复地要求

例如：

She ***kept on at*** him to buy her a new book. 她不停地要求他给她买一本新书。

(9) I hold you once more. =I have you in my arms once more.

hold *vt.*：拿住，握住，报

例如：

He was ***holing*** a baby when he entered the room. 他进屋时怀里抱着个孩子。

(10) Too soon we had to part：很快我们就分手了。

too soon 有分手太快而感到遗憾之意

part：(cause to) separate or no longer to be together(使)分开或不在一起

例如：

The war ***parted*** him from his wife. 战争使他和妻子分离。

The husband and wife had to ***part*** because of misunderstand-ing. 那对夫妇由于误会而分手。

(11) in that wonderful moment：在那美妙的一瞬间

例如：

In that wonderful moment，I left I was at the top of the world. 在那美妙的一刻，我感到我好像身在世界之巅。

(12) Something happened to my heart. =I began to have a kind of feeling that is subtle to express 某种事发生在心田。

happen to：发生于

例如：

What ***happened to*** him？他发生了什么事？

(13) keep changing partners：不断换舞伴

keep doing sth.：keep on doing sth. 继续做某事

(14) Till you're in my arms and then. = Till I hold you in my arms and then…

注释与赏析

这首歌的词曲作者是帕蒂·佩奇(Patti Page)。悠扬的曲调，迷人的舞姿，舞者产生梦幻般感觉。在如醉如痴的迷狂中，突然有人高喊："交换舞伴"。舞伴舞着离开，剩下"我"两臂空空，两眼茫茫，凝视四周，不停地交换舞伴，直到再能换到原来的舞伴。这一节歌词集中在"交换"这一动作上。交换舞伴给我带来了心里失落感。对于"我"来说，"交换"意为着"失去"。

还是在叙述心里上微妙的感觉。两人虽然共舞的时间不长，但在那美妙的一瞬间，一种感觉生于心田，那是共鸣，是共舞时和谐产生的情。对于跳舞的人来说，可能两人之间的和谐是最大的享受。难怪，许多人舞场相见，舞中生情，情中生爱。和谐的动作产生和谐的美，所以"我"要不断地交换舞伴，直到重新与原来的舞伴共舞。可是，为了爱情，"我"要打破舞场规则，不再交换舞伴。从第一节的失去舞伴到第二节中不愿失去舞伴，"我"巧妙地表达了对舞伴的爱慕之情。

这首歌旋律舒缓，略带伤感，歌词优美，有很强的抒情性，词曲达到了高度的统一。

18. Una Paloma Blanca

(白兰鸽)

1=C 4/4

Words & Music by Hans Bouwens

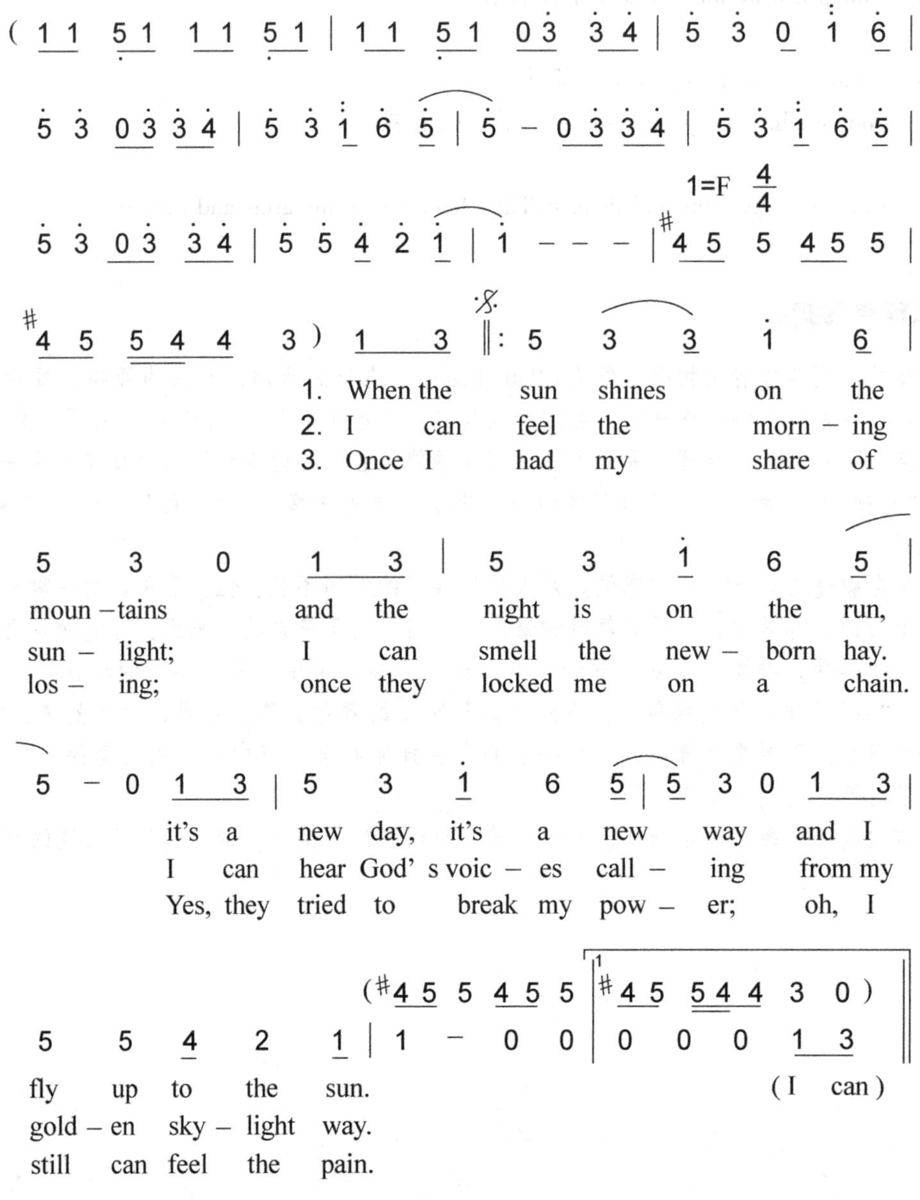

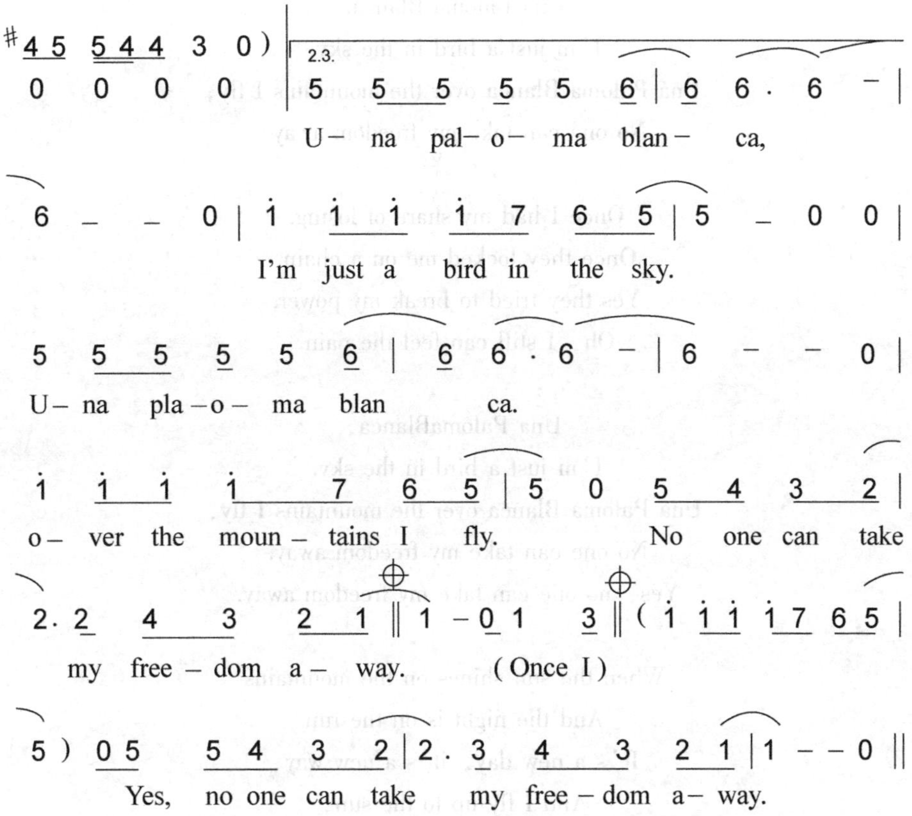

【英文歌词】

Una Paloma Blanca

When the sun shines on the mountains,
And the night is on the run,
It's a new day, it's a new way,
And I fly up to the sun.

I can feel the morning sunlight.
I can smell the newborn hay.
I can hear God's voices calling,
From my golden skylight way.

Una Paloma Blanca.
I'm just a bird in the sky.
Una Paloma Blanca over the mountains I fly,
No one can take my freedom away.

Once I had my share of losing.
Once they locked me on a chain.
Yes they tried to break my power.
Oh, I still can feel the pain.

Una PalomaBlanca,
I'm just a bird in the sky.
Una Paloma Blanca over the mountains I fly,
No one can take my freedom away.
Yes, no one can take my freedom away.

When the sun shines on the mountains
And the night is on the run
It's a new day, it's a new way,
And I fly up to the sun,

Una Paloma Blanca, I'm just a bird in the sky,
Una Paloma Blanca,
Over the mountains I fly.
No one can take my freedom away.

【参考译文】

白 兰 鸽

当太阳照耀高山上,
黑夜已经消亡,
这是新的一天,
新的生活!
我将飞向太阳!

我能感到早晨阳光，
我能闻到新晒干草，
我能听到上帝召唤之声，
声音来自金色天道。

一只白色的鸽子呀，
我只是天上一只鸟。
一只白色的鸽子呀，
我飞越群山。
没人能剥夺我的自由。

有一次我也曾不幸；
有一次他们链上我，
想毁掉我的力量，
哦，至今我仍然感到痛。

一只白色的鸽子呀，
我只是天上一只鸟，
一只白色的鸽子呀，
我飞越群山。
没人能剥夺我的自由。
没人能剥夺我的自由。

当太阳照耀在高山上，
黑夜已经消亡，
这是新的一天，
新的生活！
我将飞向太阳。

一只白色的鸽子呀，
我只是天上一只鸟。
一只白色的鸽子呀，
我飞越群山。
没人能剥夺我的自由。
没人能剥夺我的自由。

语言点解析

(1) Paloma(Spanish): dove
Blanca(Spanish): white
Paloma blanca: the white dove

(2) **On the run**: 奔逃，逃跑，忙碌，奔波
例如：
I've been on the run all day but I am not tired now. 我已奔波了一整天，但此刻还不累。
The thief was on the run when he was stopped by a policeman. 那个贼在逃跑时，一个警察拦住了他。
At a run: 跑着
例如：She came almost ***at a run***. 她几乎是跑着来的。

(3) **new-born** *adj.*: 新晒的，新生的
例如：
The cattle like to eat the ***new-born*** hay. 牲口喜欢吃新晒的干草。
This is a ***new-born*** republic. 这是一个新生的共和国。

(4) **sky-like**: 像天空一样的
这是一个合成词，由"**名词+like**"构成，表示"像……一样的"。
like: 可以组成许多合成词，像 bird-**like**，dog-**like**，doctor-**like**，pig-**like**，等等。
例如：
Panda is a ***bear-like*** animal. 熊猫是一种像熊一样的动物。

(5) I'm **just** a bird in the sky 中**just** 等于 only，merely，but.
例如：
Don't be angry with him. He is a ***just*** a child. 别跟他生气。他还是个孩子。

(6) **take away**: 拿走，剥夺
例如：Who ***took away*** my umbrella? 谁拿走了我的伞？

(7) locked me on a chain: tied me to a chain.

(8) **try to do sth.**: 企图做
try doing sth.: 做某事以试验另一事
例如：

He *tried to close* the window but he couldn't. 他想把窗户关上，但没关上。

He *tried closing* the window, but it was still very cold in the room. 他关上窗户试了试，但房间里还是很冷。

(9) **break one's power**：毁掉……的力量

break *vt*.：destroy

注释与赏析

这是一首非常欢快的歌曲，由汉斯·鲍温斯(**Hans Bouwens**)作词作曲。它歌颂自由，向往自由，给人以希望。歌中主角并非人，而是一只白兰鸽。当太阳升起并照耀群山时，这只鸽子心情异常激动，因为朝阳带来新的光耀，新的生活。同时，鸽子也讲了它差点失去自由的经历，旨在说明：无论人们怎么打算，自由乃上帝所赐，他们最终也不能够征服的。

自由是轻易剥夺不掉的，向往自由的心是不可征服的，希望人们也像白兰鸽这样乐观。

19. Love You More Than I Can Say

(爱你在心口难开)

1=C $\frac{4}{4}$

Words and Music by
Jerry Allison Sonny Cuertis

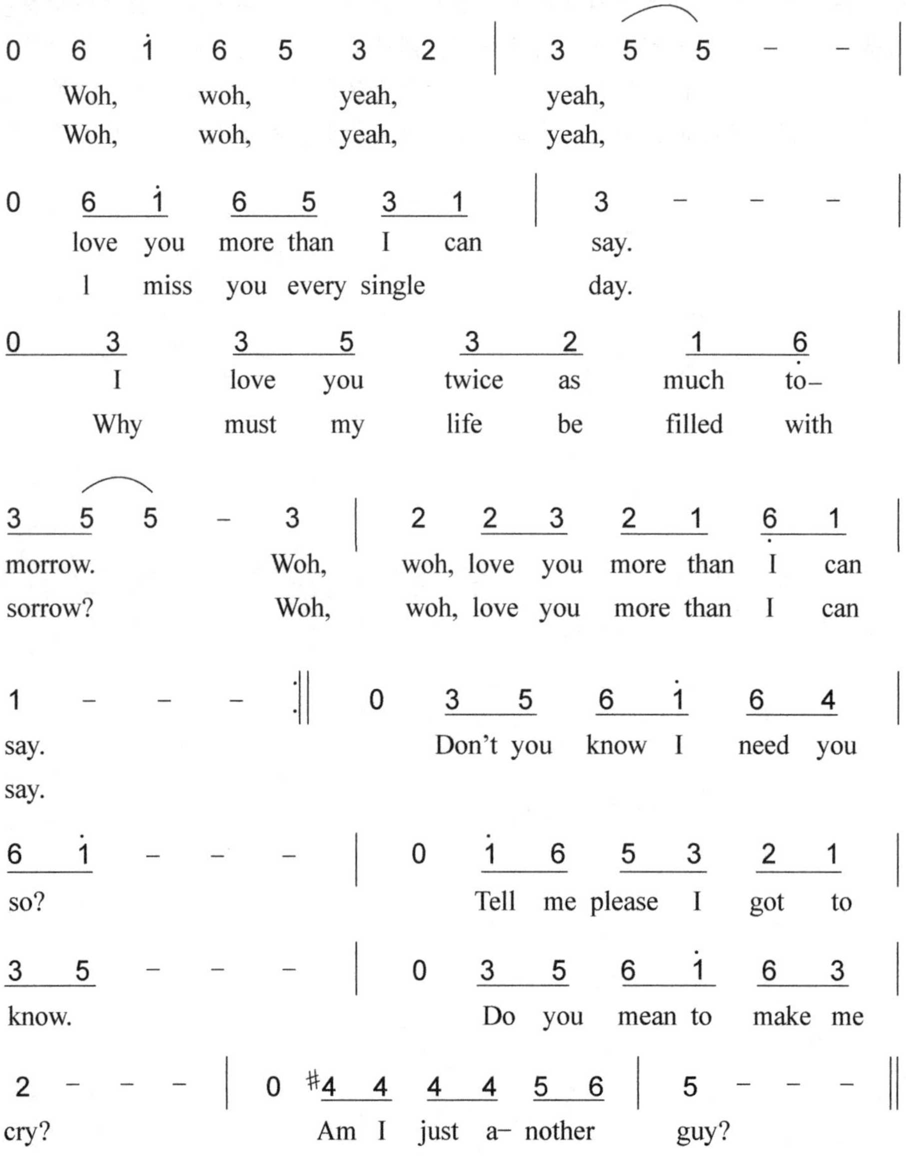

【英文歌词】

Love You More Than I Can Say

Woh-woh-yeah-yeah,
Love you more than I can say.
I love you twice as much tomorrow.
Love you more than I can say.
Woh - woh - yeah - yeah,
I'll miss you every single day.
Why must my life be filled with sorrow?
Oh, I love you more than I can say.

Don't you know I need you so?
Tell me please I get to know.
Do you mean to make me cry?
Am I just another guy?
Woh - woh - yeah - yeah,
I love you more than I can say.
I love you twice as much tomorrow.
Oh, love you more than I can say.

【参考译文】

爱你在心口难开

是呀，是呀，是呀，
爱你难用语言表达。
明天我会加倍爱你，
是呀，爱你语言难表达。
是呀，是呀，是呀，
我每天都把你思恋。
干嘛要用悲哀把生活填满？
是呀，爱你在心口难开。

你不知道我多么需要你?
告诉我，我必须要知道。
你是否想要我哭泣?
我是否成了另一人?
是呀，是呀，是呀，
爱你难用语言表达。
明天我会加倍爱你，
是呀，爱你在心口难开。

语言点解析

(1) Woh, woh, yeah: Oh, oh, yes, yes.
Yeah: yes 的变体。

(2) Love you more than I can say. =I love you so much at heart that I cannot express with words. / I love you but I am not good at expressing myself with words.

(3) I miss you every single day: I think of you every day.
single *adj*.: 单一的
例如:
She is still ***single***. 他仍是单身独处。
single 与 every, not 在一起使用，表示强调。
例如:
I read every ***single*** letter of hers 她的每一封来信我都读过。

(4) Why must my life be filled with sorrow? =Why must I fill my life with sorrow?
must: 必须，非要
例如: Why ***must*** I go there? 我干吗非要去那儿?
must 还当"偏偏"讲。
例如:
Why ***must*** the moon appear full when I miss my husband tar away? 为什么月亮偏偏在我思恋远方的丈夫时正好是圆的呢?

(5) Don't you know I need you so? =Don't you know I am in bad need of you?
Don't you...: 否定性修辞问句，不须回答。

(6) I get to know. =I have to know：I have got to know.

(7) Do you mean to make me cry? =Do you want to make me cry?

Am I just another guy? = Am I not the usual me? /Am I not the former self?

guy：fellow 口语中常用，意为：家伙；青年；人。

注释与赏析

这首歌由是杰瑞·埃利森(Jerry Allison)和桑尼·库尔梯斯(Sonny Curtis)创作的，由鲍比·李(Bobby Vee)唱红，80年代传入中国后风靡一时，至今仍被人们喜爱。

《爱你在心口难开》是用语言表达了主人公的爱。这位用唱来述说自己爱意的主人公，以不善辞令为托，却准确地对自己爱的决心作了表述，感情热烈却又恰到好处。好一个不善言辞！好一个“口难开”！简单的三段歌词，之后全部重复一遍，还是比较到位地倾诉了自己的情愿，也恰到好处地传递出自己的心声。

爱情，亘古以来一直是人类永恒的话题。歌中主人公并未使用华丽的辞藻、飞扬的文字，倒也质朴地表达出自己炽热的情感。文字不多，三次重复，或许这正是主人公言犹未尽，遗憾不能用语言完全倾露内心的真情。但只要爱心永在，心有灵犀，爱神是自会降临的。

20. Sealed with a Kiss

（以吻封缄）

1=F $\frac{4}{4}$

Words by P.Udell
Music by G.Geld

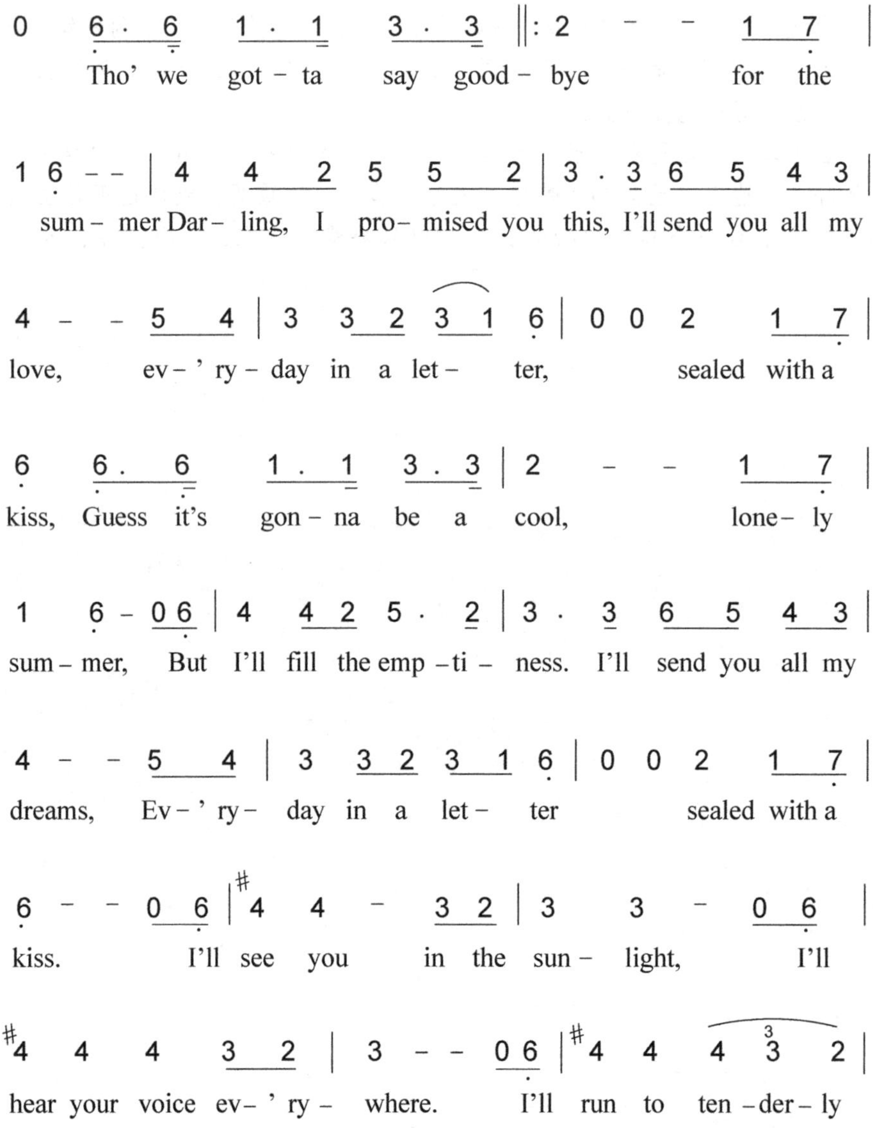

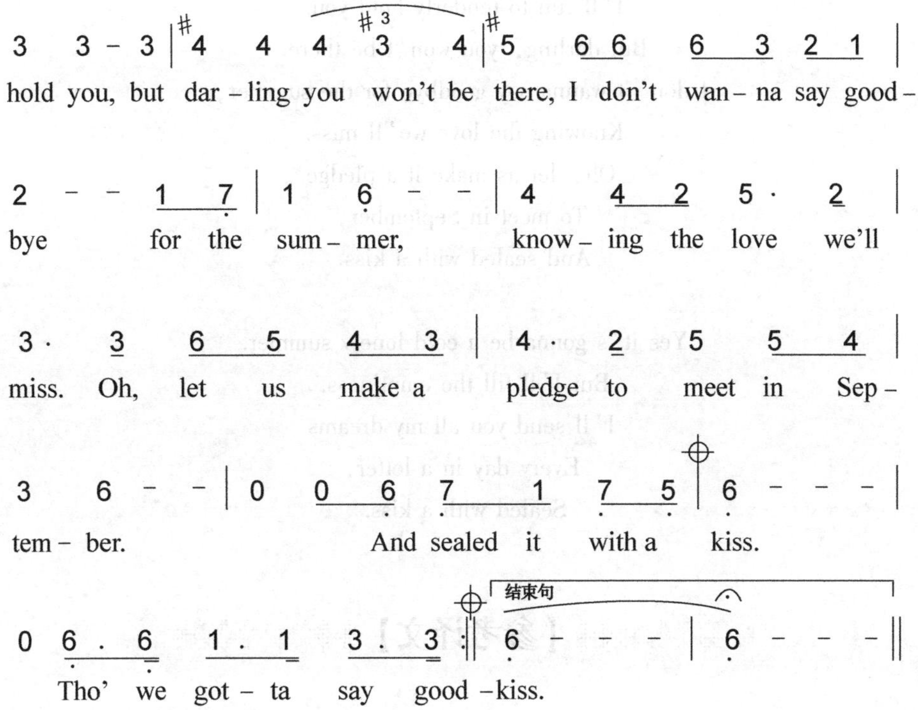

【英文歌词】

Sealed with a Kiss

Though we gotta say goodbye for the summer,
Darling, I promise you this:
I'll send you all my love every day in a letter,
Sealed with a kiss.
Yes, it's gonna be
A cold lonely summer.
But I'll fill the emptiness.
I'll send you all my dreams
Every day in a letter,
Sealed with a kiss.

I'll see you in the sunlight.
I'll hear your voice everywhere.

I'll run to tenderly hold you.
But darling, you won't be there.
I don't wanna say goodbye for the summer,
Knowing the love we'll miss.
Oh, let us make it a pledge
To meet in September,
And sealed with a kiss.

Yes it's gonna be a cold lonely summer.
But I'll fill the emptiness.
I'll send you all my dreams
Every day in a letter,
Sealed with a kiss.

【参考译文】

以吻封缄

虽然我们不得不分开度夏，
亲爱的，我答应你，
我要把爱送给你，
每天装在信封里，
以吻来封缄。
是的，今夏会是
冷酷又孤独，
但我要填补空虚：
送给你我所有梦境，
每天装在信封里，
以吻来封缄。

我将看见你在阳光里，
我将听见你的声音遍野。
我要跑过去温柔地拥抱你，
但亲爱的，你却不在。
我不想说再见，分开度夏，
知道我们会相思。

呵，咱们立个誓，
九月再相见，
以吻来封缄。

是的，今夏会是冷酷又孤独，
但我要填补空虚：
我要把爱送给你，
每天装在信封里，
以吻来封缄。

语言点解析

(1) **gotta**：have got to，have to 这是口语用法。

(2) Though we gotta say goodbye for the summer，…. =Although we have to part during the summer，…

(3) I'll send you all my love every day in a letter，sealed with a kiss：I'll write you a letter to express my love every day，and I'll seal the letter with a kiss.
seal *vt*.：盖于；封，密封
例如：He sealed the envelope and sent it to the post office. 他把信封好，送往邮局里去了。
sealed with：用……封住。Sealed with a kiss：以吻来封缄。

(4) I'll see you in the sunlight.
You 是宾语，in the sunlight 是宾语补足语，不是状语。

(5) I'll run to tenderly hold you. =(I'll see you，follow your voice) and I'll run over to hold you in my arms tenderly.

(6) But darling，you won't be there. 但亲爱的，你并不在那儿。可以看出，能见到她，听见她的声音。

(7) **fill the emptiness**：填补空虚

注释与赏析

这首歌的演唱者是鲍比·温顿(Bobby Vinton)，词曲作者分别是 P. 乌德尔(P. Udell)和

G.. 吉尔德(G. Geld)。鲍比·温顿生于1953年4月。在他成为一名歌手之前，他一直希望做一个大型乐队的指挥。然而命运并未安排他成为乐队的领导或指挥，却让他走红歌坛。1962年鲍比的歌曲《红红的玫瑰——我的爱》荣获排行榜首，之后他的许多歌曲都名列排列榜前十位之列。

《以吻封缄》是一首很具烂漫色彩的歌曲，叙离别情，但不伤感；道分手苦，但不低沉。夏天来临，主人公要与心爱的人分开一段日子，慢慢长夏，孤独又凄清，但主人公要把空虚填补：他要把没夜之梦写成书信，以吻封缄，寄给自己心爱的人。第二节用几个排比句子，幻想心上人不知的日子却处处见到她。见到她沐浴在阳光里，这是视觉在起作用；听见她的声音传遍各个角落，这是听觉在起作用；他要跑过去温柔地拥抱她，这是触觉在享受。但这只是男主人公的幻觉，不过也是伟大爱情的表现。

以吻封缄，多么热烈独到的方式，多么诗情画意的表白，轻轻的一个吻会深深地扣人心弦。过去的一吻会令人们思恋到今。有人用月亮代表他(她)的心，岂不知这封缄之吻更深情地代表恋人的心，与月亮相比，离我们更近。

21. Yesterday
(昨天)

1=G $\frac{4}{4}$

The Beatles

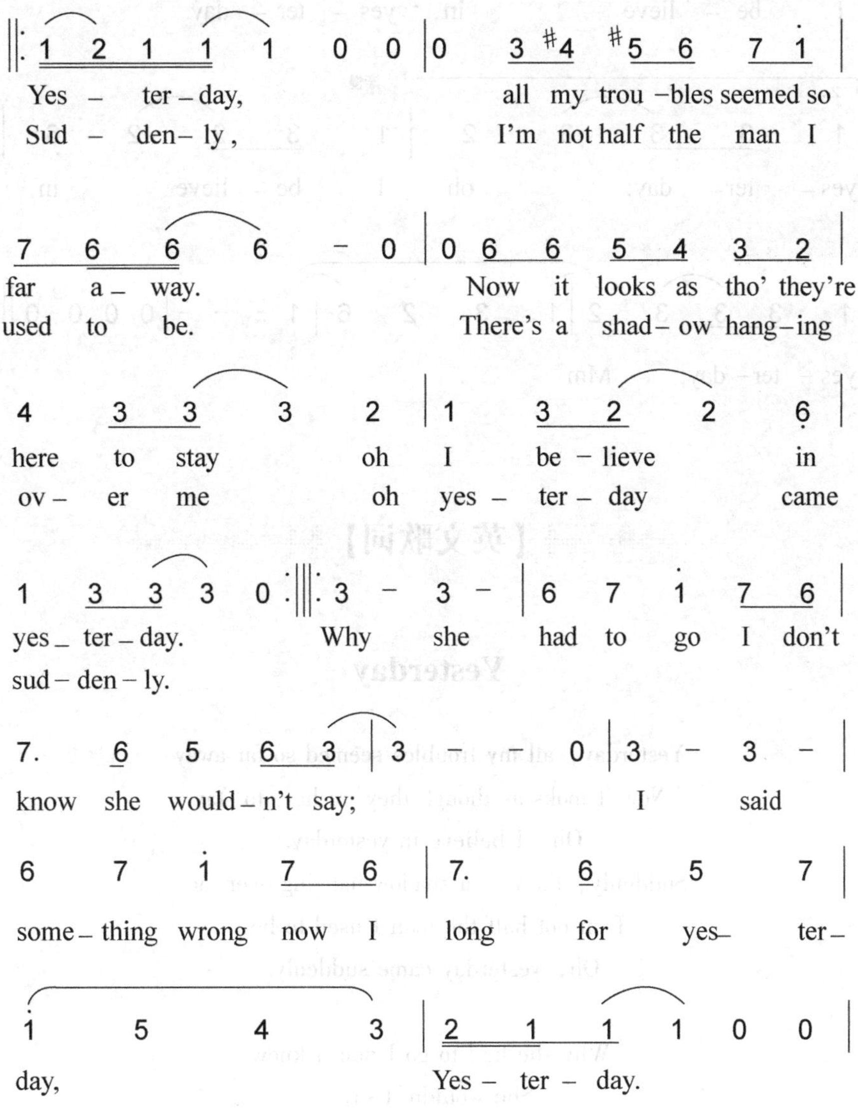

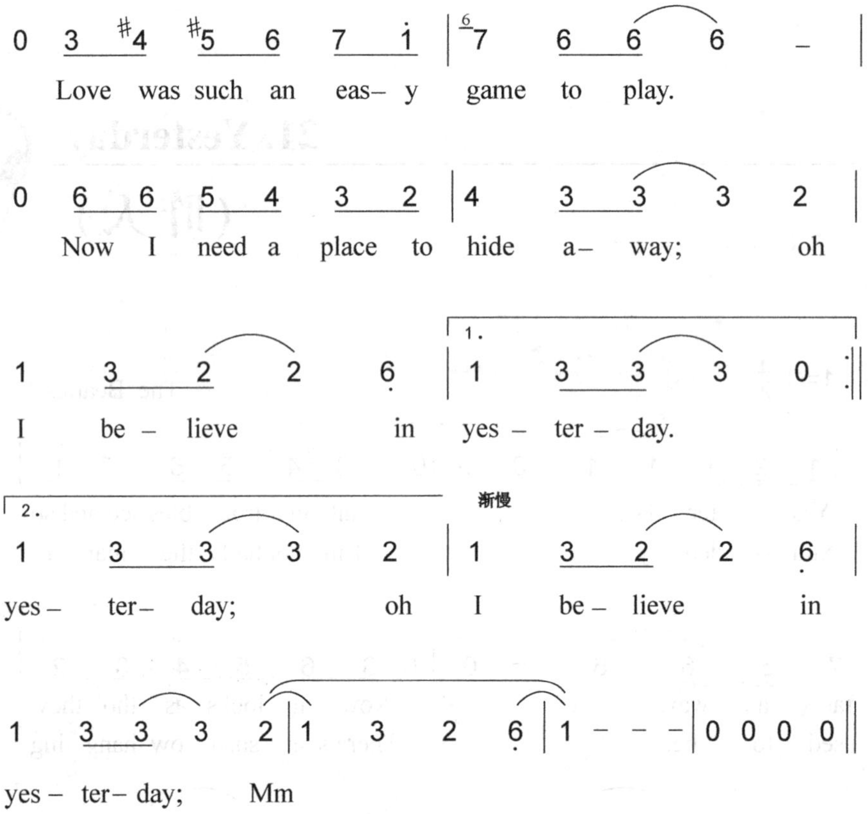

【英文歌词】

Yesterday

Yesterday, all my troubles seemed so far away
Now it looks as though they're here to stay
Oh, I believe in yesterday.
Suddenly, there's a shadow hanging over me.
I'm not half the man I used to be,
Oh, yesterday came suddenly.

Why she had to go I don't know
She wouldn't say.
I said something wrong,

Now I long for yesterday.
Yesterday, love was such an easy game to play.
Now I need a place to hide away.
Oh, I believe in yesterday.

Why she had to go I don't know
She wouldn't say.
I said something wrong,
Now I long for yesterday.
Yesterday, love was such an easy game to play.
Now I need a place to hide away.
Oh, I believe in yesterday.
Mm mm mm mm mm.

【参考译文】

昨 天

昨天，所有烦恼似乎很遥远。
今天，烦恼仿佛就在眼前，
噢，我信奉昨天。
猛然间，有个阴影笼罩着我。
我已不再是原来的我，
噢，昨天到来得太突然。
我不懂她为何要走，
她也不愿告诉我，
或许是我说错，
现在我渴望昨天。
昨天，爱情无忧无虑，
今天，我不得不躲闪，
噢，我信奉昨天。

我不知他为何要走，
她也不愿告诉我，
或许是我说错，
现在我渴望昨天。

昨天爱情无忧无虑，
今天，我不得不躲闪，
噢，我信奉昨天。
嗯……

语言点解析

(1) Yesterday, all my troubles seemed so far away: Yesterday, I didn't seem to have any troubles.

(2) Which were far away from me. 昨天，所烦恼似乎很遥远。

(3) Yesterday：此处并非指 the day before(前一天)，而是指“过去”“往日”“以前的时光”等。

(4) Now it looks as though they're here to say: Now it looks as if all my troubles still stay with me. 今天，我烦恼仿佛仍缠绕于我。

(5) Oh, I believe in yesterday. 噢，我信奉昨天。
believe in：相信(人格、价值)的存在

(6) Suddenly, I'm not half the man I used to be: Suddenly I came to realize I'm not myself as I used to be. 猛然间我意识到我已不再是自己。

(7) Why she had to go I don't know, she wouldn't say: I don't know why she went away from me, and she would not tell me the reason. 我不知她为何要离去，她也不愿告诉我理由。

(8) Now I long for yesterday: Now I look forward to yesterday. 现在我盼望昨天。
long(动词)意为：渴望，切盼(常与 for 或者 to 搭配)
long for +名词 = long to +动词原形，意为：渴望，切望
例如：
The people of the world ***long for*** the peace. 全世界人民渴望和平。

(9) Yesterday, love was such an easy game to play. = Yesterday, love was happy and lighthearted. 昨天，爱情轻松愉快、无忧无虑。

(10) Now I need a place to hide away: Now I have to escape from the reality. 今天，我需要躲避。

hide *vt*.：(动词 hid，hidden；名词)意为：把……藏起来，隐藏，躲藏。

例如：

A fox cannot ***hide*** its tail. 狐狸尾巴是藏不住的。

hide-and - seek：捉迷藏(比喻)与躲闪的人(物)打交道。

注释与赏析

《昨天》是甲壳虫乐乐队演唱的代表作品之一，于1965年9月25日发行这首单曲时就荣登英美两国排行榜首，并获得英国Ivory Novello奖。从1965年至1972年间有大约一千多位歌手演唱或翻唱过这首歌曲，这或许是世界上翻唱次数最多的歌曲。

约翰·列农1940年10月出生于英国的利物浦，16岁时结识了保罗·麦卡特尼并邀请参加了采石工乐队，1959年更名为银色甲壳虫乐队。他们冲向美国大陆后一直称为甲壳虫乐队，又因他们演唱时弹着吉他，披着长发，故而得到另一称谓——披头士乐队。由于甲壳虫乐队对英美及世界流行音乐作出了不可磨灭的贡献，因而受到世界各国青年的喜爱和崇拜，在他们的音乐生涯中多次荣获各种音乐大奖和英美排行榜的冠军。

此处选辑的《昨天》从曲式结构和节奏特点上采用了较为简单的两段式中的AABA形式，加上最后那个"姆"结尾句，实际上是最后A段结尾的重复演唱，曲式虽简单，但音乐的表现力却很丰富，具有很大的艺术容量。歌曲讲述了昨日的爱情给我带来了无比的幸福，而失去了爱的今天是多么令人难以承受。快乐美妙的昨日历历在目，从而使人更加怀恋以前。回避无爱的阴影，真好似《昔日恋情》中的某些情景再现眼前，也似《昨日再现》一样，都是昔日圣神幸福的爱的回忆。看来人们对失去的东西会加倍珍惜，爱情更是如此。

22. Yesterday Once More

（昨日重现）

1=$\frac{4}{4}$

Words & Music by Richard Carpenters

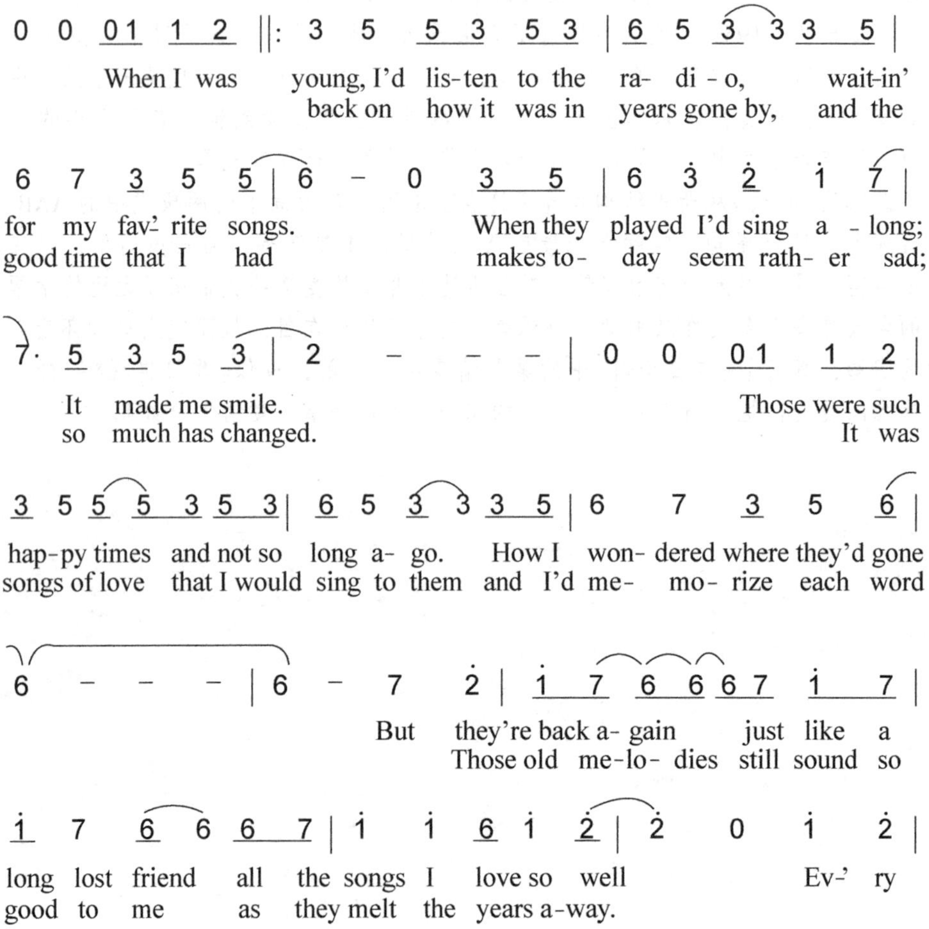

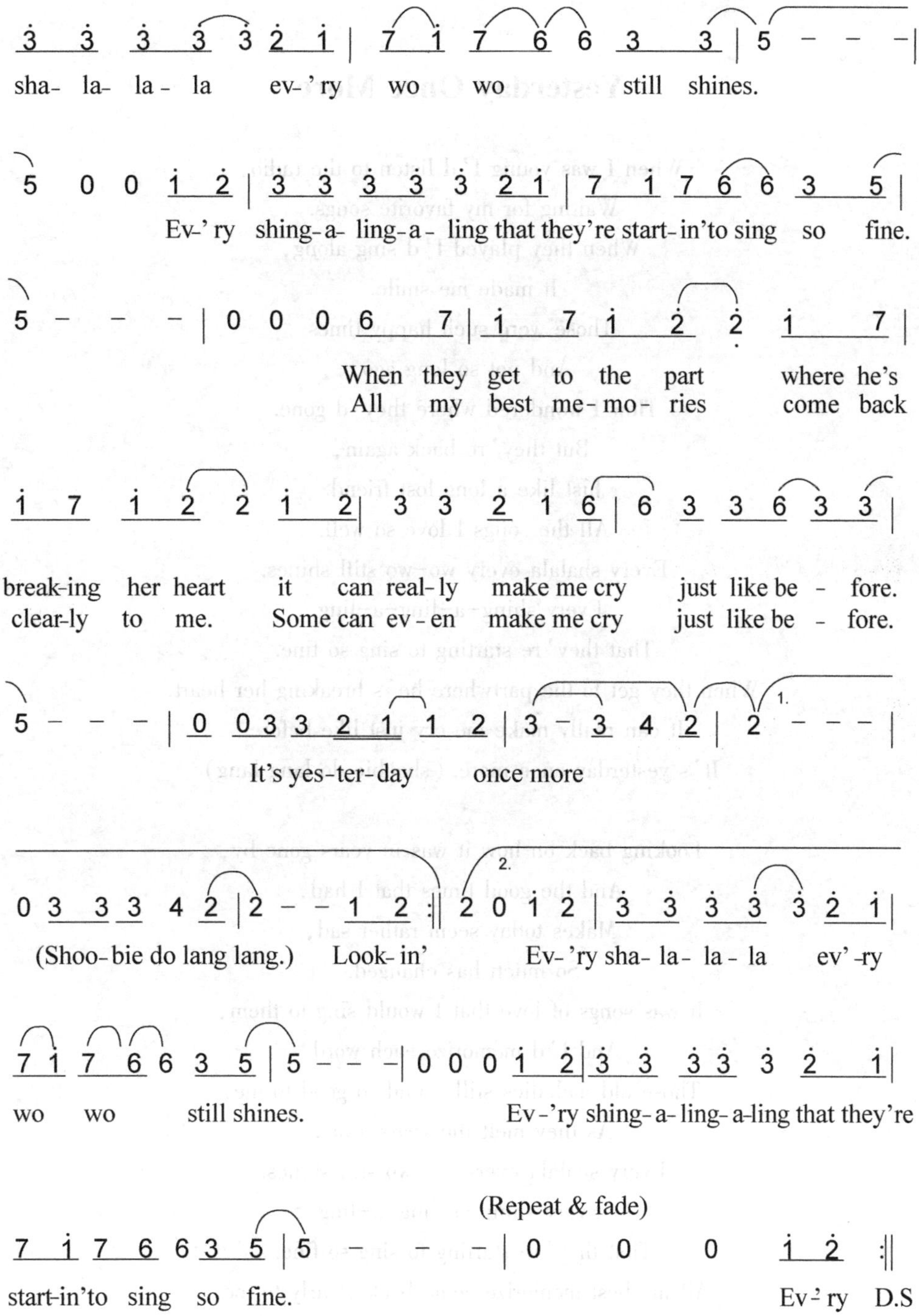
sha- la- la - la ev-'ry wo wo still shines.
Ev-'ry shing-a- ling-a- ling that they're start-in'to sing so fine.
When they get to the part where he's
All my best me-mo ries come back
break-ing her heart it can real-ly make me cry just like be - fore.
clear-ly to me. Some can ev - en make me cry just like be - fore.
It's yes-ter-day once more
(Shoo-bie do lang lang.) Look- in' Ev-'ry sha- la- la - la ev'-ry
wo wo still shines. Ev -'ry shing-a- ling- a-ling that they're
(Repeat & fade)
start-in'to sing so fine. Ev-'ry D.S

【英文歌词】

Yesterday Once More

When I was young I'd listen to the radio,
Waiting for my favorite songs.
When they played I'd sing along,
It made me smile.
Those were such happy times
And not so long ago.
How I wondered where they'd gone.
But they're back again,
Just like a long lost friend.
All the songs I love so well.
Every shalala every wo-wo still shines.
Every shing-a-ling-a-ling
That they're starting to sing so fine.
When they get to the partwhere he's breaking her heart.
It can really make me cry just like before.
It's yesterday once more. (shoobie do lang lang)

Looking back on how it was in years gone by,
And the good times that I had,
Makes today seem rather sad,
So much has changed.
It was songs of love that I would sing to them,
And I'd memorize each word.
Those old melodies still sound so good to me,
As they melt the years away.
Every shalala every wo-wo still shines.
Every shing-a-ling-a-ling
That they're starting to sing so fine.
All my best memorize come back clearly to me.
Some can even make me cry just like before.
It's yesterday once more.

Every shalala every wo-wo still shines.
Every shing-a-ling-a-ling
That they're starting to sing so fine.

Every shalala every wo-wo still shines.
Every shalala every wo-wo still shines.

【参考译文】

昨日重现

当我年轻时，常听收音机，
等待心爱的歌曲。
听到播放时便随声歌唱。
这使我欢畅。
那是多么幸福的时刻，就在不久以前！
我想知道他们曾去何处。
但我所有深爱的歌曲，
他们现在又回来，
正如老友失散又重聚。
每一句沙啦啦啦每一句喔喔仍闪烁，
每一句兴厄灵厄灵，
他们又开始唱得如此动听。
当他们唱到一个令她伤心断肠的地方，
这真能叫我哭出来，正如从前一样，
仿佛昔日又重来。

回头看，岁月如何消逝，
这些过去的好时光，
使今天显得令人哀伤。
变化多大啊！
我向他们唱爱的歌曲。
我会记住每一句歌词。
那些古老的曲调，在我听来还是那么好，
好像他们把岁月融消。
每每一句沙啦啦啦每一句喔喔仍闪烁，

每一句兴厄灵厄灵，
他们又开始唱得如此动听。
我所有美好的记忆，清晰的重现。
有一些仍能使我哭出来，正如从前一样，
仿佛昔日又重来。

每每一句沙啦啦啦每一句喔喔仍闪烁，
每一句兴厄灵厄灵，
他们又开始唱得如此动听。

每每一句沙啦啦啦每一句喔喔仍闪烁，
每每一句沙啦啦啦每一句喔喔仍闪烁。

语言点解析

(1) When they played I'd sing along. = When they sang I would sing along.
在这里，played 的意思是 sang。
sing along：跟着收音机唱。

(2) Those were such happy times, and not so long ago. = Those were such happy times of not so long ago.（指“跟着收音机唱”的好时光）

(3) **wonder**：want to know. 注意不要与 wander 弄混。**wander** 是“徘徊”“随便走”，而 wonder 是“不知道”“想知道”。
例如：
I ***wonder*** why he went there. 我不明白他为什么去了那里。
I ***wandered*** lonely as a cloud. 我独自漫游像朵孤云。

(4) All the songs I love so well. = I love all the songs so well. 我如此钟爱(深爱)这些歌曲。
so well：如此深，如此好
例如：
He speaks English ***so well***. 他的英语说得这么好！

(5) When they get to the part, =当他们唱到那一部分，……

(6) breaking her heart：使她伤心
break one's heart：令……伤心肠断

例如：

The news ***broke her heart***. 那条消息使她肝肠寸断。

(7) make me cry 使我哭泣

make sb. do sth.：让某人做某事

例如：

Nothing can ***make her cry***. 没什么东西可让她流泪。

He ***made her sing*** a Japanese song. 他逼迫她唱一支日本歌曲。

(8) Just like before：就像从前一样。

like 在这儿是个介词，应为“像……一样”。

例如：

My love is ***like*** a red，red rose. 我的爱人就像一朵红红的玫瑰。

(9) **look back on**：回顾

例如：

When I ***look back on*** my years there，I think i was lucky to beone member of that place. 当我回顾在那儿度过的岁月时，我认为，能成为那个地方的一员，我还是很幸运的。

(10) rather sad：颇为伤感

rather *adv*.：表示“颇……”“很……”

例如：

The weather is ***rather*** cold. 天气很冷。

(11) sound so good：听起来动听

sound *vi*.：用作系动词，后面接形容词，构成系表结构。

例如：

Your story souds untrue. 你的故事听起来不真实。

(12) come back clearly to me 又清楚地回到我身旁

注释与赏析

《昨日重现》20世纪70年代由美国的卡朋特乐队录制，但至今仍是大学生所需喜爱的一首校园流行歌曲。该乐队由著名的歌星卡伦·卡朋特(Karen Carpenters)与她哥哥理查德·卡朋特(Richard Capenters)组成。卡伦·卡朋彭特1950年生于美国康涅狄格州，从小在哥哥的影响下学习乐器，成了一名鼓手，并在其兄理查德·卡彭特(Richard Carpenter)组建的“卡彭特”乐队(旧译“木匠”乐队)中任主唱。大她三岁的哥哥理查德其实也是个非常有才华的音青年，担任钢琴伴奏和制作人，并创作了大量歌曲，后来在著名经纪人德纽文的帮助下，进入了美国流行乐坛。理查德由于运用多声轨重复录音技术录制并演唱披头士(The Beatles)的歌曲“Ticket to Ride”而备受瞩目，是位很有才华的音乐人。他原本也担任歌手，兼弹琴、制作及歌曲创作，但由于妹妹卡伦·卡朋特的歌声甜美出众，于是理查德甘为充当妹妹的配角，为妹妹写歌、伴奏，兄妹感情极深。

卡伦·卡朋特嗓音优美，演唱亲切自然，略带伤感，加之他们运用了多轨录音技术，因此他们的唱片无论在艺术上或技术上都非常成功，是当代流行音乐的精品。1970年一曲《靠近你》(“Close to You”)荣登排行榜首，这使卡朋特乐队一炮走红，70年代中他们不断有佳作闻世，成为无数美国青年的偶像，尼克松总统称卡朋特兄妹是最出色的美国青年。

卡伦·卡彭特的歌喉善于演绎旧伤感歌曲，怀旧歌曲如《昔日重来》《只是昨日》等；伤感歌曲如《超级明星》《与爱别》等，但她的其他歌曲，如《求求你，邮差先生》以及《唱吧》却十分轻快、流畅，不像别的歌有太多的忧郁味。

令人婉惜的是，卡伦·卡朋特年仅32岁便过早地离去。她死于神经性厌食症。以下是卡伦去世的原因，希望对那些想或者正在减肥的朋友们，能起到一些借鉴作用。

有一次，卡伦演出归来，无意中看到“Bikkboard”杂志上有对她的评价的文章，其中一段说她身体胖了点。于是，为了迎合这些低级趣味的眼光，卡伦决心减肥，她强行节食，克制食欲，并时常服用泻药，本来她的演出十分频繁，每天疲于奔波，结果身体状况每日愈下，一天比一天虚弱，比正常时的体重还少了15磅，减肥有成效了，但她却付出了生命的代价，最终因减肥而患上“精神性厌食症”。1983年2月4日，为了保持苗条身材的卡伦因治疗无效，在家人啼血沥泪的目光中，病死在洛杉矶的一家医院里，终年32岁。

23. The Sound of Silence

（寂静之声）

1=F $\frac{4}{4}$

Words & Music by
Paul Simon & Art Garfunkel

| 0 6 6 1 1 3 3 | 2 — — — |

Hello, darkness, my old friend,
In restless dreams I walked alone,
And in the naked light I saw
"Fools," said I, "You do not know
And the people bowed and prayed

0 5 5 5 7 7 2 2 | 1 — — — |

I've come to talk with you a — gain,
narrow streets of cobble — stone.
ten thousand people, maybe more.
silence like a cancer grows.
to the ne — on God they made.

0 1 1 1 3 3 5 5 | 6 — 5 — |

be — cause a vi — sion softly cree — ping
'Neath the ha — lo of a street lamp
People talking without speaking,
Hear my words that I might teach you.
And the sign flashed out its warning

0 1 1 3 3 5 5 | 6 — 5 — |

left its seeds while I was slee — ping,
I turned my collar to the cold and damp.
people hearing without listening,
Take my arms that I might reach you."
in the words that it was forming.

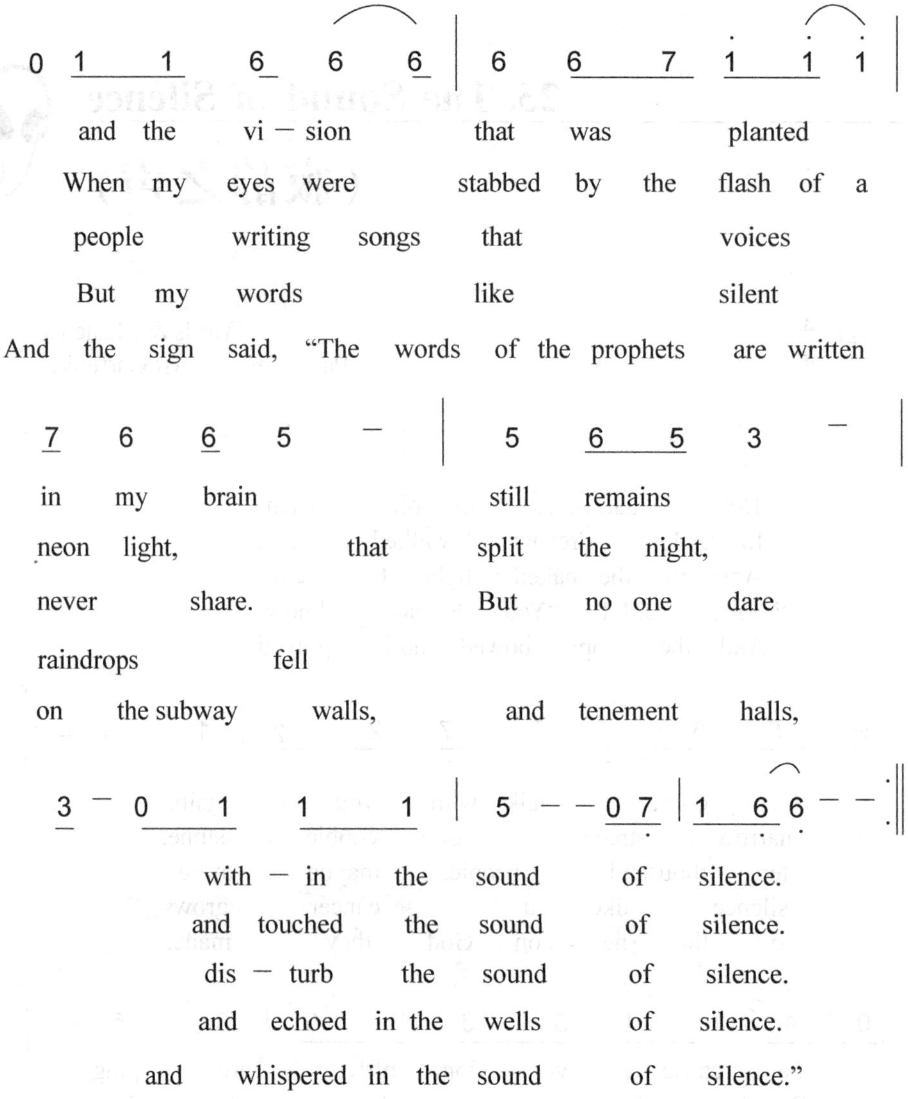

【英文歌词】

The Sound of Silence

Hello, darkness, my old friend,
I've come to talk with you again,
Because a vision softly creeping

Left its seeds while I was sleeping,
And the vision that was planted in my brain,
Still remains within the sound of silence.

In restless dreams I walked alone,
Narrow streets of cobblestone.
'Neath the halo of a street lamp,
I turned my collar to the cold and damp,
When my eyes were stabbed by the flash of a neon light,
That split the night and touched the sound of silence.

And in the naked light I saw,
Ten thousand people, maybe more,
People talking without speaking,
People hearing without listening,
People writing songs that voices never share.
No one dare disturb the sound of silence.

"Fools," said I, "You do not know
Silence like a cancer grows.
Hear my words that I might teach you.
Take my arms that I might reach you."
But my words like silent raindrops fell
And echoed in the wells of silence.

And the people bowed and prayed
To the neon god they made.
And the sign flashed out its warning,
In the words that it was forming,
And the sign said,
"The words of the prophets are
Written on the subway walls and tenement halls,
And whispered in the sounds of silence."

【参考译文】

寂静之声

你好，黑暗，我的老朋友，
我又来和你把天聊。
因为有个幻影悄悄来临，
在我熟睡时留下了它的种子。
植入我脑海的正是那幻影，
仍然萦绕在这寂静之声中。

在无尽的梦里我独自散步，
走在狭窄的鹅卵石街道上。
在昏黄晕光的街灯下，
我翻起衣领抵御寒冷与潮湿。
霓虹灯闪烁刺蛰我的眼睛，
也划破夜空触动了寂静之声。

在无遮挡的灯光下我看见
成千上万的人们。
人们无需语言即可交谈，
人们无需倾听即可领悟，
人们创作出歌曲却无人同唱，
谁也不敢扰乱这寂静之声。

我说："傻瓜，你真不知道，
寂静像癌症一样扩散。
请听听我教你的话语，
请抓住我伸给你的手臂。"
但我的话像寂静的雨滴落下来，
在沉寂的井中回想。

人们在膜拜与祈祷，
请求他们制造的霓虹灯偶像。
偶像的招牌闪烁出警言，
用独具的形式

把人们来规劝，
“先知们的预言写在地铁墙与公寓的走廊上，
也在那寂静之声中绕耳回荡。”

语言点解析

(1) Hello，darkness，my old friend，I’ve come to talk with you again. 你好，黑暗，我的老友，我又来与你聊天了。

这首歌一开始就用拟人的手法，(personification)把黑暗赋予人性，要与黑暗老朋友交谈一下。因此，作者以黑暗引出主题，因为黑暗是寂静的代表，黑暗与夜的来临是寂静的降临。

Because a vision softlycreeping，left its seeds while I was sleeping：A vision softly crept and left its seeds inside me while I was sleeping. 因为我熟睡时，幻影悄悄爬来，在我心中播下种子。

在此句中作者仍采用了拟人手法，这一手法贯穿了整个歌曲，此处把幻影拟人化，来扰乱我的睡眠和思想的宁静。

(2) **vision**：(作名词)幻影、视觉、幻想、眼光

例如：

I was haunted by her **vision**. 她的幻影萦绕着我的心。

(3) **plant**：(作动词用)种植、播种，(作名词用)植物、草木、工厂。(plant 在句中仍然是比喻的修辞用法，说明 vision 像种植一样，深深地播在我的脑海中，扰乱了我的平静)

例如：

Elm trees were ***planted*** along the road. 沿着道路和植榆树。

(4) ’Neath the halo of a street lamp，I turned my collar to the cold and damp. =Beneath the halo of a street lamp，I turned my collar to protect myself against the cold and damp air in a night. 在街灯的昏光下，我翻起衣领抵御潮湿和寒冷。

’Neath = beneath(介词)在-……之下。在诗歌和歌曲中，为了押韵或者顺口，常常使用省略首写字母或音节的形式，而以符号“’”来代替一个字节。如：’til =until，’cause = because 等等。

halo *n*.：(指环绕日、月等的)晕，晕圈；(绘于神像头上的)光环；(赋予理想化人物或事物的)光辉，光荣。

例如：

The ***halo*** of the moon tonight is bright. 今晚月亮周围的光晕非常明亮。

(5) **neon light**: coloured light 彩色霓虹灯
neon sign:(作广告用的)霓虹灯

(6) **flash n.**: 闪光、闪烁，如：a flash of lightning 闪电

(7) **split** *vi*：劈开、割裂、使分离
例如：
Tom ***spit*** the wood with an ax. 汤姆用斧头劈柴。

(8) People talking without speaking, people hearing without listening, people writing songs that voices never share. = People talking quietly with their heart, people hearing with their sense and singing songs in their heart without being heard by others. 人们无需言语即可交谈是一种心灵的默契与和谐；人们无需倾听却能听见是一种意识的理解与交流；人们创作的歌曲不能分享倾听是一种心灵之歌，别的人不能与之分享，皆源于无人敢扰乱这圣神的寂静之声。

(9) No one dare disturb the sound of silence.

(10) **dare**（作助动词，后面接不带 to 的不定式，主要用于疑问、否定或条件句中）敢、竟敢。
例如：
Who says he ***dare*** not do it? 谁说他不敢做这事?
dare 作动词用时，常用于肯定句中，随主语人称变化而变化。
例如：
Much to my surprise, he ***dares*** to try it. 令我大吃一惊的是，他竟敢做这种尝试。

(11) Silence like a cancer grows. = Silence can develop like a kind of disease. 寂静会像癌症一样扩散。（该句也是一种比喻用法。）

(12) Hear my words that I might teach you, take my arms that I might reach you. = Please listen to my words so that I might teach you, please hold my arms so that I might lead you. 请听我的话，让我教导你，请握住我的手，我为你引路。

(13) But my words like silent raindrops fell, and echoed in the wells. 我的话像寂静的雨滴落下，在沉寂的井中回响盘旋。

(14) echo *n.*（作名词用）回声、回音、回响
例如：I heard an ***echo*** in the woods. 我在森林里听到一种回声。

echo *vi.* (作动词用)回声、发回音、共鸣、附和

例如：

The mountains ***echoed*** with my shouts. 大山回应我的呼喊声。

(15) And the sign said: "The words of the prophets are written on the subway walls and tenement halls and whispered in the sound of silence." (霓虹灯)招牌说："先知们的话写在地铁墙与公寓的走廊上，也在寂静之声中轻轻回荡。"

prophet: person who knows in advance 先知，预言家

(16) **tenement** *n.*：地产、住宅、廉价公寓

注释与赏析

这首《寂静之声》是保罗·西蒙(Paul Simon)和阿特·加蓬凯尔(Art Garfunkel)创作并演唱的歌曲。俩人多次合作，多次获奖，在60至70年代的流行乐坛上曾名噪一时，被认为是男声二重唱的"黄金搭档"。此歌是1966年初时荣登美国排行榜首的冠军歌曲，两年后被用作电影《毕业生》的插曲，再一次广为流传。

《寂静之声》也有人译为《沉默之声》。这首歌蕴含着深刻的思想内含和哲理，表现了沉默寂静之中无声的喧啸。其中主要的意象为：第一段中的"幻影"；第二段中的"霓虹灯光"；第三段中的"心的交融"；第四段中的"雨滴井声"；第五段中的"先知哲言"。

我们可发现这首歌基本上含盖了两个主题，一为抨击资本主义社会的拜金主义，二为人际之间的疏离(alienation)与冷漠(apathy)造成了人类丧失了沟通的能力，其实这两个主题是互为因果的。自从"寂静的大众"这个名词出现以来"寂静"几乎与"冷漠"划下了等号，下一段话摘录自加丰科(Art Garfunkel)为西蒙第一张专辑所写的注解，从对"寂静之声"这首歌的注解，我们可以略窥一二：

《寂静之声》的主题是人与人之间无法沟通(man's inability to communicate with man)，作者看见了人沟通的范围仅止于表面与商业交易的层面(其中霓虹标志可为代表)。因为没有慎重其事的沟通(serious communication)，所以也就没有慎重其事的了解(serious understanding)——"人人言不及义(people talking without speaking)，听而不闻(hearing without listening)"，谁也不敢冒险伸手出去。(抓住我的臂膀我才能伸向你们)惊扰这寂静之声。诗人的努力也徒劳无功(……但是我的话就像雨点无声无息的飘落无数口沉默的井里)。结局令人费解。歌里告诉我们当有意义的沟通失败时，所剩的声音就只有沉默。"

《寂静之声》也有人译为《沉默之声》。这首歌蕴含着深刻的思想内含和哲理，表现了沉默寂静之中无声的喧啸。其中主要的意象为第一段中的"幻影"，第二段中的"霓虹灯光"，第三段中的"心的交融"，第四段中的"雨滴井声"和第五段中的"先知哲言"等。

可见，西蒙和加蓬格尔的这首歌曲是在向自己、向世人发问，冷静而大胆地提出社会中无声的灯光、霓虹对人们的影响，表现出某种反传统反现实的思维观念。那流畅抑扬的节奏，珠落玉盘般晶莹圆润的音符伴着霓虹的意象柔顺地流淌，也不时出现一些轻音符的跳跃

和闪动，在强拍上空半拍起唱的运用更增加了某种心理情感的迫切性、感受力和自然不断的绵续。

“寂静”真的存在吗？黑暗之中有梦幻、梦幻之中有幻影，使得大脑思维难以平静。幻影扰乱了梦的平静，灯光打破了黑色的单调，无语的交流，沉默雨滴在井中的回响，霓虹招牌的警示等等，均描绘出一个动中有静、暗中有声的彩色世界。只要有活动，就会有思想，只要你是个真正的人，就会存在于寂静的思维之中。让我们在多维的空间里纵横畅游吧！

24. Do–Re–Me
（哆唻咪）

1=C $\frac{2}{4}$

电影《音乐之声》插曲

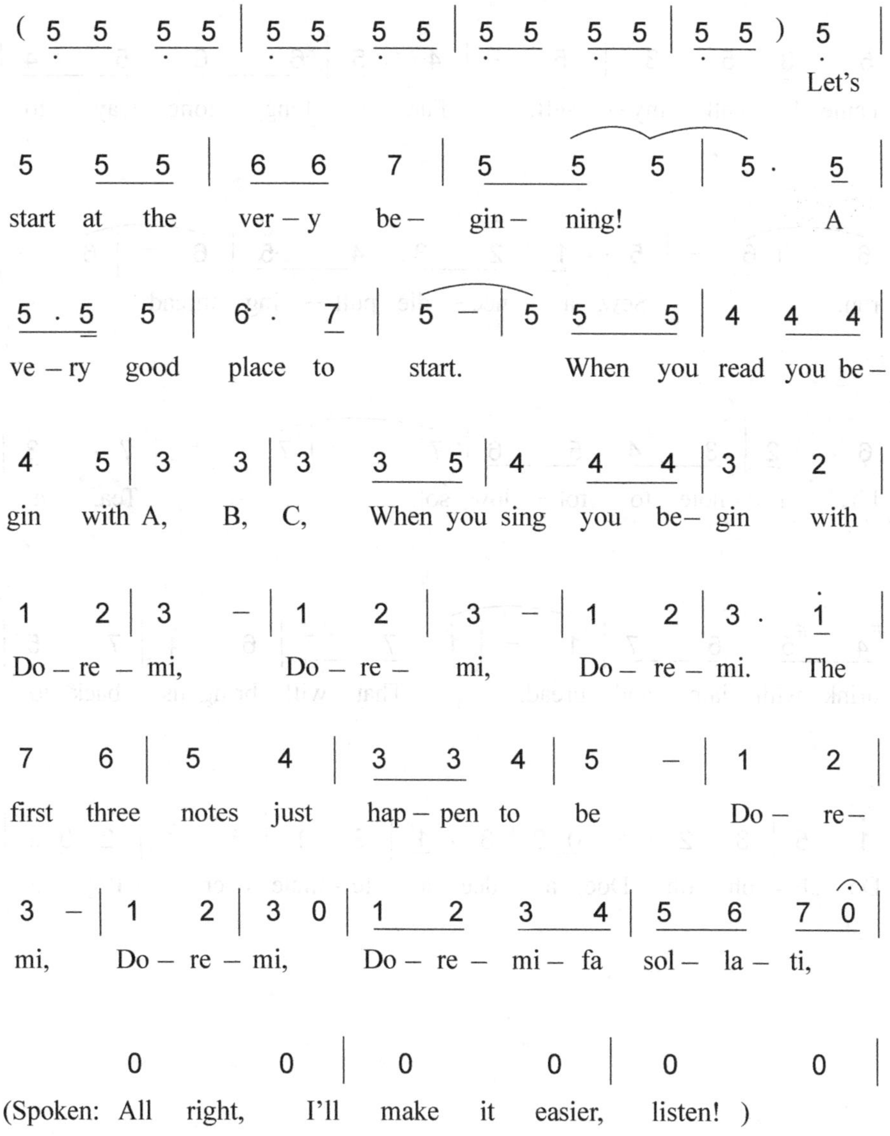

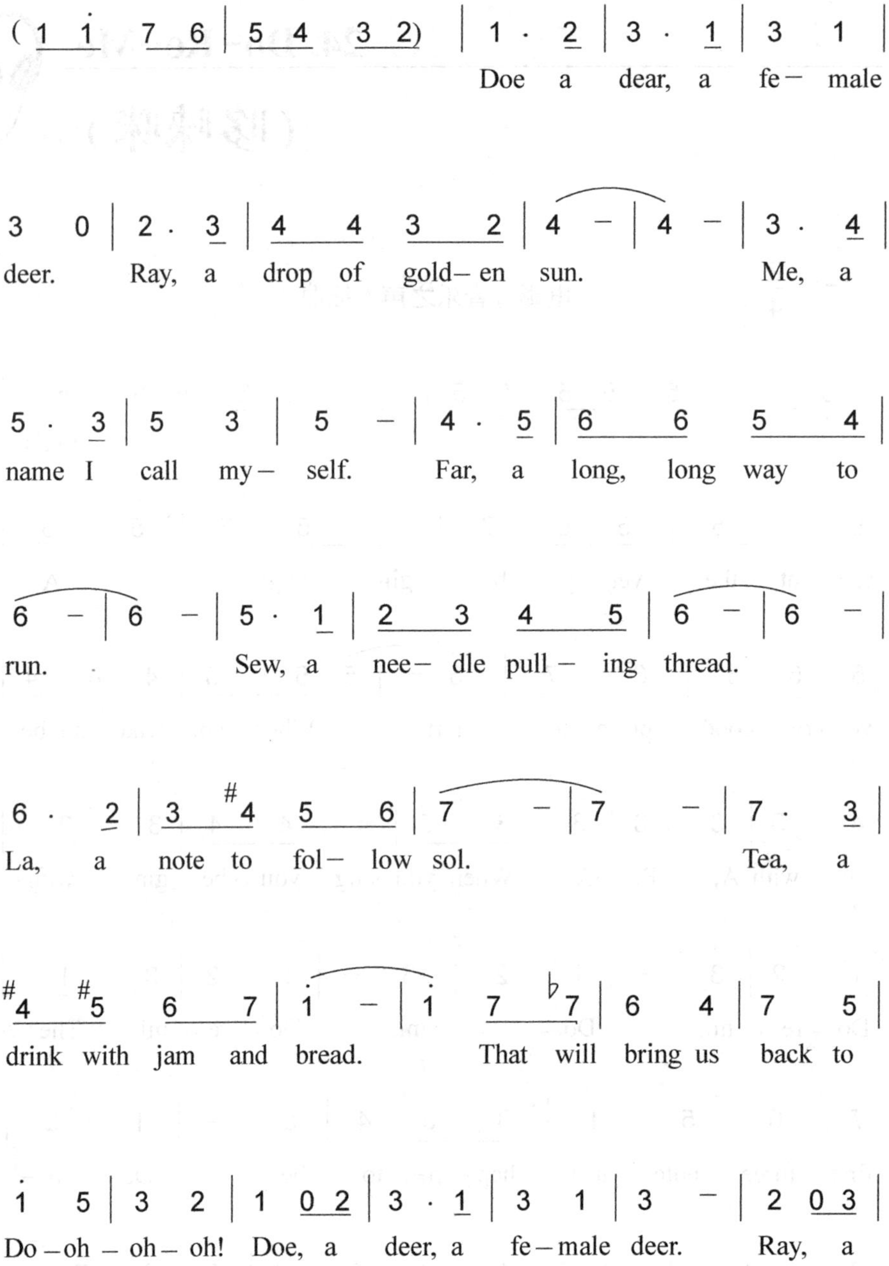
Doe a dear, a fe– male
deer. Ray, a drop of gold– en sun. Me, a
name I call my– self. Far, a long, long way to
run. Sew, a nee– dle pull – ing thread.
La, a note to fol– low sol. Tea, a
drink with jam and bread. That will bring us back to
Do –oh – oh– oh! Doe, a deer, a fe–male deer. Ray, a

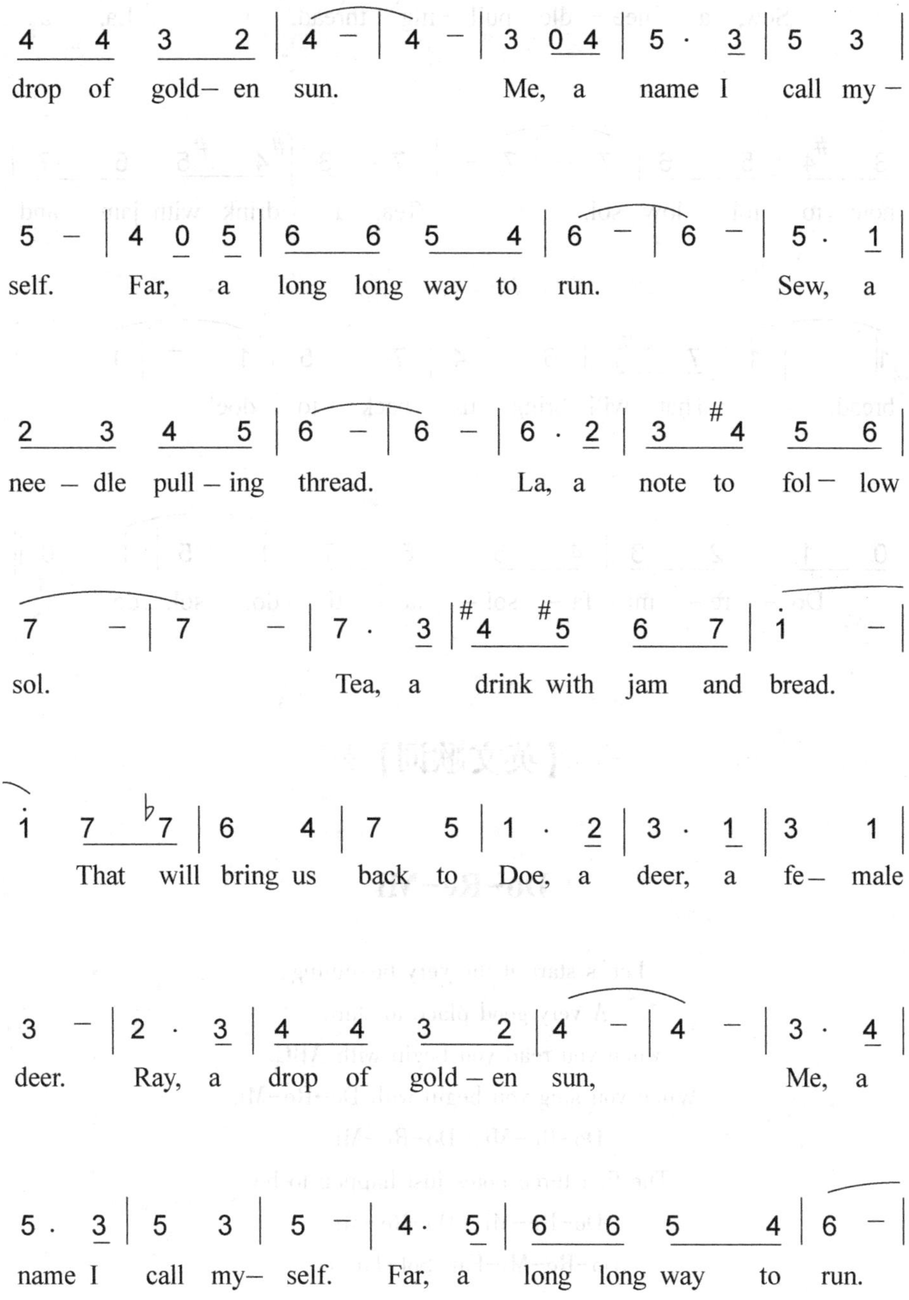
drop of gold– en sun. Me, a name I call my –
self. Far, a long long way to run. Sew, a
nee – dle pull – ing thread. La, a note to fol – low
sol. Tea, a drink with jam and bread.
That will bring us back to Doe, a deer, a fe – male
deer. Ray, a drop of gold – en sun, Me, a
name I call my– self. Far, a long long way to run.

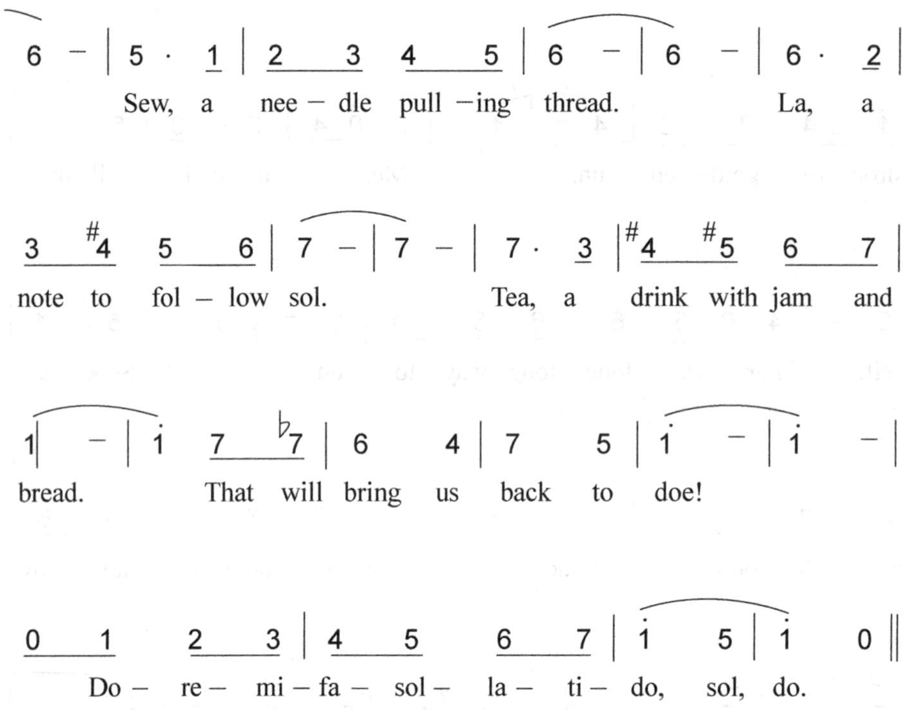

【英文歌词】

Do-Re-Mi

Let's start at the very beginning,
A very good place to start.
when you read you begin with ABC.
When you sing you begin with Do-Re-Mi.
Do-Re-Mi, Do-Re-Mi,
The first three notes just happen to be
Do-Re-Mi, Do-Re-Mi,
Do-Re-Mi-Far-Sol-La-Ti.

Doe a deer a female deer.
Ray a drop of golden sun.
Me a name I call myself.
Far a long long way to run.

Sew a needle pulling thread.
La a note to follow Sol.
Tea a drink with jam and bread.
That will bring us back to Do.
Doe a deer a female deer.
Ray a drop of golden sun.
Me a name I call myself.
Far a long long way to run.
Sew a needle pulling thread.
La a note to follow Sol.
Tea a drink with jam and bread.
That will bring us back to Do.

Doe a deer a female deer,
Ray a drop of golden sun.
Me a name I call myself.
Far a long long way to run.
Sew a needle pulling thread.
La a note to follow Sol.
Tea a drink with jam and bread.
That will bring us back to Do.
Do-Re-Mi-Fa-Sol-La-Ti-Do-Sol-Do

【参考译文】

哆—唻—咪

让我们从头来学，
一个好地方来开始。
学读书要先学 ABC；
学唱歌要先学哆—唻—咪，
哆—唻—咪，哆—唻—咪，
前三音符正好就是
哆—唻—咪。
哆—唻—咪。
哆唻咪发嗦拉梯。

"哆"是鹿，是一只母鹿；
"唻"是一束金色阳光；
"咪"是自己叫自己；
"发"是路途长又远；
"嗦"是穿针又引线；
"拉"和"嗦"后的音符；
"梯"是饮料和茶点。
然后我们回到"哆"。

"哆"是鹿，是一只母鹿；
"唻"是一束金色阳光；
"咪"是自己叫自己；
"发"是路途长又远；
"嗦"是穿针又引线；
"拉"和"嗦"后的音符；
"梯"是饮料喝茶点。
然后我们回到"哆"。

"哆"是鹿，是一只母鹿；
"唻"是一束金色阳光；
"咪"是自己叫自己；
"发"是路途长又远；
"嗦"是穿针又引线；
"拉"和"嗦"后的音符；
"梯"是饮料喝茶点。
然后我们回到"哆"。
哆唻咪发嗦拉梯哆嗦哆！

语言点解析

(1) start at the very beginning

start at：从……开始 at 指起点，接近于 from 的含义。

very *adj.*：The very beginning 中的 very 是个强调性形容词，表示"恰恰"、"正好"等义。例如：

You are the **very** person I want to see. 你正是我想见的人。

(2) **to begin with**：以……开始
例如：
He ***began with*** his class by a song. 他是以唱首歌形式开始上课的。

(3) **happen to**：恰恰，正好，恰好，碰巧
例如：
When the earthquake happened, he ***happened to*** be out. 地震发生时，他碰巧不在家。

(4) **female**：雌性的，反义词是 male

(5) a drop of golden sun：在此译为"一束金色阳光"。
a drop of：一点、一束
例如：
a drop of water(blood)一滴水(血)；
golden sun：实为 golden sunshine.
golden：指颜色像金色的；gold 指材料本身是金子的。
例如：
golden watch：指金色手表
gold ring：指用金子做的戒指

(6) a long long way **to run**：解释 far，to run 修饰 way 作定语。
例如：
I have many books ***to read***. 我有许多书要读。

(7) a needle pulling thread：a needle which is pulling
Thread 穿针引线就是在缝东西。英文里缝东西叫 sew，发音与音乐中的音符 so 相同。

(8) a note to follow "sew"
follow *vt*.：跟在……之后
例如：
He **followed** me. 他跟在我身后。

(9) bring…back to：把……带回到……。

注释与赏析

这首歌是音乐剧《音乐之声》(1965 年年初搬上银幕)里的插曲之一。同名故事片《音乐之声》描写的是生性活泼、不安心当修女的姑娘玛丽亚。故事发生在第二次世界大战前的奥

地利，实习修女玛丽亚到一个海军上校家里当家庭教师并逐渐获得七个孩子的喜爱。最后，上校也爱上了她并与她结婚。

这首歌是玛丽亚带着上校的七个孩子出去游玩时教他们唱的。有趣的是，玛丽亚让这七个孩子按年龄大小代表哆咪咪发嗦拉梯这七个音符。玛丽亚用日常生活中常见的词语帮助孩子们记音符，效果很好。

这是一首非常欢快的音乐启蒙歌曲，家庭教师玛丽亚小姐采取非常巧妙的方式来启发孩子们对每个音符的记忆。从旋律上讲，这首歌采用了“级进”的方法。老师唱，然后孩子们学唱一遍。接下去，先由孩子们在每个乐曲的第一拍顺序说出七个音符的唱名，老师接唱通俗易懂的比喻句。这些比喻句生动，形象，易学易记。然后，老师用七个音符构成不同的组合，告诉孩子们旋律就是由这些音符的不同组合和节奏的变化构成。这里，每一个乐句的基本音正好是下面这个音符。用这种方法教孩子们音乐，真是妙趣横生。

25. Sad Movies
(悲伤的电影)

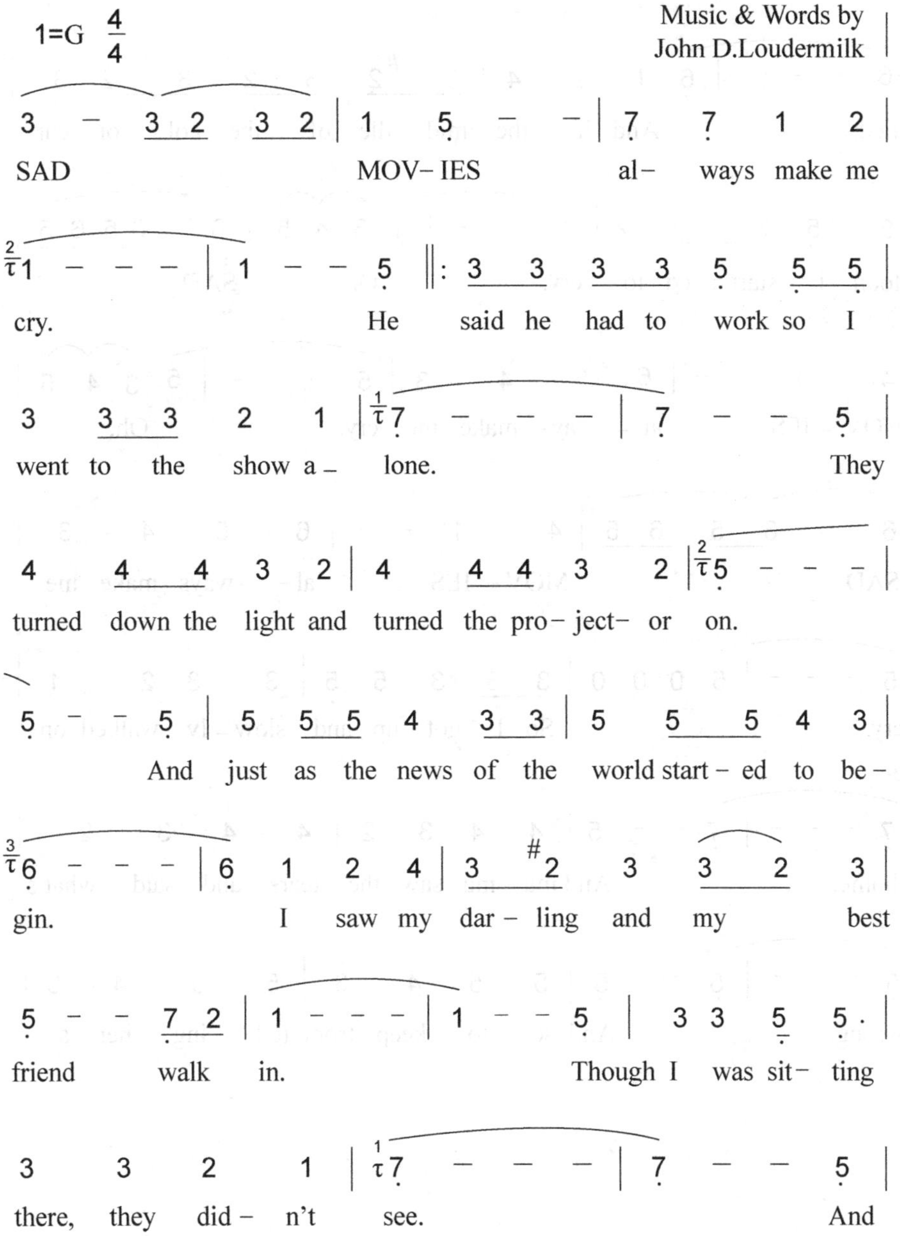

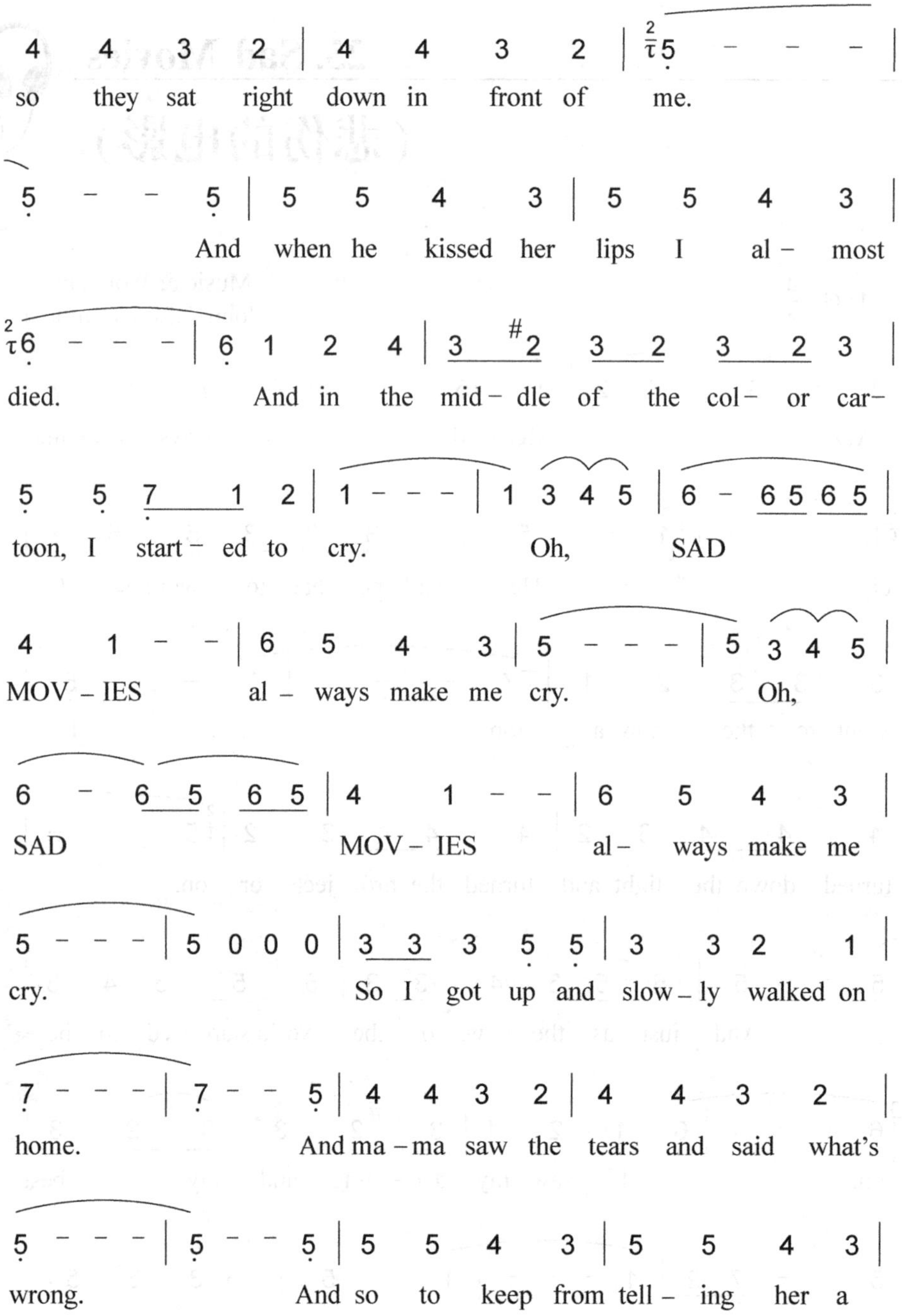
so they sat right down in front of me.
And when he kissed her lips I al – most
died. And in the mid – dle of the col – or car –
toon, I start – ed to cry. Oh, SAD
MOV – IES al – ways make me cry. Oh,
SAD MOV – IES al – ways make me
cry. So I got up and slow – ly walked on
home. And ma – ma saw the tears and said what's
wrong. And so to keep from tell – ing her a

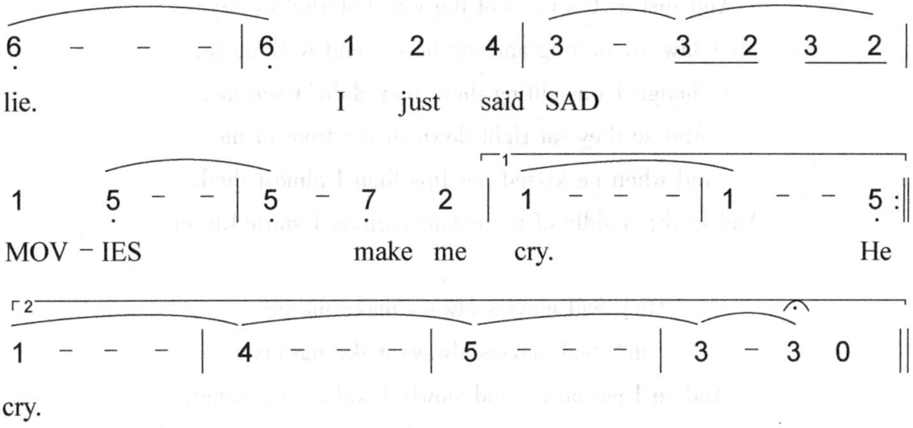

【英文歌词】

Sad Movies

Sad movies always make me cry.
He said he had to work, so I went to the show alone.
They turned down the lights and turned the projector on.
And just as the news of the world started to begin,
I saw my darling and my best friend walking in.
Though I was sitting there they didn't see me.
And so they sat right down in the front of me.
And when he kissed her lips then I almost died.
And in the middle of the colour cartoon I started to cry.

Oh! Sad movies always make me cry.
Oh! Sad movies always make me cry.
And so I got on up and slowly I walked on home,
And Mama saw the tears and said "What is wrong".
And so to keep from telling her a lie,
I just said "Sad movie makes me cry".

He said he had to work, so I went to the show alone.
They turned down the lights and turned the projector on.

And just as the news of the world started to begin,
I saw my darling and my best friend walking in.
Though I was sitting there they didn't see me.
And so they sat right down in the front of me.
And when he kissed her lips then I almost died.
And in the middle of the colour cartoon I started to cry.

Oh! Sad movies always make me cry.
Oh! Sad movies always make me cry
And so I got on up and slowly I walked on home,
And Mama saw the tears and said "Baby what is wrong".
And so to keep from telling her a lie,
I just said "Sad movie makes me cry".

【参考译文】

悲伤的电影

悲伤的电影总是让我哭。
他说他要工作，我只好独自去看电影。
他们把灯变暗，打开放映机。
就在世界新闻要开始时，我看见
我亲爱的人和我最好的朋友走进来。
我就坐在那儿，他们没看见，
于是他们正好坐在我前边。
他亲她的双唇时，我几乎晕厥。
彩色卡通演了一半，我便开始哭起来。

啊，悲伤的电影总是让我哭。
啊，悲伤的电影总是让我哭。
于是我起身慢慢走回家。
妈妈见我挂泪花，问我“怎么啦?”
于是为了不对她撒谎，
我只说：悲伤的电影总是让我哭。

他说他要工作，我只好独自去看电影。
他们把灯变暗，打开放映机。
就在世界新闻要开始时，我看见
我亲爱的人和我最好的朋友走进来。
我就坐在那儿，他们没看见，
于是他们正好坐在我前边。
他亲她的双唇时，我几乎晕厥。
彩色卡通演了一半，我便开始哭起来。

啊，悲伤的电影总是让我哭。
啊，悲伤的电影总是让我哭。
于是我起身慢慢走回家。
妈妈见我挂泪花，问我"怎么啦?"
于是为了不对她撒谎，
我只说：悲伤的电影总是让我哭。

语言点解析

(1) He said he had to work…. = He said he was obliged to work. 他说他得去上班。

have to：不得不(客观情况使他必须做某事)

must：必须(侧重于主观情况，动作执行者认为他应当去做某事)

例如：

When she was ill, she ***had to*** give up smoking. 她生病后，不得不戒了烟。

We ***must*** pay enough attention to the housing condition of the teachers. 我们必须对教师的住房条件有足够的重视。

(2) So I went to the show alone. =Therefore I went to the movies myself. 于是我独自一人去看电影。

alone：独自一人

show：表演，演出，此处指电影

(3) They turned down the lights and turned the projector on. 他们调暗了灯光，打开电影机。

they 指电影的工作人员。

turn down：调小，调暗，关小，弄小(煤气、收音机、电视机等)

例如：

It' s a midnight now. ***Turn down*** the radio. 现在已是半夜，把收音机音量调小些儿。

The meat needs soft fire now. Please **turn down** the gas. 现在这肉需要文火，把煤气关小一点。

turn off：关掉（电灯电视、收音机等）

turn on：打开（电灯电视、收音机等）

turn up：开大（电灯电视、收音机等）

（4）And just as the news of the world started to begin, …= And just as the news of the world began.

just as：就在……时

start to do(sth.)：开始做某事，表示具体动作

start doing(sth.)：表明什么样的事是从何时开始做的，表示长期习惯性动作。

例如：

Just as I was about to sleep, he came. 我正要睡觉时他来了。

He ***started to prepare*** lunch at 11 o'clock. 他 11 点时开始准备午饭。

He ***started cooking*** when he got married. 他结婚后就开始做饭了。

（5）I saw my darling and my best friend walk in. 我看见我的男友和我的闺密走了进来。

walk in：走进来

walk into：走进……

例如：

I did not notice you ***walk in***. 我没有注意到你走进来（此处 in 是副词）。

Prof. Michael is ***walking in*** his room. 迈克尔教授在他房间里行走（此处的 in 是介词）。

He ***walked into*** my room slowly. 他缓缓地走进我的房间。

see sb. do sth.：见某人做某事（侧重整个过程）

see sb. doing sth.：见某人做某事（侧重整个过程）

例如：

I saw ***her play*** with the snake. 我看她玩弄那条蛇。（指整个过程都看到）

I saw ***her playing*** with a snake. 我见她正玩弄一条蛇。（指只见她当时正在玩弄一条蛇，但其它情况不详）

"I saw my darling and my best friend walk in" 中的两人一个是自己的 darling，另一个是自己的 best friend。但却被自己的 darling 又"加班"为理由拒绝陪自己去看电影的女主人公，在影院却又看见他与自己的"闺蜜"走进电影院的全过程！好不伤心！

（6）Though I was sitting there, they didn't see. = Although I was sitting just there, they did not see me, …

这两人走进电影院到落座及以后发生的事情，主人公都看见了，而这两人却没有看见她。对主人公而言，这是他们真的没有看见？还是太"忘我""忘她"？对周围太过于不

闻不问了？

(7) And so they sat right down in front of me. = And so they sat down just in front of me.

right *adv*.：表示"恰恰""正好"。

例如：

I saw him yesterday. When we had dinner, he sat ***right*** opposite me. 我昨天见到他了。我们吃饭时，他就坐在我对面。

sitdown：坐下。

sit up：坐起来(从躺卧姿势到坐起来的姿势)

be seated：处于坐着的状态

例如：

When I went to see him, he ***sat up*** and told me to ***sit down***. But his wife remained ***seated*** on the chair without even the slightest movement. 我去看他时，他坐了起来，要我坐下。可他妻子一直坐在椅子上，一动也不动。

in front of：在……前面(边)

in the front of：在……的前部

例如：

in front of the house 在房前；

in front of a car 在汽车前；

in the front of the car 在车前部；

in the front of the classroom 在教室(内部的)前面

(8) And when he kissed her lips, I almost die. = And when he kissed her on the lips, I almost swooned.

kiss *vt*.：吻(某人、某物)

kiss sb. goodbye：吻别

例如：

I still cannot understand why she so loved her dog that she often **kissed** him passionately and talked to him. 我现在还不明白为什么她那么爱她的狗，经常热烈地亲吻他并对他说话。

He ***kissed her goodbye***. 他和她吻别。

She ***kissed*** him goodnight. 她吻他向他道晚安。

He ***kissed*** her on the forehead. 她吻她的额头。

almost *adv*.：nearly; to quite 几乎；差不多；不十分。可以用在副词、名词、形容词、动词、限定词、当初之前。

例如：

This is a kind of mistake men **almost** always make. 这是一种男人们几乎总要犯的错误。

It's ***almost*** time to go to bed. 快到上床的时候了。

Supper is ***almost*** ready. 晚饭快准备好了。

She ***almost*** died when she saw her house burning. 见到她的房子着了火，她差点昏死过去。

He is ***almost*** two metres tall. 他差不多有两米高。

Almost anybody can apply for the job. 几乎任何人都可以申请这个工作。

almost 用在 no，nobody，none，nothing，never 之前时，其意思相当于"实质上"、"实际上"。

例如：

Almost no one like her. 实际上没有人喜欢她。

(9) And in the middle of the color cartoon，I started to cry. =When the color cartoon was on，I began to cry.

color cartoon：彩色卡通

in the middle of：正在……之时；在……中央，在……中间

例如：

We were ***in the middle of*** dinner when they came. 他们来时我们正在吃饭。

I was ***in the middle of*** reading a poem when the phone bell rang.

In the middle of this century ，we fought them several times in different countries. 本世纪中期我们在不同国家跟他们打过几次仗。

I hate to be disturbed ***in the middle of*** the night. 我讨厌半夜三更时被人打扰。

Our school is ***in the middle of*** this road. 我们学校在这条路的中段。

In the middle of the room is a pot of flowers. 在屋子的中央有一盆花。

(10) So I got up and slowly walked down home. = So I stood up and slowly walked out of the cinema and walked home. 于是我站起身，缓缓走出了电影院，然后步行回家了。

walked on 中的**on** 是副词，表示"继续"。

例如：

Read ***on*** . 继续读下去。

They drove ***on*** until they came to a hotel. 他们继续开车，直到来到了一个旅馆。

The girl walked ***on*** home after she parted with her classmates. 和同学们分手后，女孩继续步行回家了。

get up：起床；起身，站起来，起立

例如：

He ***gets up*** at six very morning. 他每天早晨六点起床。

She ***got up*** and offered her seat to an old man. 她站起来，把座位让给一位老人。

(11) "What's wrong?" =What's the matter with you? 你怎么啦?

再如：

What's wrong with your pen?

(12) keep from telling her a lie, …= prevent from telling her a lie

tell a lie：撒谎；说谎

keep from doing sth.：克制自己不做某事

He ***kept from laughing***. 他忍住没笑。

I managed to ***keep myself from crying***. 我设法忍做没笑出来。

(13) I just said…= I merely(only, simply) said…

注释与赏析

《悲伤的电影》讲述了现代年轻人的爱情的另一面，是个悲剧的爱情故事。女主人公欲邀请心上人共度时光；心上人却说“不得不工作”。拿我们现在一些人的话来说，这叫“加班”。一个很好的借口，真心爱你的人不会因你加班工作而责备你，只好自己忍耐寂寞。无奈，女主人公独自一人去了影院。影院！就在这个演电影以反映人生的场所，一幕幕戏剧性场面展开了：灯光渐暗，放映机开始工作，世界新闻刚要开始，世界舞台演出的场景尚未真正开始，近处人生的戏剧已开锣，人物登场亮相——女主人公的心上人，那个自称要加班的心上人与自己最要好的女友相拥而入。这是初惊，她难以相信，她醒着？还是在做梦？

第二节又讲述了进一步发展的剧情：女主人公就坐在那儿，他们却看不见。是灯太暗？是视而不见，这后一种情况不一定对。但两人只顾注意对方、不注意周围人们，绝对是真的。更令人气恼的是：他们俩竟坐在女主人公前边的一排。这个影院不对号入座，正像这三人在他们的爱情中不对号入座一样？

这一段人生戏剧的高潮是自己的心上人开始轻吻自己最好的女友的双唇，见到这一场面，女主人公差点死去，彩色卡通刚演完一半她就开始流泪。哭什么？哭自己恋人负心？哭自己引狼入室？哭自己无能？不管为何缘故而哭，这哭是伤心的。

高潮过后，女主人公决定还是悄悄地走开，又是独自一人，步伐缓慢、沉重，泪流满面，回到家中。在这个世界上，大概最擅长观察的便是母亲。母亲见女儿流泪，关心地问：“怎么了？”女儿也懂事，不让母亲为自己过于操心，为了不撒谎还是撒了慌：她只是说伤心的电影让她哭泣。是啊，面对这种伤心事，谁能不哭泣？悲伤的电影让我哭，让你哭。让每个人都哭。

“梦幻人生”，真是梦幻！人生中充满戏剧场面，难以预料，迂回曲折，如云如雾，难以细察。有些事总的真谛难辨。工作形势有突发转突变，感情生活更难预见。有时我们全身心投入，真情可见，却突然发现，一起努力均是徒劳，我们付出，却得不到回报。错，错，错。有人说只因身处庐山不识其面目，盲目的投入迷失了自我。实则另有原因，正如一位女士评论的那样，这样的结局，即“悲伤的电影”描述的结局在某种程度上是因为自己忽略的一些生活细节并因此改变了某些事情的发展方向及本质。这是一种比较客观并且较深刻的分析。

“Sad Movies make me cry”是这首歌的主题，这一句首尾呼应，中间反复，整首歌中共出现五次。这首歌节奏舒缓，优美却充满忧伤和痛苦，令听者为之动情，令听者哀女主人公之不幸，令听者认真考虑人生和爱情，令听者思考怎么摆脱这“悲伤的电影”。

26. Auld Lang Syne

(友谊地久天长)

Words by Robert Burns

Music by William Hild

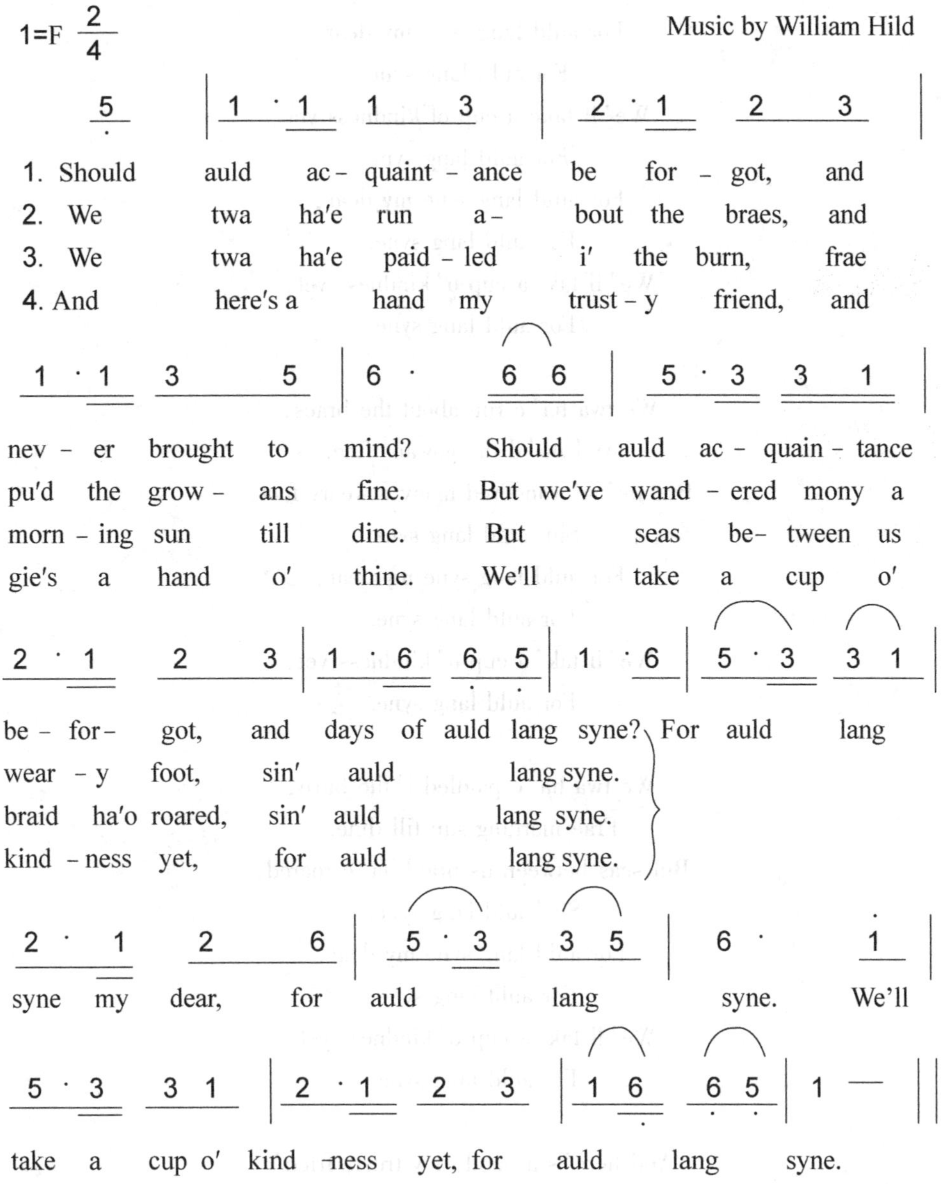

【英文歌词】

Auld Lang Syne

Should auld asquaintance be forgot
And never brought to mind
Should auld asquaintance be forgot
And days of auld lang syne
For auld lang syne my dear,
For auld lang syne
We'll take a cup of kindness yet
For auld lang syne
For auld lang syne my dear,
For auld lang syne.
We'll tak'a cup o'kindness yet,
For auld lang syne.

We twa ha'e run about the braes,
And pu'd the gowans fine.
But we've wandered mony a weary foot,
Sin'auld lang syne.
For auld lang syne my dear,
For auld lang syne.
We'll tak'a cup o'kindness yet,
For auld lang syne.

We twa ha'e paidled i'the burn,
Frae morning sun till dine.
But seas between us braid ha'e roared,
Sin'auld lang syne.
For auld lang syne my dear,
For auld lang syne.
We'll tak'a cup o'kindness yet,
For auld lang syne.

And here's a hand, my trusty frien'

And gie's a hand of thine.
We'll tak's a cup of kindness yet,
For auld lang syne.
For auld lang syne my dear,
For auld lang syne.
We'll tak'a cup o'kindness yet,
For auld lang syne.

【参考译文】

友谊地久天长

怎能忘记昨天朋友,
心中能不怀想?
昨天朋友岂能相忘,
过去的好时光。
为了过去的好时光,
友谊万岁!
举杯痛饮同声唱,
友谊地久天长。

我们曾经终日游荡,
在故乡的青山上,
我们也曾历尽苦辛,
到处奔波流浪,
在过去的好时光。
友谊万岁!
举杯痛饮同声唱,
友谊地久天长。

我们曾终日逍遥,
荡浆在碧波上,
但如今却劳燕分飞,
远隔大海重洋。
为了过去的好时光。
友谊万岁!

举杯痛饮同声唱，
友谊地久天长。

我们往日情意相投，
让我们紧握手，
让我们举杯畅饮，
为了过去的好时光。
友谊万岁！
友谊万岁！
举杯痛饮同声唱，
友谊地久天长。

语言点解析

（1）曲中的歌词保持了原貌，从下面可以找到他们对应的部分：

① auld lang syne = long long ago

auld = old；lang syne = long since，long ago

② o：of

③ tak'：take

④ We twa ha'e run about the braes = We two have run about small hills.

⑤ pu'd：pulled

⑥ mony：many

⑦ i'the burn：in the rivulet（small stream）

⑧ sin'：since

⑨ frae：from

⑩ gie's：give us

（2）Should auld acquaintance be forgot，and never brought to mind?

auld acquaintance：老朋友

nodding acquaintance：点头之交

（3）**bring … to mind**：想起……

例如：

The picture ***brought*** his fond memory of the past ***to mind***. 这张照片勾起了他对过去时光的美好回忆。这里有两个不需要回答的修辞问句，加重了这首歌的主题思想：无论时间过了多久，无论彼此相隔多远，老朋友永远也不能忘掉。

例如：

Should we so hurry as to kill a hen in order to get more eggs? 我们应不应该为获取更多的蛋而急于把母鸡杀死呢?

(4) for auld lang syne: 为了过去的好时光
for our friendship: 为了我们的友谊

(5) tak' a cup o' kindness=take a cup of kindness 喝一杯友谊的酒

(6) run about the braes=wandered around the small hills
run about: 跑遍
例如:
We ***ran about*** many places to look a kind of bird that could talk. 为寻找一种能说话的鸟儿,我们曾跑遍许多地方。

(7) wandered mony a weary foot=wandered to many places and our feet got weary. 意思是说历尽辛苦,四处奔波,表明人生沧桑、去日苦多。

(8) Sin' auld lang syne. =Since long long ago. 自从很久以前,意思是说离过去的好时光已很久远

(9) the burn 与下几行中的 seas between us braid 形成对照,一边是儿时的小溪,一边是汹涌澎湃的海洋。这个对照很重要,如今朋友们各在一方,远隔重洋,更知过去友谊之珍贵,更加怀念过去的好时光。

(10) frae morning sun till dine: from morning till noon 自早晨到中午,形容以前曾无忧无虑,乐不知疲。

(11) But seas between us braid ha' e roared. =But the seas broad between us have roared. 指我们之间大海大洋咆哮不止,说明我们彼此远离,与以前趟水而过的小溪形成对比。

(12) Here' s a hand: 我已伸出我的手。有的版本为 there' s a hand。

(13) Gie' s a hand of thine: =Give us your hand 给我们你的手。

注释与赏析

这首歌原本是苏格兰诗人罗伯特·彭斯(Robert Burns 1759~1796)的一首诗,歌唱真挚持久的友谊。后经威廉·希尔德(William Hilde)整理为歌词并谱了曲。1940 年美国电影《魂

断蓝桥》(Waterloo Bridge)采用这首歌作主题曲，并传遍世界各地。

《魂断蓝桥》描写了英国青年军官洛伊上尉和芭蕾舞演员玛拉的爱情故事，故事发生在第一次世界大战期间。一天，英国军官洛伊为躲避空袭，在防空洞中认识了玛拉。两人一见钟情。夜渐深，酒店乐队领班向客人们宣布演奏最后一支曲子并祝人们回家时一路平安。在舒缓、优美的“auld Lang syne”乐曲中，大厅里的蜡烛一支支熄灭。这支曲子在影片中反复出现，始终把洛伊和玛拉的爱情连在一起。当天晚上，洛伊奉命出征。玛拉因私自离开剧团与洛伊会面而被解职。后因贫困交加，被迫沦为妓女。一天，她正在滑铁卢桥上拉生意，不料突然看见洛伊，原来洛伊并没有阵亡。洛伊带玛拉回家，准备结婚。婚礼前夕，玛拉悄然离去，来到滑铁卢大桥上，带着美好的回忆和遗憾，投身车轮下自尽。这个善良的、不愿给洛伊家族带来耻辱、渴望幸福又不愿把不幸强加给自己心上人的姑娘，就这样结束了自己的生命。

这首歌名也被译为“过去的好时光”“一路平安”和“友谊万岁”等。在国外，朋友聚会结束时常演唱这首歌，作为最后一个节目，甚至在国内的许多大学里，大学生们在毕业时，大都选唱这首歌曲，作为纪念以前美好时光的怀旧歌曲及对未来时光的美好祝愿。

彭斯这首诗原本已很出名，经配曲传唱后更加受人喜爱。可以说，《魂断蓝桥》用它作主题曲后更把它推向世界各地，使它家喻户晓，传唱于全球。这首歌歌唱人类最美好的事物——友谊。随着人们年龄的增长，生活中的各种艰辛尽已尝遍，人们四处奔波，疲惫不堪，有的甚至远隔重洋，想一想过去的好时光，这种想象，回忆本身便是一种享受。这首歌令人产生一种怀旧感。但伤感过后，人们更加珍视现在和将来，更知友谊在人生中的作用。

27. Love Story

（爱情故事）

1=C $\frac{4}{4}$

Words by Carl Sigman
Music by Francis Lai

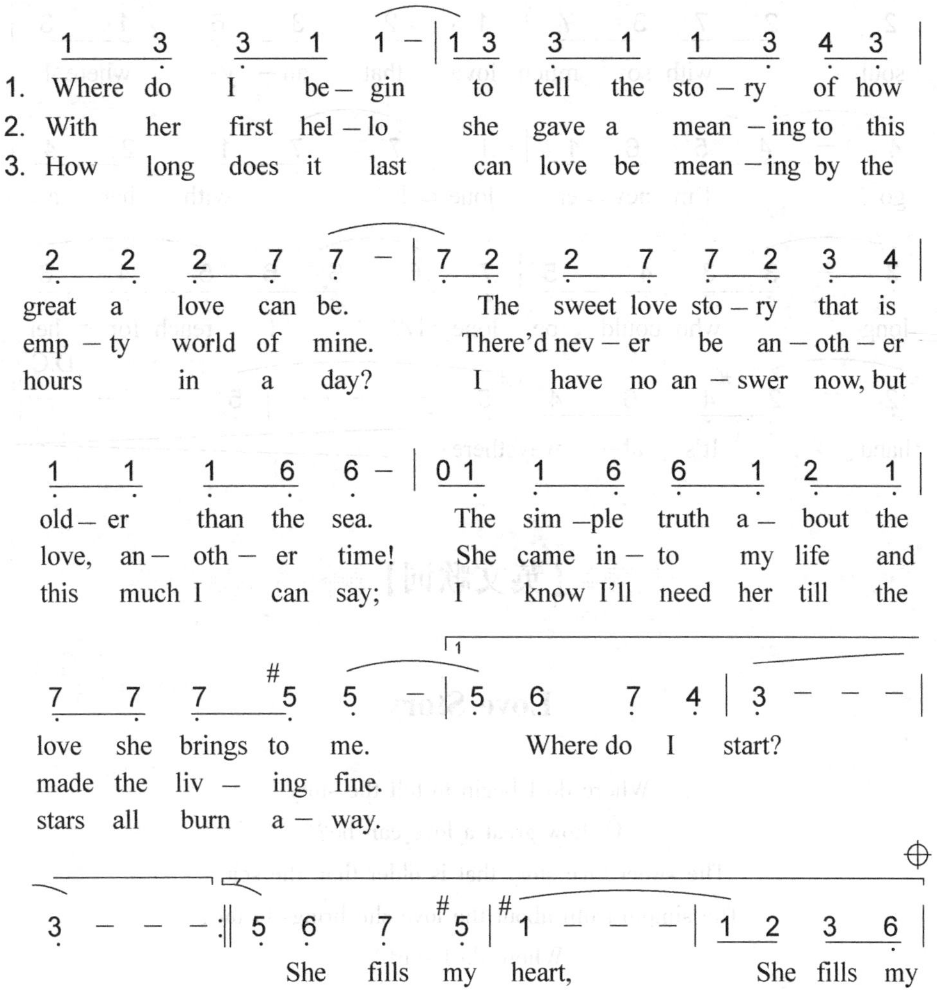

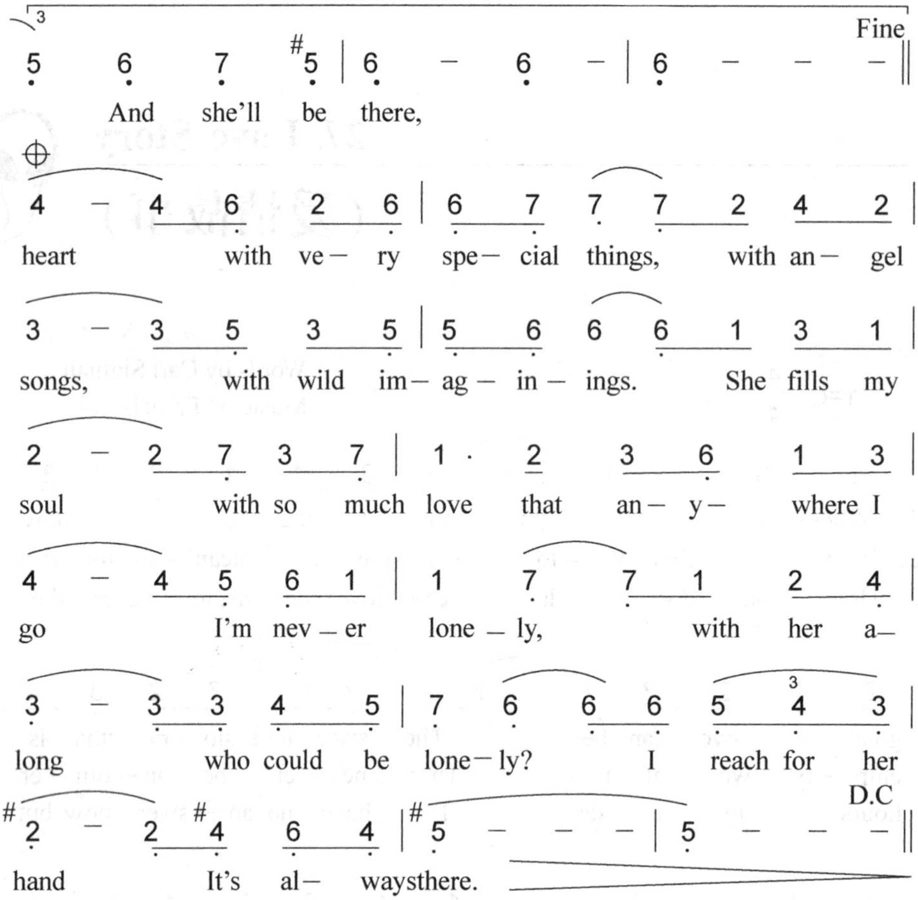

【英文歌词】

Love Story

Where do I begin to tell the story
Of how great a love can be?
The sweet love story that is older than the sea.
The simple truth about the love she brings to me,
Where do I start?

With her first hello,
She gave a meaning to this empty world of mine.
There'll never be another love, another time.

She came into my life and made the living fine.
She fills my heart.

She fills my heart with very special things,
With angel's souls,
With wild imaginings.
She fills my soul with so much love
That anywhere I go, I'm never lonely.
With her along, who could be lonely?
I reach for her hand.
It's always there.

How long does it last?
Can love be measured by the hours in a day?
I have no answers now, but this much I can say.
I know I'll need her till the stars all burn away
And she'll be there.

【参考译文】

爱情的故事

从何讲述这个故事,
细说爱情是多么伟大,
这甜蜜爱情故事
比大海还古老。
她给我带来爱情的朴素真理。
我从何说起?

用第一声"哈罗",
她把情义注入我这空虚的世界。
再也没有另一个爱人,没有另一次。
她走入我的生活,使我快乐。
她充满我心窝。

她充满我心窝,用很特殊的方式,

用天使之歌，
用丰富想象。
她用这么多爱充满我心灵，
不论走到哪里，我从不寂寞。
与她在一起，谁会寂寞？
我拉她的手
它总在那里等候。

这爱会持续多久？
爱能否按一天的小时计算？
我现在没有答案，但我可以说这么多
我知道我需要她，
直到天荒地老，
她会仍在那里等候。

语言点解析

(1) Where do I begin to tell the story of how great a love can be…
Where do I begin：从何说起。
Tell the story of：讲述……的故事。
a love：一次爱情。用 a 把 love 具体化。
begin to tell：开始讲述
例如：
Where do I ***begin to tell*** the story of how I fell in love with her? 我从何说起我是怎样爱上她的呢？

(2) The simple truth about the love she brings to me. =She brings to me the simple truth about the love.
the simple truth：朴素的真理，真谛

(3) **bring…to**：把……带给……
例如：
She ***brings to*** me the simple truth about friendship. 她给我带来有关友谊的朴素真理。

(4) There'll never be another love another time. 这样的爱只有一次，没有另一次，也没有另一人。

(5) She came into my life and made the living fine.

come into one's life：走入某人的生活。

例如：

She ***came into my life*** and I felt that even the whole world was smiling. 她进入我的生活，我感到整个世界都在微笑。

(6) **make the living fine**：使生活快乐

例如：

Reading is one of the ways to ***make the living fine***. 读书是使生活快乐的方式之一。

(7) with angel songs, with wild imaginings

这两行都是 She fills my heart 的继续。

angel songs：天使们唱的歌

wild imaginings：丰富的想象

(8) She fills my soul with so much love that anywhere I go I'm never lonely. =Her love fills my heart to such an extent that no matter where I go I never feel lonely.

soul：灵魂，实指 heart

heart and soul：全心全意

例如：

We still need to serve the people ***heart and soul***. 我们仍须全心全意地为人民服务。

(9) I reach for her hand. =I extend(hold out) my hand to take her hand.

reach for：伸手去够(拿)

例如：

He ***reached for*** the book. 他伸手去够书。She fell into the river when she reached for a beautiful flower. 他伸手去够一朵漂亮小花时掉进了河里。

(10) Can love be measured by the hours in a day? =Love cannot be measured by the hours in a day.

measure by：用……测量

(11) I know I'll love her till the stars all burn away… =I know I'll love her till the end of the world…

虽然… the stars all burn away 是不可能实现的事情，这与 I'll love you still till the seas go dry(我要爱你到大海干枯。)异曲同工。"要想不让我爱你，除非是高山夷为平地"也是同一意思。这样的用法在中外诗歌中还有许多例子。

注释与赏析

这是美国影片《爱情故事》(1970 年)的同名主题歌，由卡尔·西格曼(Carl Sigman)作词，弗朗西斯·莱依(Francis Lai)作曲。这部电影传入中国后深受欢迎，主题音乐家喻户晓。《爱情故事》于 1971 年获“金球”奖。该主题曲贯穿全片，旋律优美动听，歌词真挚感人。《爱情故事》的内容梗概如下：大银行家之子奥利佛与面包师之女詹妮弗相爱，遭到父亲的坚决反对。奥利佛情笃意深，与家庭脱离关系，毅然与詹妮弗结婚；靠打短工度日，生活清苦，但爱情甜蜜。詹妮弗放弃了自己喜爱的音乐事业，支持奥利佛攻读法律。奥利佛以优异的成绩受聘为律师，生活开始好转。奥利佛的父亲也要回心转意是，詹妮弗却患上了血癌。奥利佛悉心照料詹妮弗。最后詹妮弗在奥利佛怀中安然告别人世。

《爱情故事》的情节也摆脱不了流行套路，影片在基本大团圆的情况下结束，在人类情感恢复和谐之时给观众一个伤感却合理的结局。从一个侧面也告诉人们，对待爱情不应有门第之见，否则爱情悲剧便会跌出，人类美好情感遭到破坏。

《爱情故事》的同名主题歌的歌词十分感人，它告诉人们，伟大爱情的作用是多么无与伦比，其强大的威力能让任何事物，任何艰难险阻瞬间变得十分渺小，不足称道。男女的结合，爱神的降临，会赶走生活上的空虚，精神的压抑，世界从此变得幸福而甜蜜。驰骋的想象，天使的歌声互相充盈着对方的心灵。无论何时，无论何地，只要爱相随，谁会感到寂寞？即使人的肉体可以化去，但人的灵魂不灭，真挚的爱情永恒。即使一人升入天堂，另一方仍会认为其存在，分分秒秒将其铭刻在心底。这就是真爱，它让你生生死死相爱，岁岁年年相守。

28. Right Here Waiting (此情可待)

1=♭D 4/4

Words & Music by Richard Mark

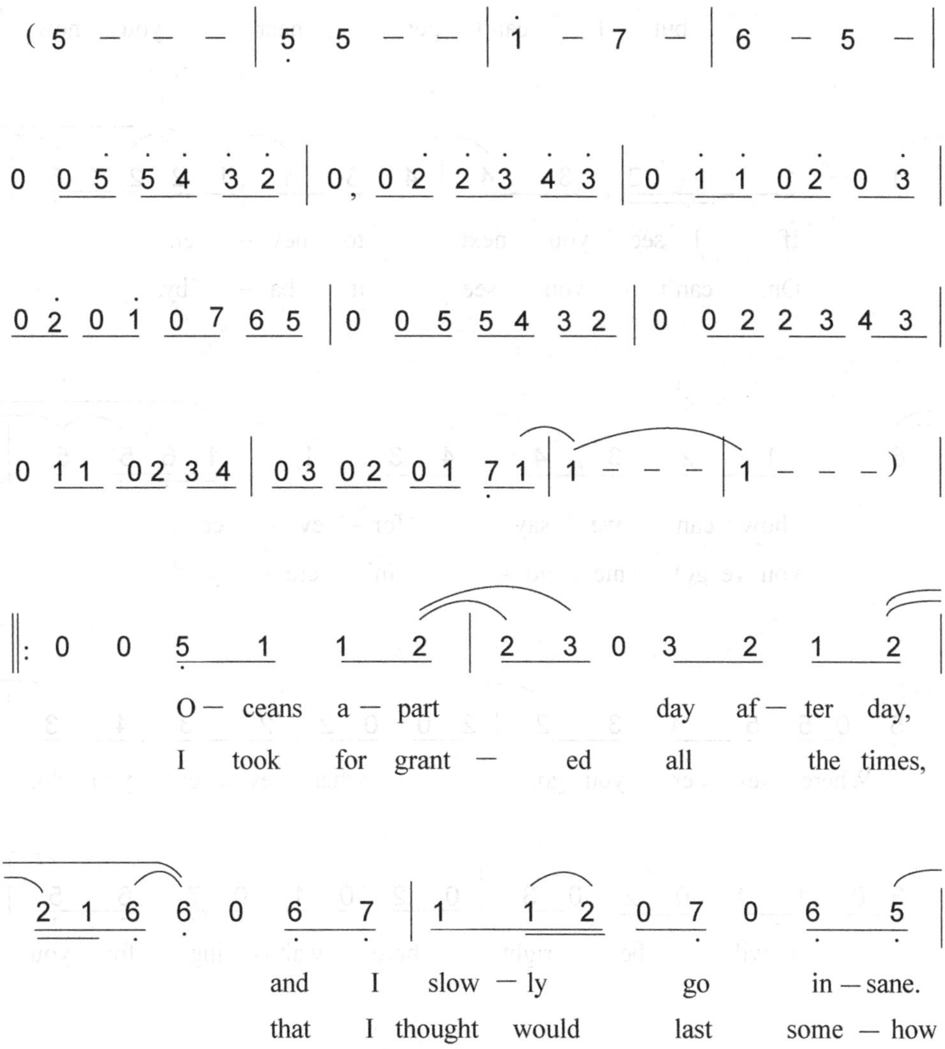

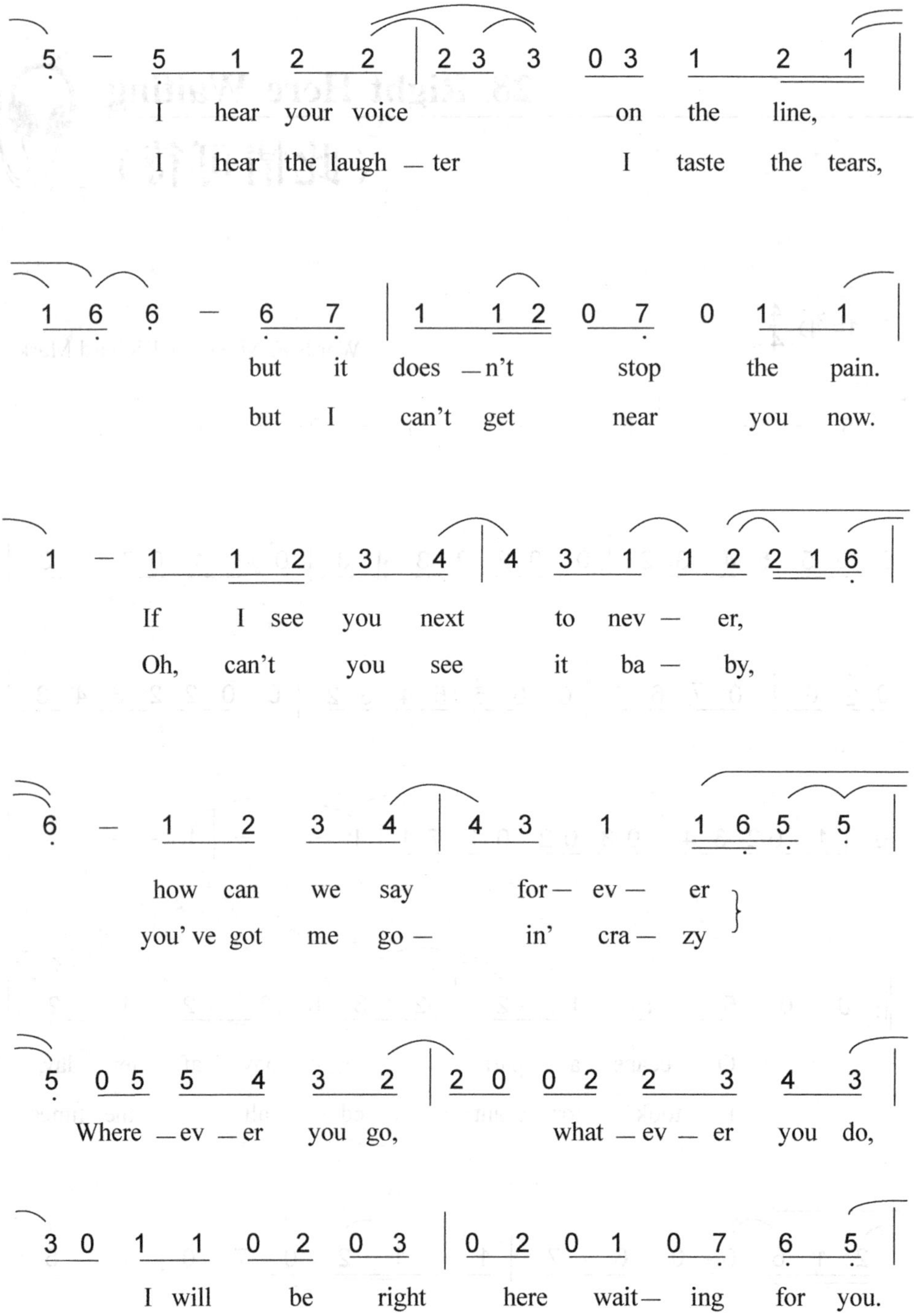
I hear your voice on the line,
I hear the laugh — ter I taste the tears,
but it does — n't stop the pain.
but I can't get near you now.
If I see you next to nev — er,
Oh, can't you see it ba — by,
how can we say for — ev — er
you' ve got me go — in' cra — zy
Where — ev — er you go, what — ev — er you do,
I will be right here wait— ing for you.

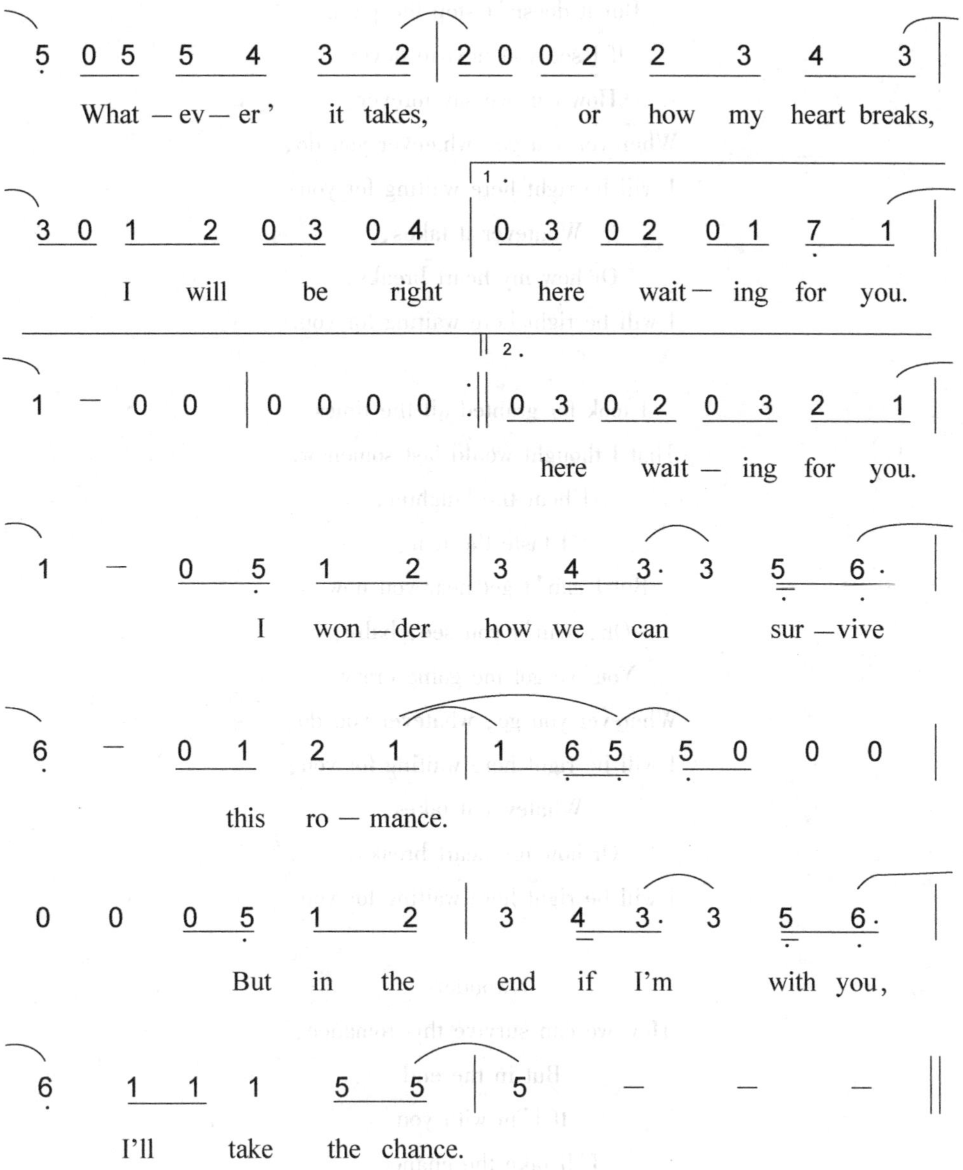

【英文歌词】

Right Here Waiting

Oceans apart, day after day,
And I slowly go insane.
I hear you voice on the line,

But it doesn't stop the pain.
If I see you next to never,
How can we say forever?
Wherever you go, whatever you do,
I will be right here waiting for you;
Whatever it takes,
Or how my heart breaks,
I will be right here waiting for you.

I took for granted all the times
That I thought would last somehow.
I hear the laughter,
I taste the tear,
But I can't get near you now.
Oh, can't you see, baby,
You've got me going crazy?
Wherever you go, whatever you do,
I will be right here waiting for you;
Whatever it takes,
Or how my heart breaks,
I will be right here waiting for you.

I wonder
How we can survive this romance,
But in the end
If I'm with you
I'll take the chance.
Oh, can't you see it, baby,
You've got me going crazy?
Wherever you go, whatever you do,
I will be right here waiting for you;
Whatever it takes,
Or how my heart breaks,
I will be right here waiting for you.
Waiting for you.

【参考译文】

此情可待

远隔重洋，日复一日，
我慢慢地变得要失常。
电话传来你的声音，
但这不能停止我的悲伤。
如果再也不能与你相见，
又怎能说我们到永远？
无论你在何地，无论你做何事，
我就在这里等候你。
不管怎么样，
或不管我多哀伤，
我就在这里等候你。

我一直认为，
你我会情长意久。
我听见你的笑声，
我品尝眼泪，
但此刻不能接近你。
哦，宝贝，难道你不懂，
你已使我发疯？
无论你在何地，无论你做何事，
我就在这里等候你。
不管怎么样，
或不管我多哀伤，
我就在这里等候你。

我试问，
我们如何熬过这浪漫情。
但到最后，
如果我与你同在，
我要抓住这机会。
哦，宝贝，难道你不懂，
你已使我发疯？

无论你在何地，无论你做何事，
我就在这里等候你。
不管怎么样，
或不管我多哀伤，
我就在这里等候你。
等候你。

语言点解析

(1) Oceans apart, day after day = Oceans are apart, day in day out

day after day：日复一日

apart：隔开；相隔

take sth. apart：拆开某物

apart from：除去；除了(某事物)以外……都、全、没、没有等

例如：

Day after day she waited in vain for him to call her. 日复一日，她等等他给她打电话，但徒劳无获。

These two villages are 5 kilometers ***apart***. 这两个村庄相隔五公里。

He is **taking** the radio ***apart***. 他正把收音机拆开。

Apart from a few spelling mistakes, your composition is quite good. 除了几个拼写错误外，你的作文挺不错。

(2) And I slowly go insane. = And I gradually go mad.

insane：精神失常的；疯狂的；愚蠢的

例如：

He is an ***insane*** man. 他是个精神失常的人。

(3) I hear your voice on the line. = I hear your voice from the phone receiver.

on the line：在电话上

(4) But it doesn't stop the pain: But hearing your voice on the line does not stop the pain of missing you.

(5) **next to never**：近乎于永不

next to：在……一旁；在……后面；跟在……之后，几乎，近乎；近于

例如：

He sat ***next to*** Mary on the sofa yesterday evening. 昨天晚上，他紧挨着玛丽坐在沙发上。

The Yellow River is the longest in China **next to** the Yangtse River. 在中国，黄河是仅次于长江的最长的河。

Doing this proved ***next to*** impossible without a ladder. 要做这事没有梯子可以说是不行的。

(6) How can we say forever: How can we say we'll love forever.

(7) Wherever you go, whatever you do: No matter where you go and no matter what you do, 疑问句+ever: 无论……。

(8) I will be right here waiting for you. =I will be nowhere else but here waiting for you.

right *adv.*: 恰恰；就

例如：

Right below the tree there sat an old man. 就在这树下坐着一个老头儿。

(9) Whatever it takes. =No matter what takes place.

(10) Or how my heart breaks. =Or no matter how my heart breaks.

One's heart **breaks**: (某人)伤心至极、心碎。

例如：

He heart **broke** when he told her they were through. 当他告诉她他们之间的关系已经结束时，她心碎了。

(11) I took for granted all the times that I thought would last somehow. =I all the times took for granted that, I thought, would last somehow.

I thought 是插入语。that 指他们之间的爱情。That would last somehow 是 take for granted 的宾语，所以说这个句子还可以这样理解：I thought I always believed that that (our love) would last somehow. 若不这样理解，这两行歌词就不易看懂。

take sth for granted: 信以为真，认为某事属实

例如：

I ***take it for granted*** that you love me. 我真以为你爱我。

all the times: always

somehow: 不知何故；以某种方式；通过某种途径

例如：

Somehow, I don't feel he can pass the exam. 不知什么原因，我觉得他通不过考试。

We must stop him investigating this matter ***somehow***. 我们得想个办法不能让他调查这件事。

(12) I hear the laughter. =I hear you laugh on the phone.

(13) I taste the tear. =I taste my tear.

(14) But I can't get near you now: But I can't get close to you now.

get near: 接近

例如:

In that remote place, it was not easy to ***get near*** a human being. 在那个遥远的地方，接近人是一件很难的事。

(15) Can't you see?: 难道你看不出?

例如: *Can't you see* he loves you? 你看不出他爱你吗?

(16) You've got me going crazy: You've made me crazy.

go crazy: go mad; go insane. 发疯，精神错乱

get sth. (sb.) doing: 使(某人、某物)做某事

例如:

He ***got the clock working***. 他又让钟表走起来。

Can you ***get him talking***? 你能让他开口说话吗?

(17) I wonder =I want to know

(18) How we can survive this romance. =How we can live longer than this love affair

survive *vi.* & *vt.*: 继续生存或存在; 经历某生物而幸存，比某人长命。

例如:

The ship sank, only 134 people ***survived***. 船沉下去了。只有134人幸存下来。

My classmates ***survived*** the earthquake. 我的同学们经历了地震并从中逃生。

Most women **survive** their husbands. 大部分妇女都比自己的丈夫活是时间长。

romance: love story; love affair 爱情故事。Romance本指具有传奇色彩的浪漫故事，曾是一种流行的文学形式。男子为寻求自己的爱情，历尽风险，跋山涉水，最终到达目的地，大部分能获得追求的爱情。这首歌中把他们之间的爱情说成是romance，因为他们远隔重洋，虽因有电话比浪漫传奇故事中的恋人略占优势，但从性质而言，这远隔重洋的爱情与古代传奇故事里的爱情无异; 差别是，昔日的骑士变成今天打电话的人。

(19) But in the end, if I'm with you, I'll take the chance.

In the end: at last; finally 终于; 最后

例如:

He tried different jobs; ***in the end*** he became a teacher. 他试过不同的工作，但最后他当了教师。

take the chance：抓住这机会；冒这次险

take a chance：冒险，碰运气

take chances：冒险

注释与赏析

这首歌的词曲作者及演唱者均为理查德．马克斯(Richard Marx, 1964—)。这首歌创作并演唱于1989年，夺得排行榜冠军。Richard Marx 是美国歌坛近年来最走红的抒情歌手之一。在1989年，他被评为美国十大歌星之一。无论从曲调上讲，还是从内容上看，这首歌曲都是一首佳作。

相恋的人远隔重洋，日复一日地思恋着。起码主人公是这样的。这里首先摆出了地点和时间两个意象。地点是无限大的，时间是以日计算的。遥远的距离与每日的思恋形成大与小的对比，充分表现了主人公对身在远方的恋人的焦渴的思恋。他思恋她都到了快要精神失常的地步。电话虽能传声，但它怎能缓解不见面的悲情？真是：电话响，声音清，此时此刻难为情。相恋不相见，怎能谈永远？

主人公的态度是值得称赞的，是很感动人的。他不管所爱之人身在何处，也不管她在干什么，他都要等待她，这个声明是需要勇气的，是可以此见其真诚的，因为这是一般恋人不愿说的：Whenever you go, whatever you do, —这 Wherever you go 还可以接受，而 whatever you do 则不然，因为它可以包含着对爱情的背叛。Wherever you go, whatever you do. I' ll be right here waiting for you. 这不是一般人能轻易说出口并愿承受的。还有，“不管怎么样，或不管我多哀伤，我就在这里等候你”。这里指，不管发生什么事，仍然可能包括对方背叛爱情。不管我多哀伤仍然可能包括因对方背叛爱情而使他不悦、悲伤，他仍然期待她回来。这就是他对爱的表白。

他一直认为他们情谊会久长，但它久居异地，这不是已有偏离的倾向？电话上可听对方的声音，但边接电话边流泪，自己把自己的眼泪尝，因见不到恋人而流出的眼泪可能不仅是咸的而且还是苦的。不能接近恋人，几乎使主人公发疯。这就是他的爱情，即便是单相思，也是伟大的爱情。

主人公也慢慢地发现，他怀疑他这爱情是否能成。在一段歌词中他几乎用了表明他对爱情把握不大的疑虑：他想知道如何能熬过这烂漫情，又想：但最终如果他能与她在一起，他要抓住这机遇，这里同时暗含此义：可能最终也见不到对方。他又问：难道你不懂你已使我发疯？

不管对方是不是要回来，我们已听到主人公求爱若渴、感情真挚、语言典雅的表白，听起来让人感觉舒服，为之动情，替他渴盼，盼望他爱的人回到他身边来。

这首歌最令人难忘的是这一段歌词：

无论你在何地，
无论你做何事，
我就在这里等候你。
不管怎么样，
或不管我多哀伤，
我就在这里等候你。

这段歌词共唱了三遍，其用意是显而易见的。

真正地爱一个人可能就是这样的，两人若真相爱了，可能真的“不管你做过何事，从今以后我就爱你，你不许再做别的事。”

29. I Do It for You
(一切为你)

Words & Music by
Bryan Admas & Robert Jonh Lange

1=G 4/4

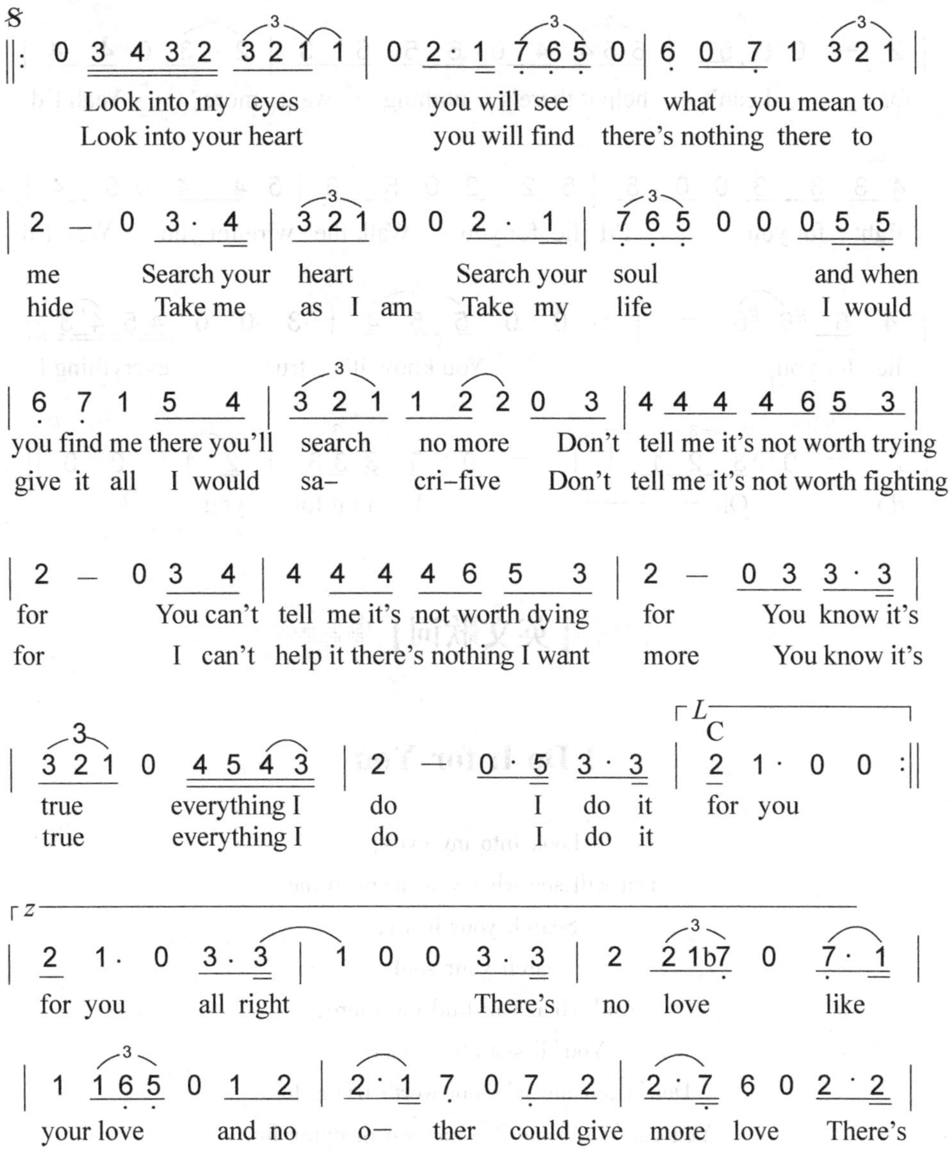

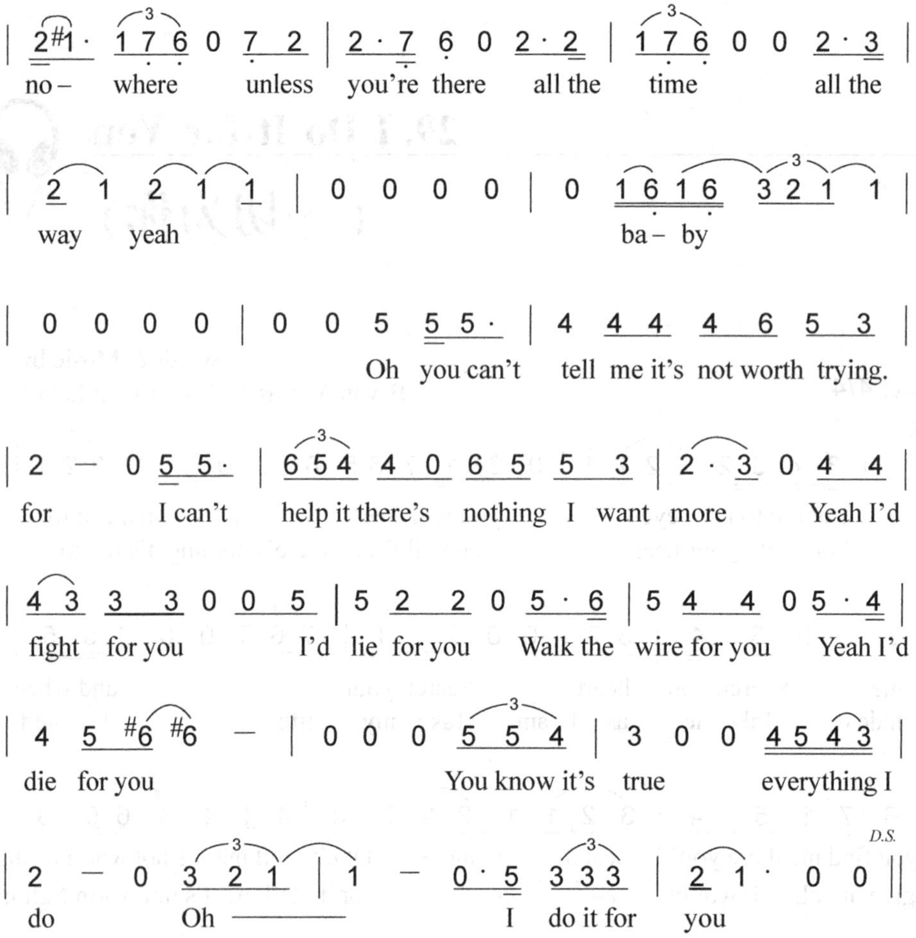

【英文歌词】

I Do It for You

Look into my eyes,
You will see what you mean to me
Search your heart,
Search your soul,
And when you find me there,
You'll search no more.
Don't tell me it's not worth trying for.
You can't tell me it's not worth dying for.

You know it's true,
Everything I do,
I do it for you.

Look into your heart.
You will find there's nothing there to hide.
Take me as I am,
Take my life.
I would give it all I would sacrifice.
Don't tell me it's not worth fighting for.
I can't help it there's nothing I want more.
You know it's true,
Everything I do,
I do it for you
All right,
There's no love like your love,
And no other could give more love.
There's nowhere unless you're there
All the time, all the way.
Yeah, baby.
Oh, you can't tell me it's not worth trying for.
I can't help it there's nothing I want more.
Yeah I'd fight for you.
I'd lie for you.
Walk the wire for you.
Yeah I'd die for you.
You know it's true,
Everything I do
Oh! I do it for you.

【参考译文】

一切全为你

请看着我的眼睛,
你会明白你对我意味着什么。

寻求心相连，
寻求意相投，
当你在那儿发现我，
你就会别无寻求。
别说那不值去奋争，
别说那不值去牺牲，
你真的很清楚，
我做的一切
全为你。

透视你的心灵，
你会发现纯真的一片情。
人诚挚，
情意切，
我会抛弃所有，
我会以死为代价。
别说那不值去奋争，
真没办法我别无他求。
你真的很清楚，
我做的一切
全为你。

噢，你的爱最深厚，
有谁能付出更多的爱。
没办法，除非你伴我左右，
直到永远。

噢，宝贝。
你不能告诉我那不值去奋斗，
真没办法我别无他求。
耶，我愿为你拼搏，
为你献身，
为你铤而走险，
耶，我愿为你献身。
你真的很清楚，
噢，我做的一切
全为你。

语言点解析

(1) Look into my eyes, you'll see what you mean to me. 请看着我的眼睛，你会明白你对我意味着什么。

(2) **look into**：窥探，调查

(3) Search your heart, search your soul. 寻求心相连，寻求意相投。
soul *n.*：意为：精力，热情；人；典型；鬼魂

(4) Don't tell me it's not worth fighting for. =Please don't tell me that it's not worth fighting for. 别说那不值得去奋争。
be worth doing：(词组)值得干某事
fight *vi.* (fought, fought)意为打仗，进行战争；奋斗，斗争
例如：
We have been **fighting** for freedom. 我们为自由而奋斗。
fight 作名词意为"战斗"时，应与下列词语区分开来：
war：主要指国家间的战争。
battle：war 中的各个战役。
combat：比 battle 小的战斗。
fight：私人的战斗，打架。
struggle：肉体上、精神上的战斗、拼搏。

(5) So, take me as I am, take my life. =So, I'm as honest and devoted to your love as I treat my life. 因此，我对你的爱忠贞如一，正像对待我自己的生命一样(即：人诚挚，情意切)。

(6) I would give it all, I would sacrifice. =I would give all my love to you and I would give up everything if necessary. 我会全抛一片情，如果有必要，我会以死为代价。

(7) There is no way unless you're there all the time. 没办法，除非你伴我左右。
unless *conj*：if…not 如果不，除非
例如：
I shall come ***unless*** it rains (i. e. , I shall come if it doesn't rain). 如果不下雨，我会来的。

(8) I can't help it, there's nothing I want more：It can't be helped, I want nothing more than fighting for your love. 真没办法，我只为爱而奋斗。

(9) I can't help it. =It can't be helped. 真没办法。

Help 与 can 连用，意为：回避，忍受。

例如：

He didn't speak more than he could ***help***. 他绝口不谈那些不适宜的话。

(10) I'd lie for you, walk the wire for you. =I'd give all my life for you, I'd rush (ahead) into danger for you. 我愿为你献身，为你付出一切。

注释与赏析

这首《一切全为你》歌曲是1991年摄制的每个影片《绿林王子罗宾汉》("Robin Hood: Prince of Thieves")中的主题歌，主要由布莱恩·亚当斯和罗伯特·约翰·兰格作词作曲，并由布莱恩·亚当斯亲自担任影片插曲的主唱。此歌一经唱出就轰动欧美，后传唱于世界各地，获得了诸多殊荣。如它在美国热门排行榜上连续7周第一，在英国则持续9周第一以及夺下了欧洲其他九个国家排行榜的冠军。获得了葛莱美最佳影视歌曲奖和全美音乐奖的最佳单曲奖。

布莱恩·亚当斯1975年出生于加拿大，从小酷爱音乐，十几岁时便开始了音乐演唱生涯。他同人合作，为许多乐队创作歌曲。1980年他开始到美国发展音乐事业，经过自己锲而不舍地艰苦努力，逐渐打开了市场，获得了成功。他不仅作词作曲，有谁还参加演唱，被认为是一位多才多艺的当代流行歌星。

影片《绿林王子罗宾汉》描写了一位在英国12世纪是劫富济贫绿林侠盗的传奇故事。为片配制的此歌也体现出为爱情做出一定牺牲的挚爱精神，表现了绿林英雄有血有肉的普通人的一面。罗宾汉是西方文化传统中绿林人物的典型代表。与中国同类题材的描述有所不同，如我国绿林好汉的典型代表《水浒传》中的英雄们几乎没有多少爱情的叙述，青一色的中国式的好汉，是一种事业上的硬汉子。而西方以罗宾汉为代表的好汉们即追求事业上的成功，也追求情感上享受的两栖奋斗者。"别说那不值去奋争，别说那不值去牺牲，你真的很清楚，我做的一切全为你。"歌中即没有豪言壮语，也没有浩荡气魄，所包含的唯有执着的爱。

30. Sing
(唱吧)

1=A 4/4

Words & Music by Joe Raposo

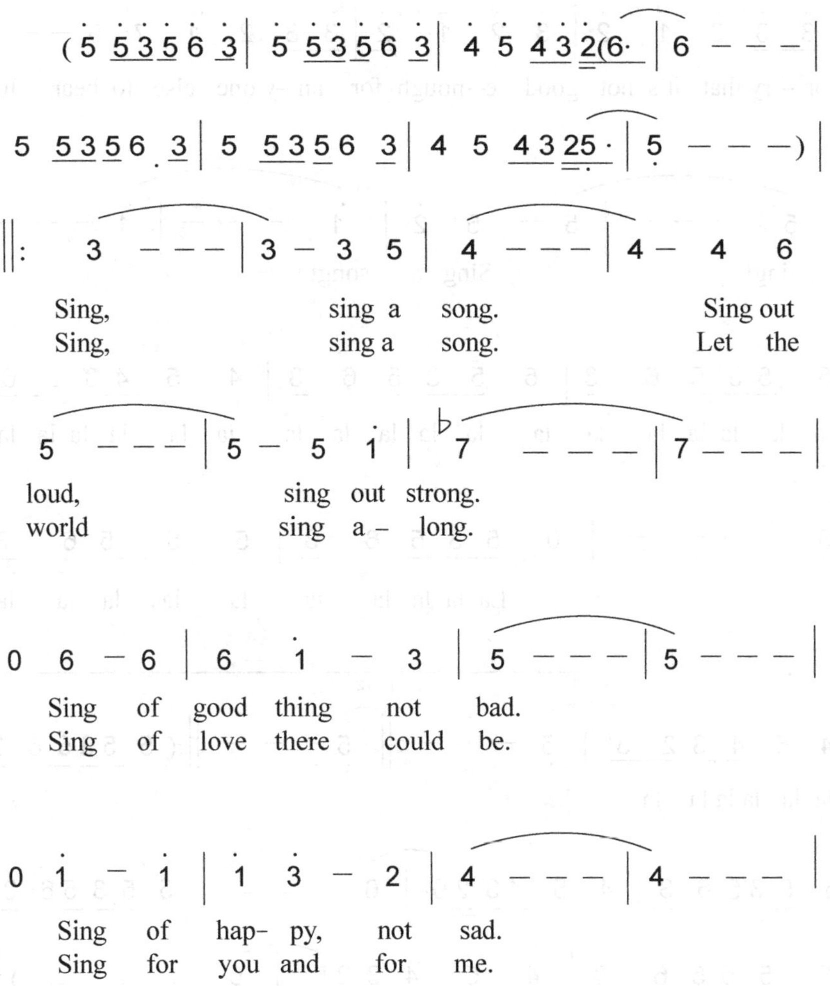

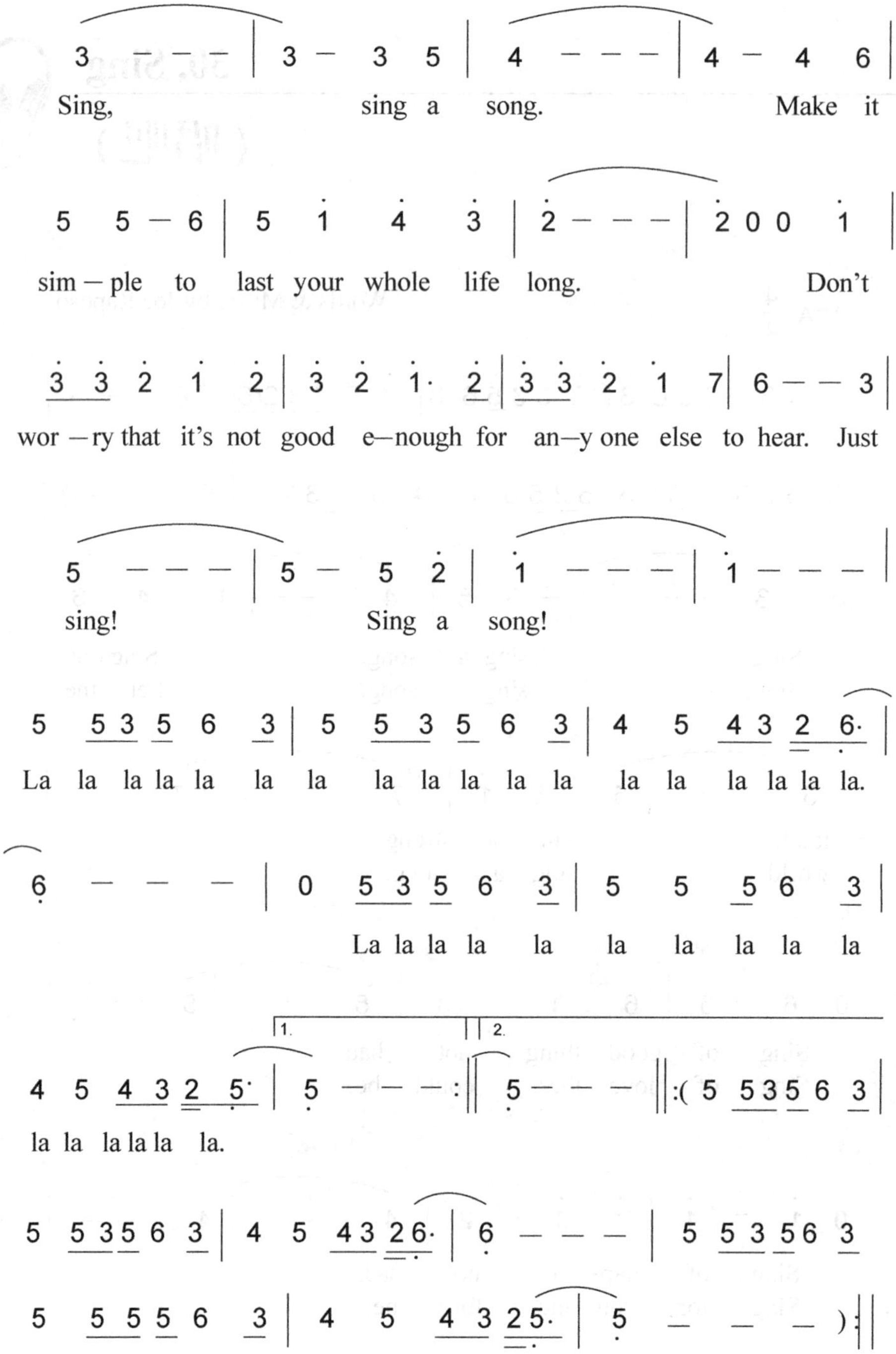
Sing, sing a song. Make it
sim — ple to last your whole life long. Don't
wor — ry that it's not good e—nough for an—y one else to hear. Just
sing! Sing a song!
La la la la la la la la la la la la la la la la la la.
La la la la la la la la la la
la la la la la la.

【英文歌词】

Sing, sing a song.
Sing out loud, sing out strong.
Sing of good things not bad.
Sing of happy not sad.

Sing, sing a song.
Make it simple to last
Your whole life long.
Don't worry that it's not
Good enough for anyone
Else to hear.
Just sing, sing a song.

Sing, sing a song.
Let the world sing along.
Sing of love there could be.
Sing for you and for me.

Sing, sing a song.
Make it simple to last
Your whole life long.
Don't worry that it's not
Good enough for anyone
Else to hear.
Just sing, sing a song.

【参考译文】

唱　吧

唱，放声唱，
声音要高，
还要有力量。

唱美好不唱悲伤。

唱，放声唱，
要一生一世
轻松欢畅。
莫怕唱得不够好，
别人会听到。
你就唱，放声唱！
啦，啦，啦……

唱，放声唱，
让整个世界也跟着唱。
唱可能有的爱，
为你我都欢快。

唱，放声唱。
要一生一世轻松欢畅。
莫怕唱得不够好，
别人会听到。
你就唱，放声唱！

你就唱，放声唱！

语言点解析

(1) **sing out** 唱出来，原意为“大声叫喊”“大声讲出”
例如：
You should ***sing out*** your thoughts. 你应把自己的思想讲出来。

(2) Sing out loud, sing out strong 中的 loud 和 strong 分别等于 loudly 和 strongly.

(3) Sing of happy, not sad. =Sing of happy things, but bot sad things.
sing of：歌唱……
例如：
They ***sang of*** their friendship。他们歌唱友谊。
We ***sing of*** his great deeds. 我们歌唱他的丰功伟绩。

(4) Make it simple to last your whole life long.

It 是形式主语，真正的主语是 to last your whole life long，意思是唱歌能使你一生一世轻松，这样一件事非常 simple.

(5) Don't worry that it's not good enough for anyone else to hear.

enough to 是足以……做……

例如：

The water is not hot ***enough to*** drink. 这水太凉，不能喝。

He is old ***enough to*** take care of himself. 他够大了，可以自己照顾自己了。

(6) **else** 要放在 somebody，nobody，anybody，something，nothing，anything，somewhere，no where，anywhere 这些词的后边，但如果想表达别人，其他人"用 other。如 other people：别人(但不可以说 else people)。

(7) Just sing，sing a song!

Just：可译成"就""尽管"，意思是不顾虑任何东西。

例如：

Don't be afraid. ***Just*** do it. 别害怕，放心去做。

(8) Let the world sing along.

the world：指人们

sing along：意为"随着唱"，"跟着唱"。

例如：

When I sang that old song，many middle aged people ***sang along*** without being a aware of it. 我唱起那首老歌时，许多中年人不知不觉地随着唱起来。

(9) Sing for you and for me.

for：表示"为"

例如：

He sang ***for*** the soldiers. 他为士兵们唱歌。

注释与赏析

《唱吧》这首歌曲的词曲作者是杰欧·罗伯素(Joe Raposo)。除了众多伤感和怀旧的歌曲之外，本歌曲是卡伦·卡彭特演唱的一首十分轻快、流畅的流行歌曲，而不像别的歌具有太多的忧郁味。

本歌的曲调和歌词内容比较崇尚释放和追求人生中的快乐情感。歌中建议人们在面对困难的时候，要乐观向上，始终以一种积极的心态去放松心情、放大美好，去带给人们幸福和快乐。表达了作者和歌唱者对美好、幸福生活的向往和追求。

31. My Heart Will Go On

(我心永恒)

1=F 4/4

♩=112

Words by Will Jennings
Music by James Horner

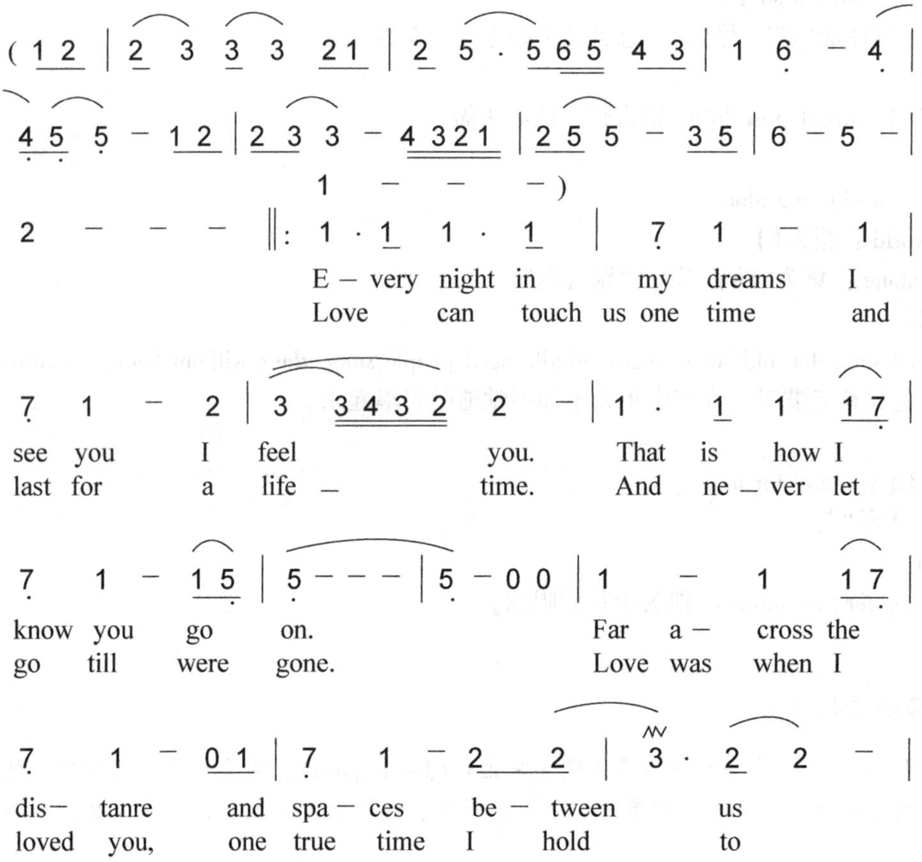

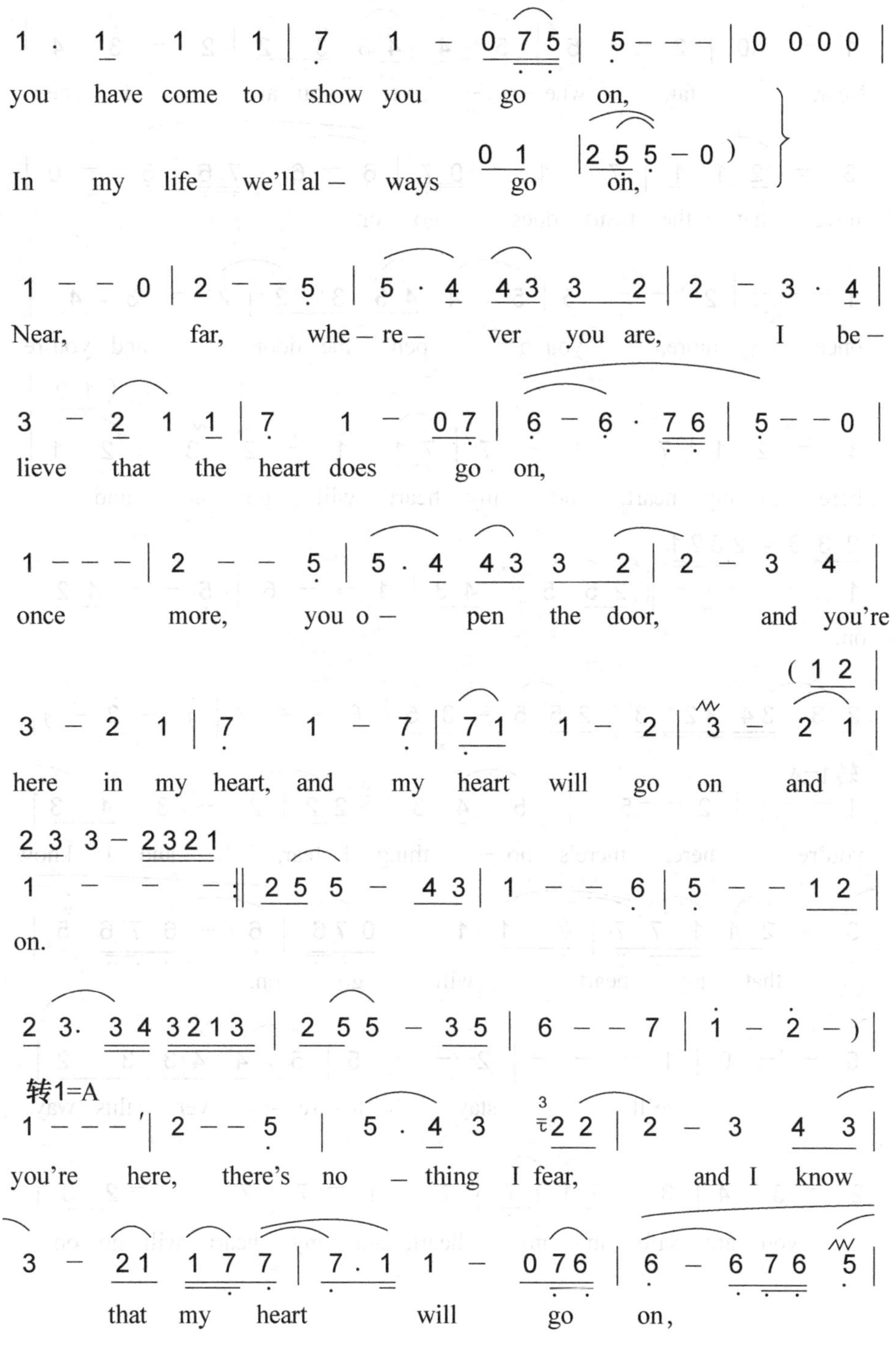
you have come to show you go on,
In my life we'll al – ways go on,
Near, far, whe – re – ver you are, I be –
lieve that the heart does go on,
once more, you o – pen the door, and you're
here in my heart, and my heart will go on and
on.
转1=A
you're here, there's no – thing I fear, and I know
that my heart will go on,

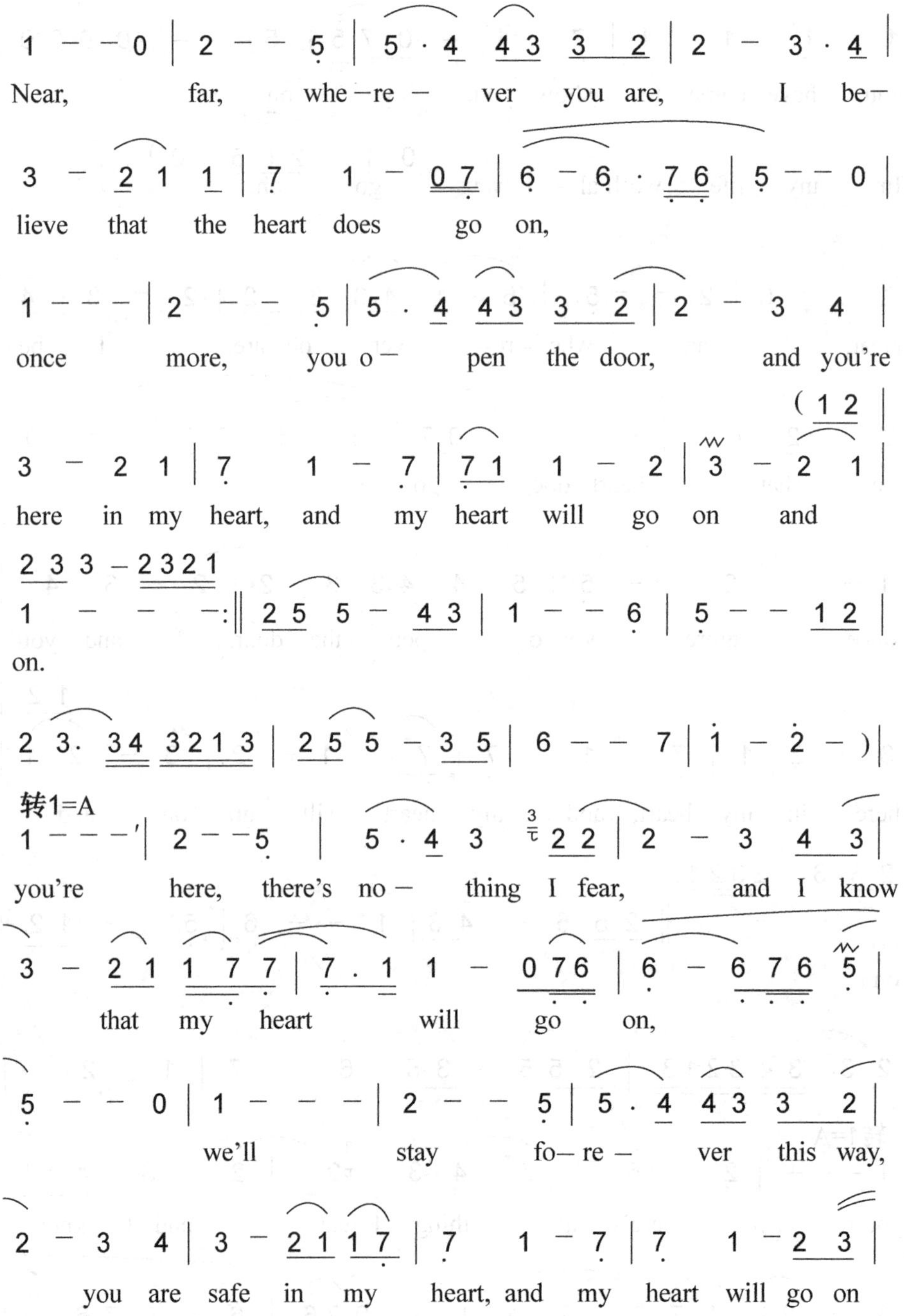
Near, far, whe-re - ver you are, I be-
lieve that the heart does go on,
once more, you o- pen the door, and you're
here in my heart, and my heart will go on and
on.
转1=A
you're here, there's no- thing I fear, and I know
that my heart will go on,
we'll stay fo- re - ver this way,
you are safe in my heart, and my heart will go on

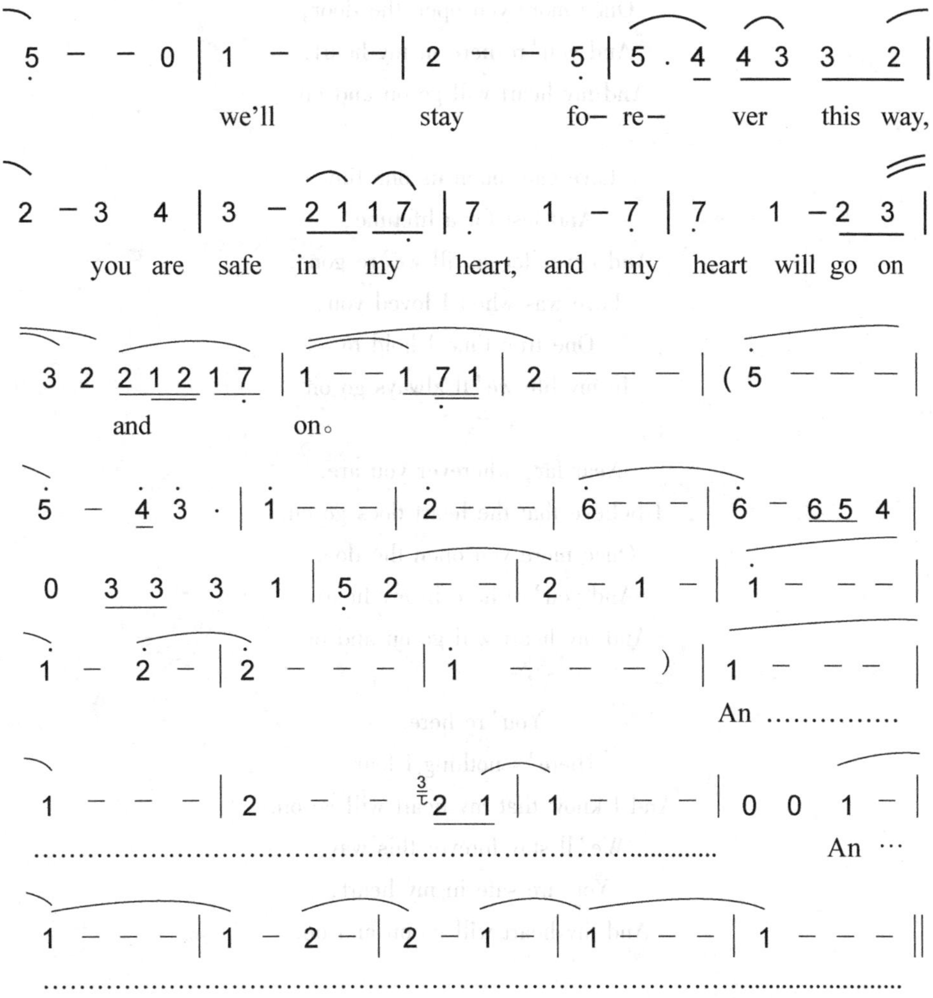

【英文歌词】

My Heart Will Go on

Every night in my dreams,
I see you, I feel you.
That is how I know you go on.
Far across the distance and spaces between us,
You have come to show you go on.
Near far wherever you are
I believe that the heart does go on.

Once more you open the door,
And you're here in my heart,
And my heart will go on and on.

Love can touch us one time
And last for a lifetime,
And never let go till we're gone.
Love was when I loved you,
One true time I hold to
In my life we'll always go on

Near far, wherever you are.
I believe that the heart does go on.
Once more you open the door.
And you're here in my heart.
And my heart will go on and on.

You're here.
There's nothing I fear,
And I know that my heart will go on.
We'll stay forever this way.
You are safe in my heart,
And my heart will go on and on.

【参考译文】

我心永恒

每天夜里
我梦见你，感觉到你。
就这样我知道你还好。
穿越你我之间的距离和空间，
你来告诉我你还好。
远，近，不管在哪里，
我相信这心将永恒。
再一次，你打开这门，

你来到我的心里,
我的心将永恒,永恒。

爱触击我们一次,
便永远如此,
永不放松直到我们去世。
爱就是我爱你,
一次便成终身。
在我们一生中永恒。

远,近,不管在哪里,
我相信这心将永恒。
再一次,你打开这门,
你来到我的心里,
我的心将永恒,永恒。

有你在,
我什么也不怕,
我知道我的心将永恒。
我们就这样永远相爱。
你安全地待在我心里,
我的心将永恒,永恒。

语言点解析

(1) That is how I know you go on. =That is the way how I know you are getting on. (i. e. By dreaming of you in my dreams, I know how you go on.) how I know you go on 是个表语从句。
go on:在此处是 get on, get along 的意思。
go on 主要还有以下几条意思(时间)过去,流逝,经过;发生;继续

(2) I believe that the heart does go on. =I believe that my heart continues to love you.
does:用在动词前,表示强调。go on 在此为"继续""永恒"之意。
...the heart does go on:译成"这颗心永恒"。

(3) One more, you open the door and you've here in my heart.... =Once again, you open the door of my heart and you come into it.
once more:再一次

注意**more**组成的其他词组：
no more：不再；也不；和-------一样不；不超过
more and more：越来越
more or less：差不多，几乎；大致；大约；或多或少
more than happy (glad, willing) to do sth：非常乐意或做某事
What is more：而且；此外；还有，更有甚者

(4) Love can touch us one time and last for a lifetime, =Love can touch us once and leave an everlasting influence.

(5) **for a lifetime**：一生一世，终生

(6) And never let go till we're gone. =And never let it go till we are dead.

(7) Love was when I love you, one true time I hold to. =It was love when I loved you, I cherish and remain loyal to this one true time.
hold to sth.：不放弃或不改变(原则等)忠于某事物
例如：
I will **hold to** my love for him. 我不会改变对他的爱。
hold组成的其他词组有：
hold sb. to sth.：使某人遵守诺言
hold sth. together：使……团结一致
hold up sth：以武力或暴力威胁抢劫
hold with sth：(用于否定或疑问句)容忍或赞成某事物

(8) In my life we'll always go on.
in one's life：在……一生中
例如：
For the first time ***in my life***, I earned 500 dollars a day yesterday. 我一生中，昨天第一次在一天之内挣了500美元。

(9) You're here, there's nothing I fear. =With you here, there is nothing I fear. Or: I fear nothing because you are here.

(10) We'll stay for ever this way. =We'll go on loving each other like this forever.

(11) You're safe in my heart. =Nobody can hurt you when you are in my heart.

(12) **safe**：安全；平安；无危险；不会或不致受到伤害、损失

例如：

Don't be afraid. You'll be *safe* here. 别害怕，在这里你会很安全。

She was *safe* though frightened by the tiger. 尽管受到老虎的惊吓，她并没受到伤害。

注释与赏析

这首歌是美国电影巨片《泰坦尼克号》的主题歌，由韦尔·杰宁斯(Will Jennings)作词，杰姆斯·奥纳(James Horner)作曲，加拿大歌星席琳·迪翁(Celine Dion)演唱，获1998年第70届奥斯卡最佳歌曲奖。这首歌曲调优美、激昂，歌词动人，深受世界各地青年喜爱，尤其风靡于各国大学校园。

1912年，在当时称得上有史以来最大的客轮"泰坦尼克号"从英国出发，首航横渡大西洋。这艘客轮曾视为不会沉没的巨轮，因为即使是部分密封舱被破坏，其余的仍然能照常工作。不料，4月14日，"泰坦尼克号"与冰山相撞，5个密封舱进水，开始沉没，船上1517名乘客遇难，幸存、获救者仅712人。这个故事多次被搬上银幕，其情节大致如下：一位穷酸青年画家杰克赌赢了一张船票，乘船回家。他在甲板上见一女子要跳海自尽，他劝阻成功，两人慢慢地产生好感，直到那女子罗丝以身相许。船沉之时，他们彼此把生的机会让给对方。最后，杰克冻死于冰海，罗丝获救。这部影片采用了罗丝回忆往事的倒叙手法。

主题歌"我心永恒"很有激情，内容感人，整首歌与电影中的音乐融为一体，使影片颇具感染力。我既能听到这"不会沉没"的巨轮起航时气势磅礴的雄伟交响乐，又能听到巨轮撞上冰山时那种大跌大宕的旋律；既能感觉到恋人缠绵的柔情，又能感受到巨轮沉没时的悲哀。在Celin Dion最后几句近乎呐喊的高亢声中，我们听到的不仅仅是几行简单的歌词，而是令天地为动容、令听众为之心颤的宣言书。Dion本人曾说："在演唱时，我的心在颤抖，在流泪，几乎无法控制自己的声音。"

尽管《泰坦尼克号》描写了一个并不令人信服的爱情，不过这一曲"我心永恒"却是公认的旷世杰作并被反复传唱，愿世上每人都会得到"我心永恒"里面所表达的这种爱情。

32. Endless Love

(无尽的爱)

1=$^{\flat}$B $\frac{4}{4}$

中速

Words & Music by Lionel Richie

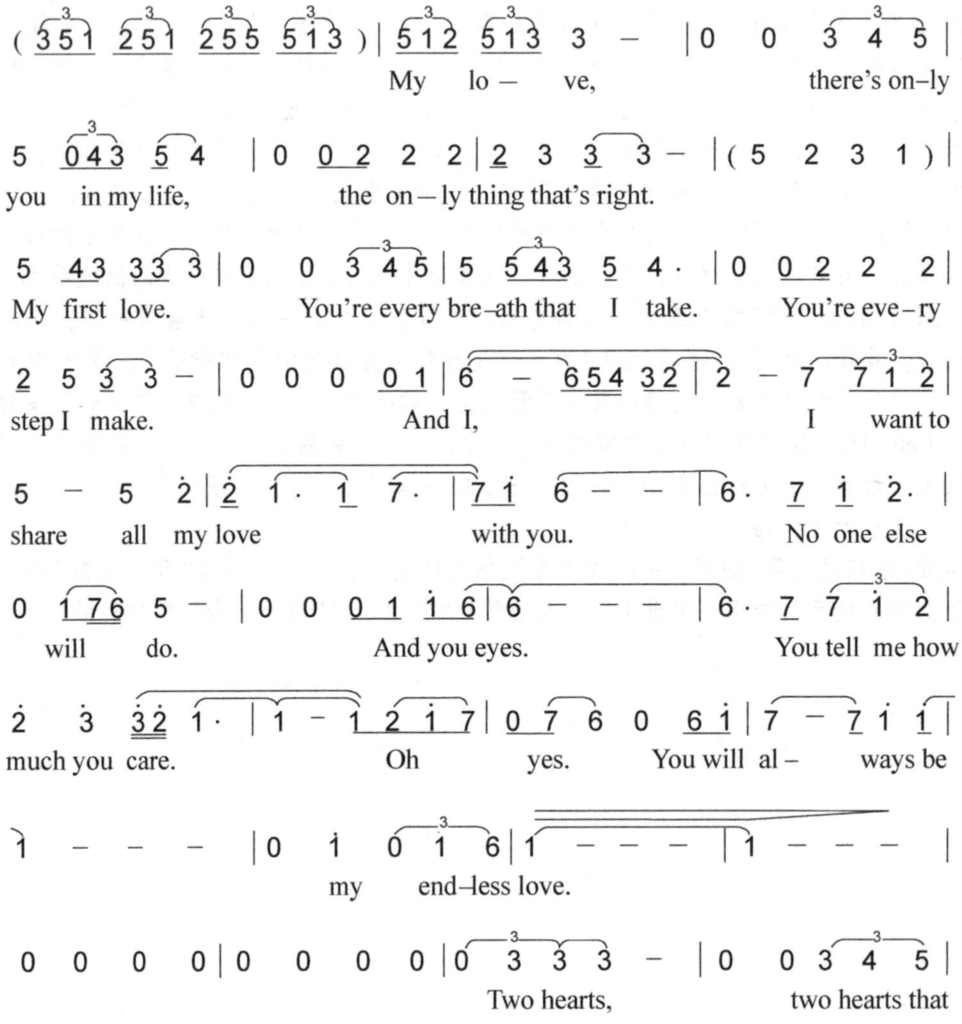

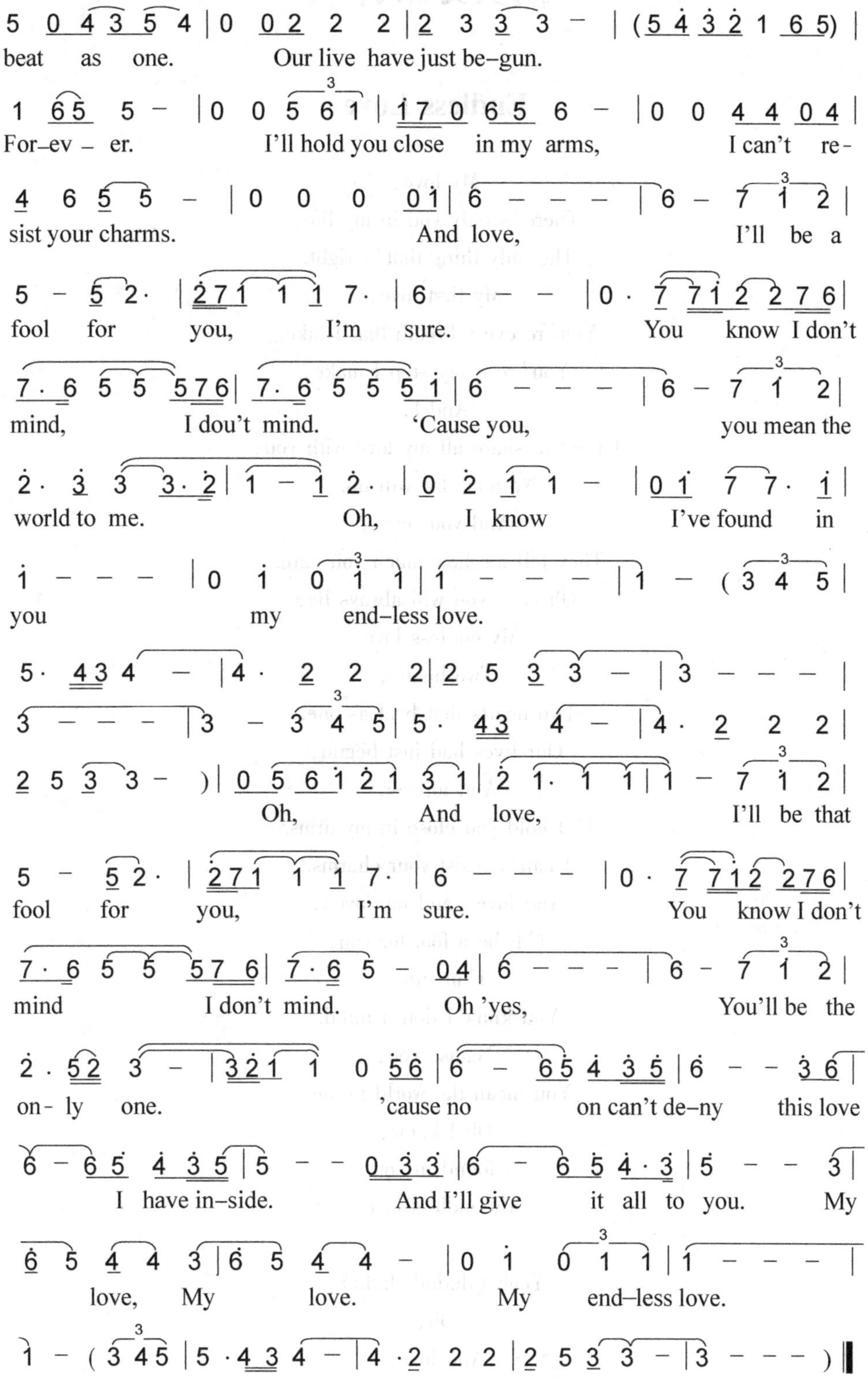
beat as one. Our live have just be-gun.
For-ev - er. I'll hold you close in my arms, I can't re-
sist your charms. And love, I'll be a
fool for you, I'm sure. You know I don't
mind, I dou't mind. 'Cause you, you mean the
world to me. Oh, I know I've found in
you my end-less love.
Oh, And love, I'll be that
fool for you, I'm sure. You know I don't
mind I don't mind. Oh 'yes, You'll be the
on- ly one. 'cause no on can't de-ny this love
I have in-side. And I'll give it all to you. My
love, My love. My end-less love.

【英文歌词】

Endless Love

My love,
There's only you in my life,
The only thing that's right.
My first love,
You're every breath that I take.
You're every step I make,
And I,
I want to share all my love with you;
No one else will do.
And your eyes,
They tell me how much you care.
Oh yes, you will always be,
My endless love.
Two hearts,
Two hearts that beat as one.
Our lives had just begun,
And forever.
I'll hold you close in my arms.
I can't resist your charms.
And love (and my love).
I'll be a fool for you,
I'm sure.
You know I don't mind.
'cause you,
You mean the world to me.
Oh I know,
I found in you,
My endless love.

Yeah (dudududu),
Oh,
And love,

I' ll be that fool for you,
I' m sure.
You know I don' t mind.
Oh 'yes,
You' ll be the only one,
Because no one can' t deny,
This love I have inside.
And I' ll give it all to you,
My love,
My love,
My love,
My endless love.

【参考译文】

无尽的爱

我的爱，
你是我生命中的唯一，
你使我的生命有意义。
我的初恋，
我与你心心相印，
朝夕相伴。
我愿与你共享全部的爱，
只愿与你同行。
你的目光告诉我，
你多么爱我，
你将是我无尽的爱。

我们的生活已经开始，
两颗心连在一起跳动。
你的魅力让我倾倒，
我要永远将你紧紧拥抱。
为了爱，我宁愿痴心，
你知道我对此毫不介意，
因为你是我的整个世界。

噢，我知道，
你将是我无尽的爱。

噢，为了爱，
我宁愿痴心；
我确信是为了你。
你知道，我毫不介意，
哦，是的。
你将是我爱的唯一，
谁也无法否认。
我对你的爱，深深印在心底，
将全部奉献给你。
无尽的爱。

语言点解析

(1) There is only you in my life：You are only one in my life. 你是我生命中的唯一，我的心中只有你。

(2) The only thing that's right：You are the only one who I makes my life meaningful and full. 只有你时我的生命有意义放光彩。

(3) You are every breath I take, you are every step I make：Wherever I am, I think of you; whatever I do, I do it for you. 我与你息息相通，心心相印，一切为了你。

(4) I want to share all my love with you. 我愿与你共享我全部的爱。

(5) **share with**：与……分享，共享
例如：
Please ***share*** your newspaper ***with*** me. 让我看看你的报纸吧。
I'll ***share*** my last pound ***with*** you. 我将与你同舟共济。

(6) Two hears that beats as one. 两颗心息息相通，心心相印。

(7) I can't resist your charms：我无法抗拒你的魅力。

(8) I'd be a fool for you. =I seem to be foolish in front of you. 在你面前，我看起来像个痴情的

傻瓜。

(9) 'Cause you, you mean the world to me: because you are, everything to me. 因为你是我的一切。

(10) I don't mind: I don't care how foolish I am in front of you. 在你面前，尽管我显得痴情，可是我却毫不在意。

(11) I'm sure: I'm certain 我相信。

例如：I'm sure you are the top student in your class. 我相信你一定是班里的优秀生。

注释与赏析

这首歌曲由莱昂内尔·里奇作词谱曲，戴安娜·罗丝与莱昂内尔·里奇联手演唱。这是一部美国影片《无尽的爱》主题歌，歌曲也由此而得名。

唯有你能使这世界变得美好，唯有你能照亮黑暗，使我的生命有意义。这是歌中主人公对自己爱人的肺腑之言。是啊，大千世界，人海茫茫，而唯有一个人，让自己如此心动，占据整个心扉。为了这份至爱，为了这份人间真情，将自己无尽的爱全部奉献。愿天下所有的爱侣爱意无限。

整首歌表达了作者对爱的理解，对爱的执着，并赋予了爱情这一永恒主题以新意。歌中表达了主人公对爱情专一的追求和向往，“你是我生命中的唯一”道出了他的心声。

33. Nothing's Gonna Change My Love for You

（痴心不改）

1=D 4/4

Words & Music by
George Benson

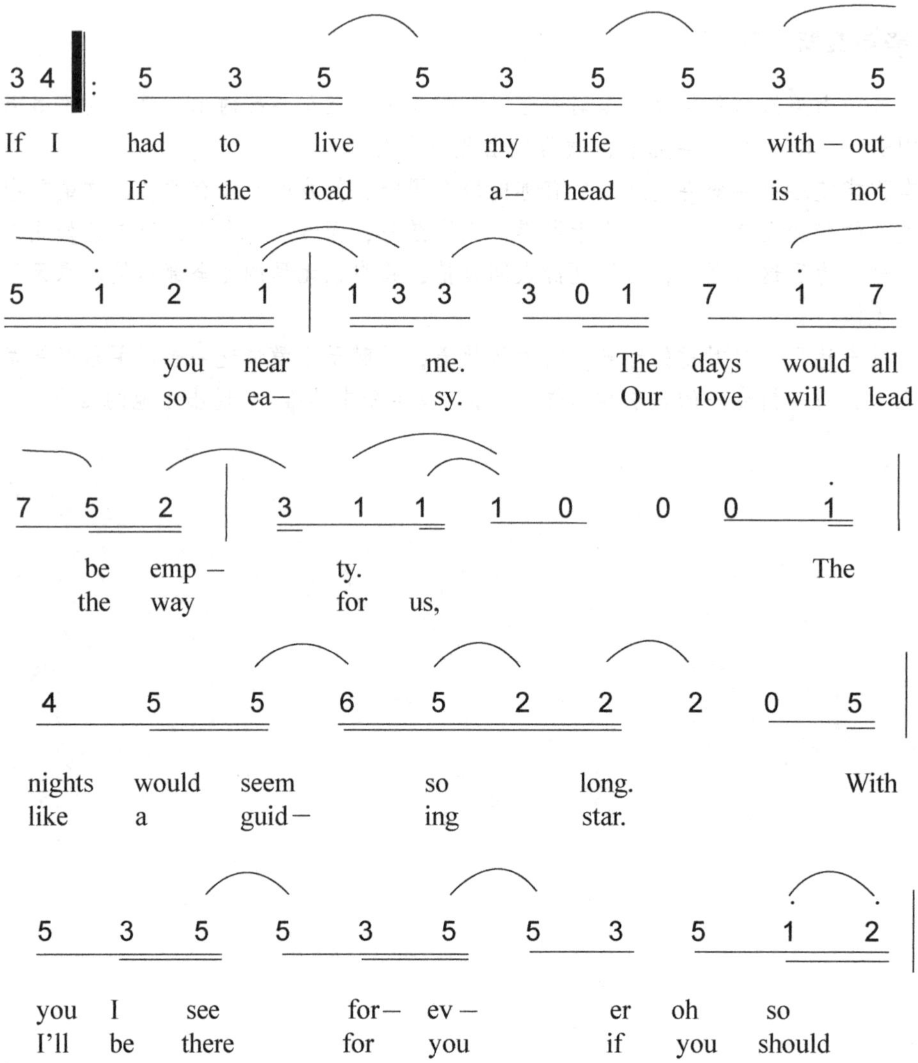

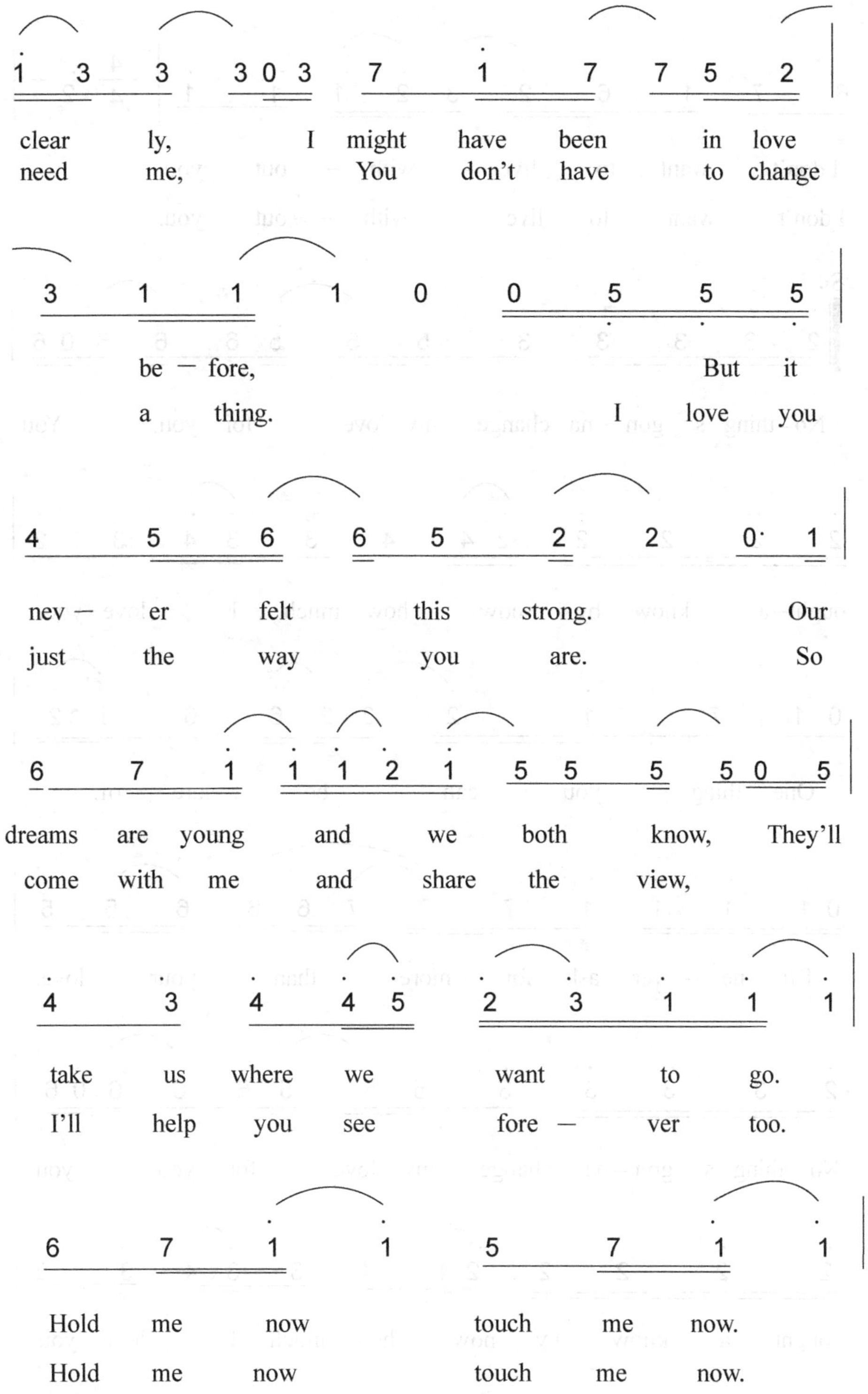
clear ly, I might have been in love
need me, You don't have to change
be — fore, But it
a thing. I love you
nev — er felt this strong. Our
just the way you are. So
dreams are young and we both know, They'll
come with me and share the view,
take us where we want to go.
I'll help you see fore — ver too.
Hold me now touch me now.
Hold me now touch me now.

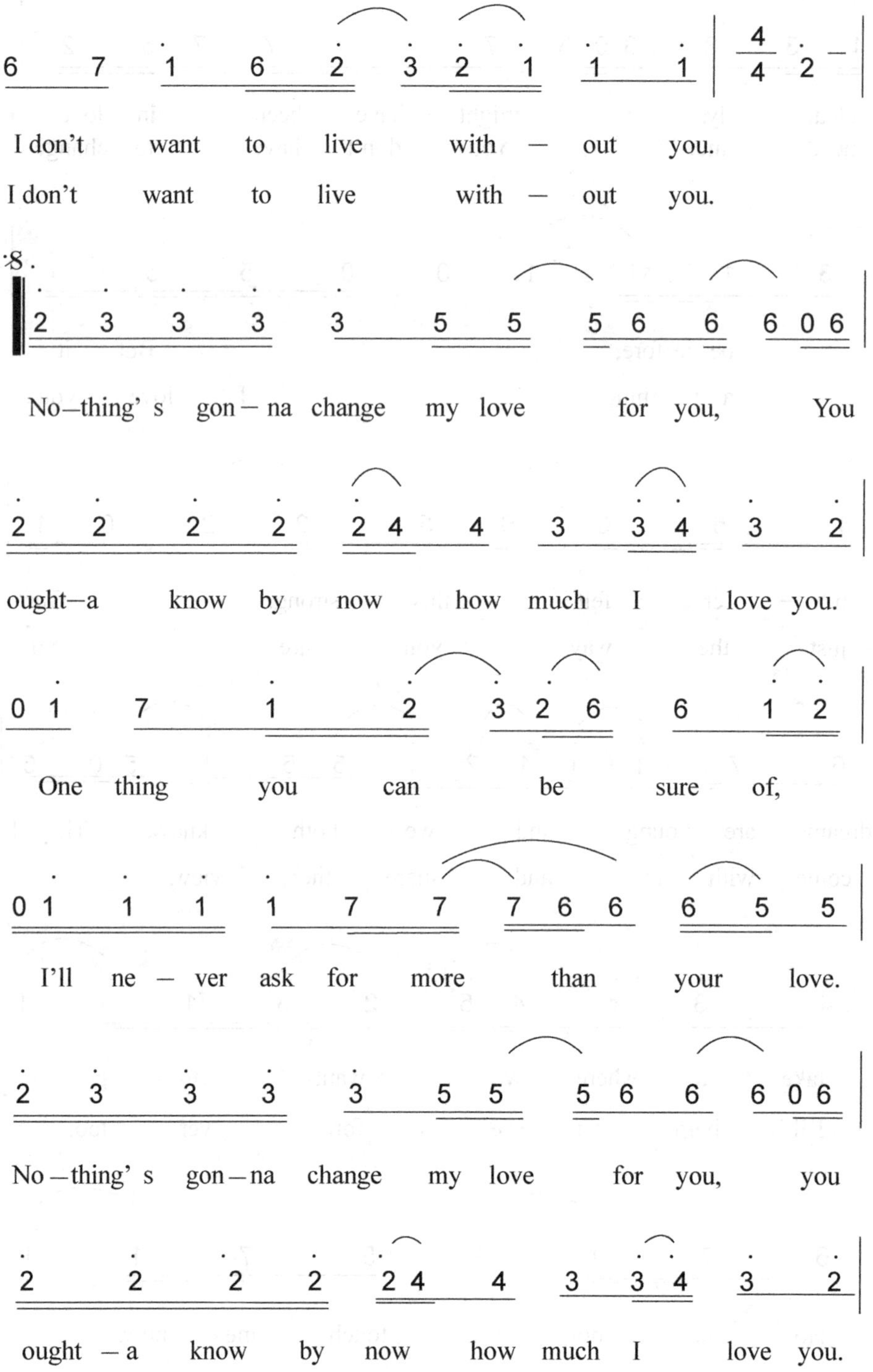
I don't want to live with — out you.
I don't want to live with — out you.
No—thing' s gon — na change my love for you, You
ought—a know by now how much I love you.
One thing you can be sure of,
I'll ne — ver ask for more than your love.
No —thing' s gon—na change my love for you, you
ought —a know by now how much I love you.

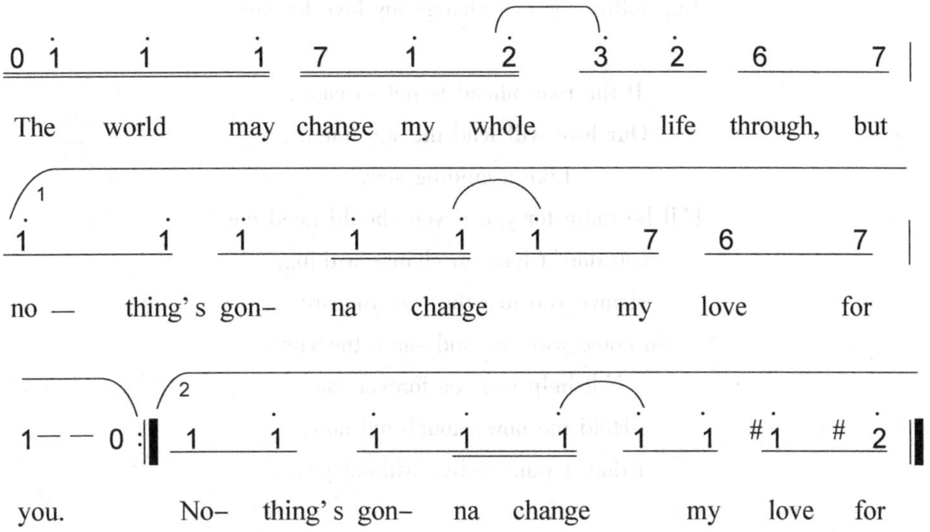

【英文歌词】

Nothing's Gonna Change My Love for You

I had to live my life.
Without you near me the days would all be empty.
The nights would seem so long
With you I see forever, oh so clearly.
I might have been in love before.
But it never felt this strong.
Our dreams are young and we both know
They'll take us where we want to go
Hold me now, youch me now.
I don't want to live without you.

Nothing's gonna change my love for you.
You oughta know by now how much I love you.
One thing you can be sure of,
I will never ask for more than your love.
Nothing's gonna change my love for you.
You oughta know by now how much I love you.
The world may change my whole life through.

But nothin' gonna change my love for you.

If the road ahead is not so easy,
Our love will lead the way for us.
Like a guiding star.
I'll be there for you if you should need me
You don't have to change a thing.
I love you just the way you are.
So come with me and share the view.
I'll help you see forever too.
Hold me now, touch me now.
I don't want to live without you.

Nothing's gonna change my love for you.
You oughta know by now how much I love you.
One thing you can be sure of,
I will never ask for more than your love.
Nothin' gonna change my love for you.
You oughta know by now how much I love you.
The world may change my whole life through.

Nothing's gonna change my love for you.
You oughta know by now how much I love you.
One thing you can be sure of,
I will never ask for more than your love.
Nothin' gonna change my love for you.
You oughta know by now how much I love you.
The world may change my whole life through.

【参考译文】

痴心不改

如果我的生活中没有你,
白昼将会多么空虚!
夜晚将会多么漫长!

与你同在使我清楚地感到：
即使我曾坠入情网，
此时的爱将胜过以往。
我们怀着美好的梦想，
它将引导我们去那向往的地方，
拥抱我，别离开我，
我的生活不能没有你。

我将始终对你痴心不改，
你该知道现在我多么爱你。
唯一请你记住的是：
你的爱就是我最大的心愿。
我将始终对你痴心不改。
你该知道现在我多么爱你。
这世界会改变我的全部生活，
但我将始终对你痴心不改。

如果前面的道路布满荆棘，
爱会指引我们共同前进，
无论何时需要我，
我将与你在一起。
你的一切都无需改变，
我爱的就是现在的你。
让我们在一起，分享彼此的爱。
我也要让你憧憬未来。
拥抱我，别离开我，
我的生活不能没有你。

我将始终对你痴心不改，
你该知道现在我多么爱你。
唯一请你记住的是：
你的爱就是我最大的心愿。
我将始终对你痴心不改
你该知道现在我多么爱你，
我将始终对你痴心不改。

我将始终对你痴心不改，
你该知道现在我多么爱你。

唯一请你记住的是：
你的爱就是我最大的心愿。
我将始终对你痴心不改。
你该知道现在我多么爱你。
这世界会改变我的全部生活，
但我将始终对你痴心不改。

语言点解析

（1）**gonna**：going to 美国俚语

（2）The days would all be empty. 白昼将会多么空虚。

（3）With you I see forever oh so clearly I might have been in love before，but it never felt this strong. 与你在一起，我会清楚地感到即使我曾坠入过情网，此时的爱将胜过以往。
居中 it 指“be in love”，指以往的爱(我现在所拥有的情感比以往任何时候都强烈)。

（4）hold me now，touch me now. 拥抱我，抚摸我。
hold *vt.*：抱着、抓、拿在手里。
例如：
She was ***holding*** her baby in her arms. 它双臂抱着婴儿。

（5）**ought-a**：ought 一词的结尾辅音与 to 一词开头的辅音相同，所以前面一词的辅音[t]失去爆破，后面 to 的元音[u]清读，所以发[ə]音，故歌中 ought to 写成了 ought-a，发音为[ɔ：tə]。Ought 一词为情态动词，后面只接不定式。

（6）One thing you can be sure of. =You can be sure of one thing. 唯一请你记住的事情。
此句为倒装句，目的是强调 one thing.

（7）I love you just the way you are. 我爱的就是现在的你。
the way：作主从连词，引导出方式状语，意思是“用……方式”“以……方式”

（8）So come with me and share the view. 让我们在一起，分享彼此的爱。
view：这个短语中的 view 指“观点、见解、意见”。句中的意思应为“the love for each other”（彼此的爱）。

注释与赏析

乔治·本森(George Benson)1943年3月2日生于美国宾夕法尼亚，是一位著名的黑人爵士吉他手和歌唱家。《对你痴心不改》是他为一部电影作词曲并演唱的插曲。

这首歌是二段式乐曲，同时又是两段歌词。第二段乐曲是歌曲的副。整首歌曲流畅动听，词句真挚感人。歌曲的结尾部分重复了副歌三遍，给人留下了难忘的印象。由于副歌的曲调很优美，词曲结合得天衣无缝，所以，即使只听了一遍，我们也无法忘记那迷人的旋律和动人的词句。

34. Puff the Magic Dragon

(帕夫神龙)

1=D $\frac{4}{4}$

Words by Leonard Lipton
Music by Peter Y arrow

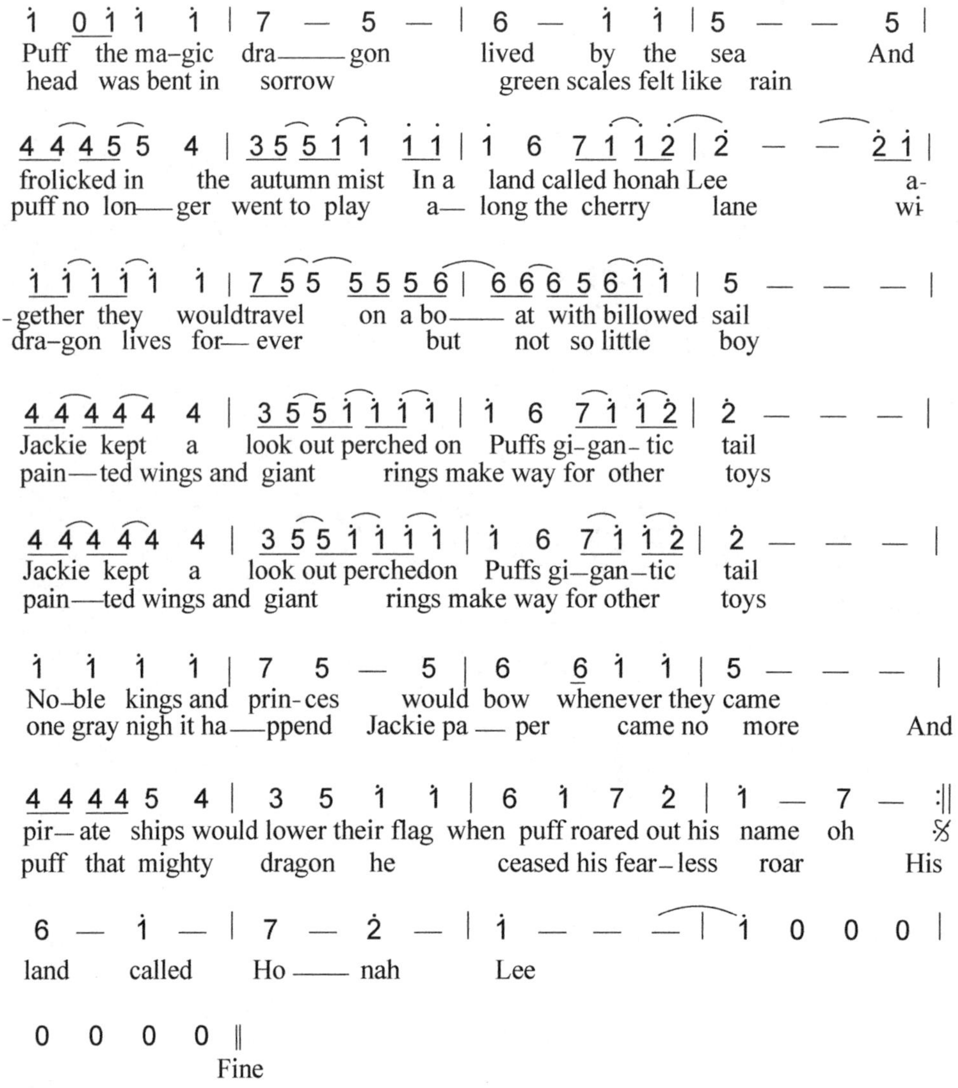

【英文歌词】

Puff the Magic Dragon

Puff, the magic dragon lived by the sea,
And frolicked in the autumn mist in a land called Honah Lee.
Little Jackie Paper loved that rascal puff.
And brought him strings and sealing wax and other fancy stuff.

Puff, the magic dragon lived by the sea.
And frolicked in the autumn mist in a land calledHonah Lee,
Puff, the magic dragon lived by the sea,
And frolicked in the autumn mist in a land called Honah Lee.

Together they would travel on a boat with billowed sail
Jackie kept a lookout perched on puff's gigantic tail,
Noble kings and princes would bow whenever they came,
Pirate ships would lower their flag when puff roared out his name. Oh!

Puff, the magic dragon lived by the sea
And frolicked in the autumn mist in a land called Honah Lee.
Puff, the magic dragon lived by the sea,
And frolicked in the autumn mist in a land called Honah Lee.

A dragon lives forever but not so little boys
Painted wings and giant rings make way for other toys.
One grey night it happened, Jackie Paper came no more
And puff that mighty dragon, he ceased his fearless roar.

His head was bent in sorrow, green scales fell like rain,
Puff no longer went to play along the cherry lane.
Without his life-long friend, puff could not be brave,
So puff that mighty dragon sadly slipped into his cave. oh!

Puff, the magic dragon lived by the sea,
And frolicked in the autumn mist in a land calledHonah Lee,

Puff, the magic dragon lived by the sea
And frolicked in the autumn mist in a land called Honah Lee.

【参考译文】

帕夫神龙

帕夫，一种海边的魔龙。
常在有雾的秋天到陆地上来玩耍的我们叫它荷拉里。
小杰克·派博很喜欢它。
常带给他一些细线，封蜡和很多奇特的材料。

帕夫，一种海边的魔龙。
常在有雾的秋天到陆地上来玩耍的我们叫它荷拉里。
帕夫，一种海边的魔龙
常在有雾的秋天到陆地上来玩耍的我们叫它荷拉里。

他们一起驾着小船航行探险，乘风破浪，
杰克站在帕夫的大尾巴上了望
当他们到来时，尊贵的国王和王子也要向他们鞠躬行礼。
当帕夫大声叫出他的名字，连那些海盗船也要降下旗子。

帕夫，一种海边的魔龙
常在有雾的秋天到陆地上来玩耍的我们叫它荷拉里。
帕夫，一种海边的魔龙
常在有雾的秋天到陆地上来玩耍的我们叫它荷拉里。

一条龙是永生的，但那小男孩不是
美丽的风形成巨大的环为另一些玩具开路
在一个灰色的晚上终于发生了，杰克·派博再也没有来。
帕夫，这条大龙停止了他威严的吼叫。

帕夫变得悲哀，阴暗的心情就下雨天。
帕夫不再前往美丽的陆地玩耍。
失去了多年的伙伴，帕夫不再勇敢。
最后，帕夫这条大龙悲伤地躲进了它的洞穴。

帕夫，一种海边的魔龙。
常在有雾的秋天到陆地上来玩耍的我们叫它荷拉里。
帕夫，一种海边的魔龙。
常在有雾的秋天到陆地上来玩耍的我们叫它荷拉里。

语言点解析

(1) Puff, the magic dragon lived by the sea, and frolicked in the autumn mist in a land called Honalhlee. =Once there was a magic dragon called Puff, who lived by the land called Honalhlee. 帕夫这条曾住在海边的神龙常在哈纳里国的秋雾中戏水。

magic *adj.* & n. 有魔力的，不可思议的；魔法(术)

frolic *vi.*：(frolicked, frolicked; frolicking)嘻玩，玩乐；欢闹。

(2) Little Jackie Paper loved that rascal Puff, and brought him strings and sealing wax, and other fancy stuff. 小顽童杰克．佩帕很喜欢淘气的帕夫，常给他线绳、封蜡及其它玩艺儿。

rascal *n.* 流氓、无赖、恶棍，小淘气。

例如：

You little ***rascal***！你这个小淘气！

sealing wax：封蜡(一种固体物质，红色，成块出售，由于融化后凝结得快，常用来封东西)。

stuff *n.*：物质、材料、东西

例如：

He collected all the ***stuff*** for painting. 他收集了画画的全部材料。

What is this sticky ***stuff***？那黏黏的东西是什么？

与**staff** 职员的区别：这两个词都是集合名词。

例如：

My brother is on the editorial ***staff***. 我弟弟是编剧部的职员。(staff 后不加"s")

(3) Together they would travel on a boat with billowed sail: They would travel together on boat with billowed sail. 他们常同船杨帆出航。

billow n. & v. 巨浪，波涛；(波浪似地)翻腾，使翻腾

例如：***billowing*** smoke and flames 滚滚的烟火

(4) Jackie kept a look-out perched on Puff's gigantic tail. =Jackie kept a look-out rested on puff's very great tail. 杰克站在帕夫的大尾巴上向远处眺望。

look-out *n.*：守望，警戒

例如：

They are on the ***look-out*** for a storm. 他们在警戒暴风雨。

(5) **perch** *n.* & *v.* 有利地形，高位；停歇，栖息

(6) Pirate ships would lower their flags when Puff roared out his name. 当帕夫吼出名字海盗船会把旗降下。

roar *v.* (猛兽)吼、咆哮、(人等)大笑。

roar out 大声叫出。

例如：

The lion ***roared*** . 狮子咆哮了。

(7) A dragon lives forever, but no so little boys：A dragon lives forever, but little boys can't live forever. 神龙能万寿，小孩却不能。

(8) Painted wings and giants rings make way for other toys. 彩色双翼和巨大金环被其他玩具所代替。

make way for：……为……让路；让路给……

例如：

When the professor came into the hall, the students ***made way for*** him. 当教授走进大厅，学生们为他让路。

(9) One grey night it happened, Jackie Paper came no more. = It happened one grey night that Jackie Paper didn't come any more. 在一个灰暗的夜里杰克·佩帕不再来。

(10) And Puff that mighty dragon, he ceased his fearless roar. 勇猛的帕夫停止了他无畏的吼叫。

(11) **cease** v. t.：停止。

cease 与**stop** 的区别：

例如：

cease talking 停止说话

cease to talk 停止说话

Cease fire! 停火!

stop talking 停止说话

stop to talk 停下来去说话

(12) His head was bent in sorrow, green scales fell like rain. 神龙忧伤地垂下了头，绿色鳞片雨点般地脱落。此句是个比喻句子，用 like，是明喻(simile)鳞片像雨点般往下落。

bend *vt.* & *vi.*：(bent, bent)弯，曲，朝向
scale *n.* 鳞片

注释与赏析

彼特、保罗和玛丽是美国蜚声歌坛的民谣三重唱组合，他们制作与演唱的歌曲受到了青年人的喜爱。在20世纪六七十年代摇滚、爵士盛行的美国，像他们这样以民谣为主的重唱组的确少见。他们为民族的传统、特色保存着一片春天的记忆，发扬和光大了一个民族最具生命力的东西。这首典型的《帕夫神龙》正是彼特、保罗和玛丽三重唱的一首具有代表性的民谣歌曲。

《帕夫神龙》这首神龙传说的故事式歌曲，主要以人神的交往表现古时人们渴求友谊、重情重义的愿望。故事讲述了一个儿童和一条住在海边的神龙之间建立友谊共同玩耍，互赠礼物的过程。龙是神，可以万寿无疆，而孩子只是血肉之躯，不能长生不老，不能永远与神龙一块嬉戏。人有自己的劳动和生活方式，需要去创造财富，因此，孩子长大后不能与神龙再交往下去了。失去伙伴的友情，神龙也失去了神力，不再勇猛，伤心地回到水下洞穴去了。过去的民谣传说没有今天新闻或故事那种一触即发扣人心弦的情节悬念，但却充满了真实挚诚的情感。

其实Puff的真正主题是“the loss of innocence(失却的纯真)”，有歌评这样说：“这首歌主要是谈小孩子长大的过程，及对环境的感受。歌词中的Puff实为一虚构的奇异龙，用此来影射孩子小时侯很喜欢小玩具，长大后就把奇异龙甩掉，因为孩子已慢慢长大，对这种虚构的东西已不再有兴趣了”。

歌中用大量的篇幅描绘Jackie和Puff一起出行时的威猛：连王孙贵胄都要向他们弯腰行礼，海盗船也要退让三分。这与男孩离开puff后，神龙的形单影孤、郁郁寡欢形成鲜明对比。反差如此之大。何故？歌中的神龙当是小男孩最喜欢的一件玩具，孩童了无羁绊的心灵为它插上了想象的神奇外衣。在想象的奇境中，他们纵横驰骋，白纸被染上污迹，失去孩童可贵纯真的同时，想象力也折断了翼翅。每每看到小学生瘦小稚嫩的双肩上架着一只宽厚的书包，蹒跚着沉重前行时，我们便不禁为他们而悲哀。

成长本是不可逆转的过程，每个人都要经历从boys to men的过程，这本是自然规律；然而，丧失想象力却是可悲的。人们在谈the loss of innocence的时候，其实是在追忆追悼着童真而失却的自由自在的想象力。

孟子曰：“大人者，不失其赤子之心者也。”(有德行的人，是保留了儿童般纯洁之心的人)这里的赤子之心，在当代的大环境中是否可以理解为充满自由想象的心灵呢？当我们再度品味这听似简单的“儿歌”时，千年古训仿佛在耳边响起，发人深思。愿我们都保持一颗纯洁真诚的赤子之心，在心田珍藏一片让想象力自由飞升的空间。

35. Casablanka

（卡萨布兰卡）

1=D 4/4

Words & Music by Bertie Higgins

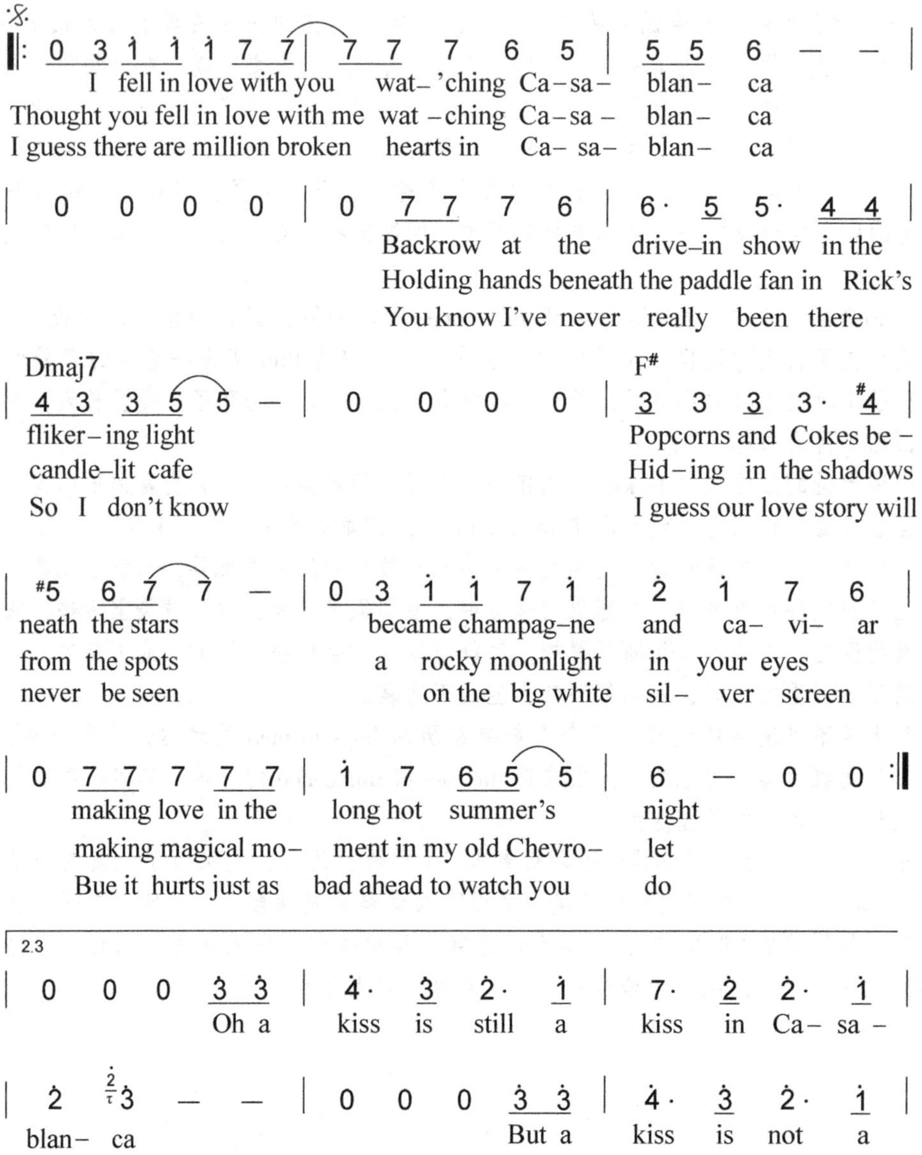

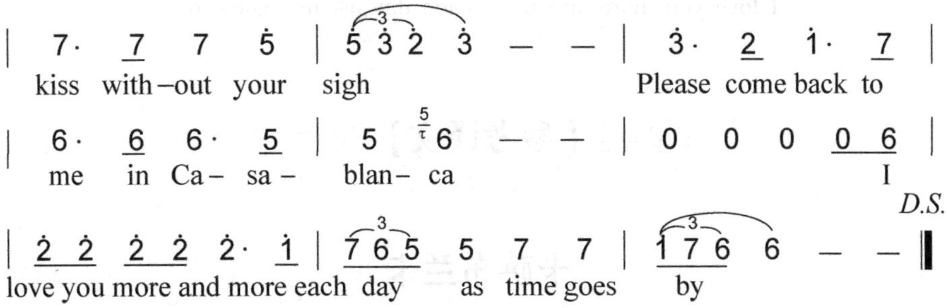

【英文歌词】

Casablanca

I fell in love with you watching Casablanca,
Back row of the drive–in show in the flickering light,
Popcorn and cokes beneath the stars
Became champagne and caviar
Making love on a long hot summer's night

I thought you fell in love with me watching Casablanca
Holding hands' neath the paddle fans in Rick's candlelit cafe
Hiding in the shadows from the spots
Moroccan moonlight in your eyes
Making magic at the movies in my old Chevrolet

Oh! A kiss is still a kiss in Casablanca.
But a kiss is not a kiss without your sigh.
Please come back to me in Casablanca.
I love you more and more each day as time goes by.

I guess there're many broken hearts in Casablanca.
You know I've never really been there.
So, I don't know.
I guess our love story will never be seen
On the big wide silver screen.
But it hurt just as bad when I had to watch you go.

I love you more and more each day as time goes by.

【参考译文】

卡萨布兰卡

看着《卡萨布兰卡》这部片时，
我爱上了你。
当时汽车电影院的后排灯光闪烁不定。
爆米花和可乐在星光下变成了香槟和鱼子酱。
我们在漫长的而燥热的夏夜里尽情欢笑。

我以为在看《卡萨布兰卡》时，
你爱上了我。
在点着烛光的里克咖啡馆里的吊扇下牵手。
我们躲在阴影里，你的眼里映着摩洛哥的月光。
随着电影在我那辆旧雪佛莱里变着魔术。

噢！卡萨布兰卡的亲吻依旧。
但没有了你的叹息，那吻已不成吻。
请来卡萨布兰卡找我。
随着时光流逝，我一天比一天更爱你。

我猜，在卡萨布兰卡有很多伤心人。
你知道我从未真的到过那里。
所以我不是很清楚，
我想我们的爱情故事永远都不会让人知晓，
更不会被搬上银幕。
但当我不得不看着你离去，我也感受到那种伤痛。
随着时光流逝，我年复一年地更加爱你。

语言点解析

(1) **fall in love with sb.**：爱上了某人；两人彼此相爱

例如：They ***fell in love*** **with** each other during the journey. 他们在旅途中彼此相爱了。

(2) Back row at the drive-in show：We were sitting at the back row in a drive-in show. 我们依偎在汽车影院的后排座位上。

(3) In the flickering light：在闪烁的灯光下，这里指放映电影时，晚隐时现的灯光。

(4) Popcorn and cokes beneath the stars became champagne and caviar. =While watching Casablanca, we were so happy and gay that the popcorn and cokes tasted as good as champagne and caviar. 看电影时，我们喝着可乐，吃着爆米花，就像喝上了香槟和吃鱼子酱一样让人开心。

beneath the stars：in the open air 在闪烁的星空下，这里指露天的汽车影院。

(5) **holding hands**：手牵着手

(6) **in Rich's candle-lit cafe**：在烛光闪闪的吕克饭店里

(7) **in the shadows**：在阴影里

(8) A kiss is not a kiss with your sign. =A kiss is meaningless to me if it's not your kiss. 只有你的亲吻才对我有意义。

(9) Please come back to me. 这里用了祈使句，表达了主人公对爱人情真意切的呼唤，“快回到我的身边吧!”

(10) I love you more and more each day as time goes by. 随着时光的流逝，我对你的爱与日俱增。

more and more：increasingly 越来越

例如：

I'm becoming ***more and more*** interested in classical music. 我对古典音乐越来越感兴趣。

注释与赏析

这首歌曲由作者 Bertie Higgins 在 1986 年录唱，内容涉及一部老电影《卡萨布兰卡》以及其中的一首插曲“As Times Goes By”(年复一年)，歌词还引用了《年复一年》中的句子。

这首歌曲在 80 年代后期风行一时。歌中唱出了两个青年因看电影《卡萨布兰卡》而产生恋情，又因分离而伤感的内容。在那夏日漫长的夜晚，他们双双在汽车影院里吃着赛过鱼子酱的爆米花，喝着胜过美味香槟的可口可乐，手牵着手，在月光下看电影《卡萨布兰卡》，一次次动情的亲吻，伴他们度过了美好的时光。但时过境迁，这一切已成追忆，表达了作者对昔日美好浪漫爱情的渴望。

36. Take Me Home, Country Road

（乡村路，带我回家）

1=G $\frac{2}{4}$

Words & Music by
B.Danoff,T.Nivert,& J.Denver

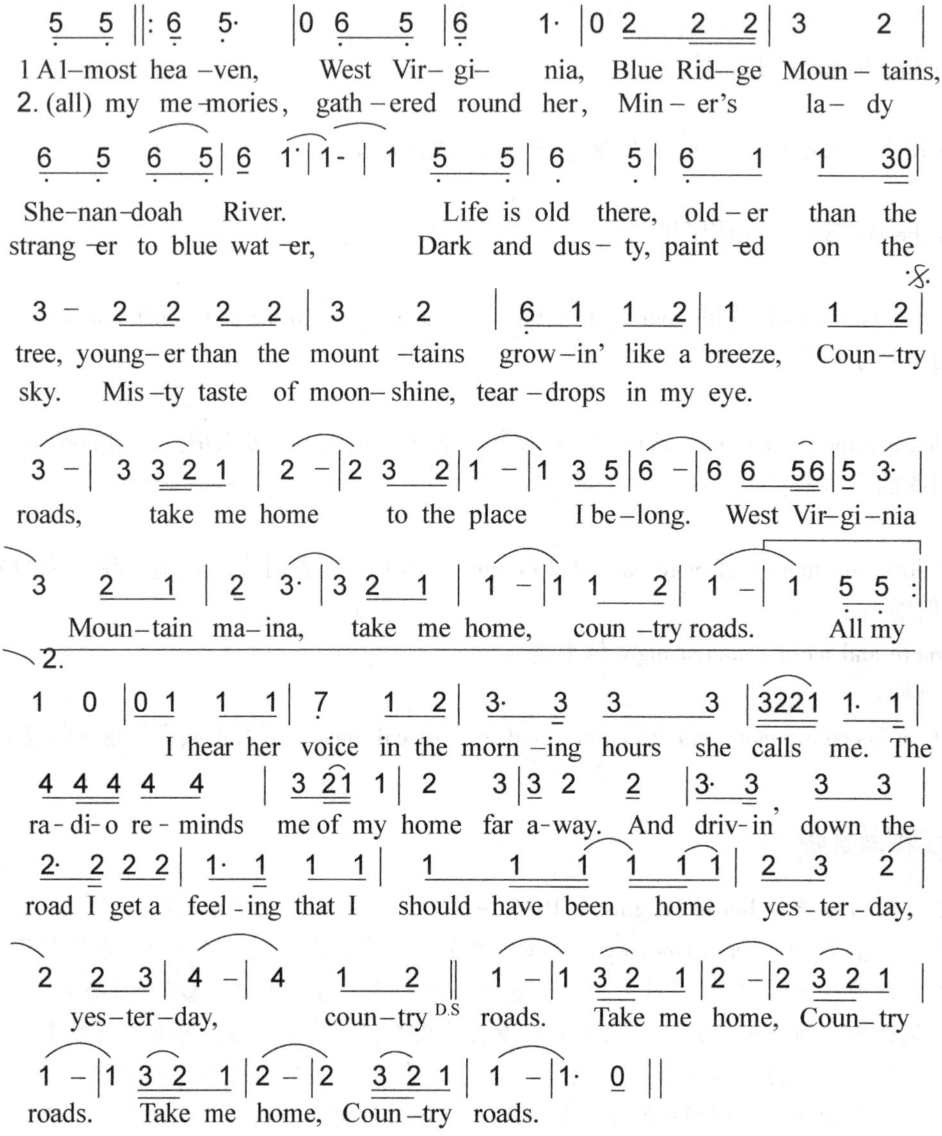

【英文歌词】

Take Me Home, Country Roads.

Almost Heaven, West Virginia,
Blue Ridge Mountains, Shenangoah River.
Life is old there, older than the trees,
Younger than the mountains,
Growing like a breeze.

Country Roads, take me home,
To the place I belong.
West Virginia, Mountain mama,
Take me home, Country Roads.

All my memories, gathered round her,
Miner's lady, stranger to blue water,
Dark and dusty, painted on the sky,
Misty taste of moonshine, teardrops in my eye.

Country Roads, take me home,
To the place I belong,
West Virginia, Mountain mama,
Take me home, Country Roads.

I hear her voice in the morning hours she calls me.
The radio reminds me of my home far away.
And driving down the road I get a feeling that
I should have been home yesterday, yesterday.
Country Roads, take me home,
To the place I belong.
West Virginia, Mountain mama,
Take me home, Country Roads.

Country Roads, take me home,
To the place I belong.

West Virginia, Mountain mama,
Take me home, Country Roads.
Take me home now, Country Roads.
Take me home now, Country Roads.

【参考译文】

乡村路，带我回家

西弗吉尼亚，总如天堂一般，
那儿有蓝岭山脉，谢南多亚河。
生命在那里比树木更长久，
又如同山脉那般年轻，
像清风一样飘逝。

故乡的路，带我回家吧，
回到我期盼已久的归宿，
西弗吉尼亚，大山母亲，
带我回家吧，故乡的路。

我所有的记忆都围绕着她。
她是矿工的妻子，从未见过深邃的大海，
黑暗与灰尘在天空中绘出颜色，
在那朦胧的月光下，泪水涌出我的眼睛。

故乡的路，带我回家吧，
回到我期盼已久的归宿，
西弗吉尼亚，大山母亲，
带我回家吧，故乡的路。

清晨我听见一个声音在对我呼唤，
收音机里的声音让我想起了遥远的家，
沿着公路行驶，我心中产生这样的感觉：
也许我昨天就该回到家中，就在昨天！

故乡的路，带我回家吧，

回到我期盼已久的归宿，
西弗吉尼亚，大山母亲，
带我回家吧，故乡的路。

故乡的路，带我回家吧，
回到我期盼已久的归宿，
西弗吉尼亚，大山母亲，
带我回家吧，故乡的路。
带我回家吧，故乡的路。
带我回家吧，故乡的路。

语言点解析

(1) Almost heaven west Virginia, Blue Ridge Mountains, Shenandoah River. = West Virginia where there are mountains and Shenandoah River is almost heaven.

(2) Life is old there, older than the trees; younger than the mountains, growing like a breeze：这几行在说：那里生活久远，指很早便有生命存在，与树比，比树老，与山比，则比山年轻，徐徐生长如清风。

like a breeze：像微风一样

例如：

Smile is like sunshine and ***like a breeze***. It makes others happy. 微笑如阳光，又如清风，令人高兴。

(3) … to the place I belong = … take me to the place where I belong

(4) All my memories ***gather round*** her. = All my memories center on her.

例如：

All his memories ***gather round*** the years when he was in the countryside. 他所有的记忆全是关于他在农村时的那些岁月。

(5) miner's lady = a miner's wife 矿工的太太

stranger to blue water. = a person who has not seen seas.

stranger to：对……陌生的人

例如：

I am a ***stranger to*** art. 我是个不懂艺术的人。

(6) The radio reminds me of my home far away.

the radio 可能是汽车上的收音机，可能是收音机里放的音乐或歌曲使他更怀恋家乡。

remind sb. of sth .：提醒，使人想起

例如：

Don't *remind* him *of* the cause of his anger—that would be pouring oil on flames. 不要向他提起他发怒的原因，那会使他怒气更旺。

(7) driving down the road. = while I was driving along the road

(8) I get a feeling that I should have been home yesterday, yesterday.

should have done sth.：表示"本当做……"

例如：

You ***should have gone*** there. 你本应当去那儿。

注释与赏析

这首歌是约翰·丹佛(John. Denver)(1943—1997)的成名作。此歌创作于1971年，使丹佛一跃成为著名乡村音乐歌星。他创作的其他著名歌曲还有《乘喷气机远去》《海上的微风》《阳光照在我肩上》《安妮之歌》《又一次回家》。

乡村路，带我回家。多么深挚的乡恋情！是啊，天堂般的西弗尼亚，那里有崇山峻岭，有清澈的河流；那里生命常在，树木参天，青山不老，一切都缓缓生长，如徐徐微风，吹拂着浓浓的乡情。这天堂般的家乡，怎能使人不怀恋？

乡村路，带我回家。鸟恋旧林，人思故乡，这是有史以来难以抹掉的乡情。游子思归，欲归之处不仅是那西弗吉尼亚，更重要的是回到山里的妈妈身旁。还家路上，汽车奔驰，所有的记忆全是围绕自己的生母亲娘。这山里的妈妈，一个矿工的太太，从未走出深山，从未见过大海，皮肤黝黑，尘土沾襟，清楚的记忆，模糊的印象，似隐似现。这便是养育自己成人的山里母亲。想起这山里纯朴的母亲，怎不令人潸然泪下？

这乡村路非常寻常，它连接了山村与外边的世界。它把游子送出深山，又把游子带回家园。外边的世界很精彩，但怎能令游子留恋不归？难怪几位外国朋友听见这首歌顿起归思，难怪有那么多人对它深深地喜爱。

37. Say You，Say Me

（说你，说我）

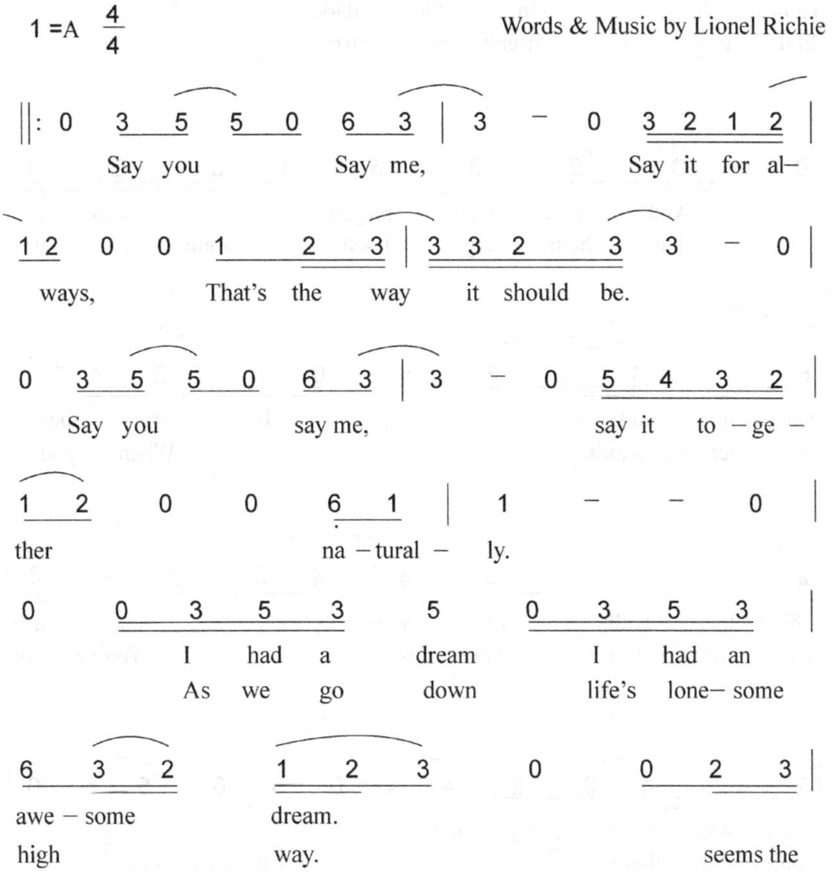

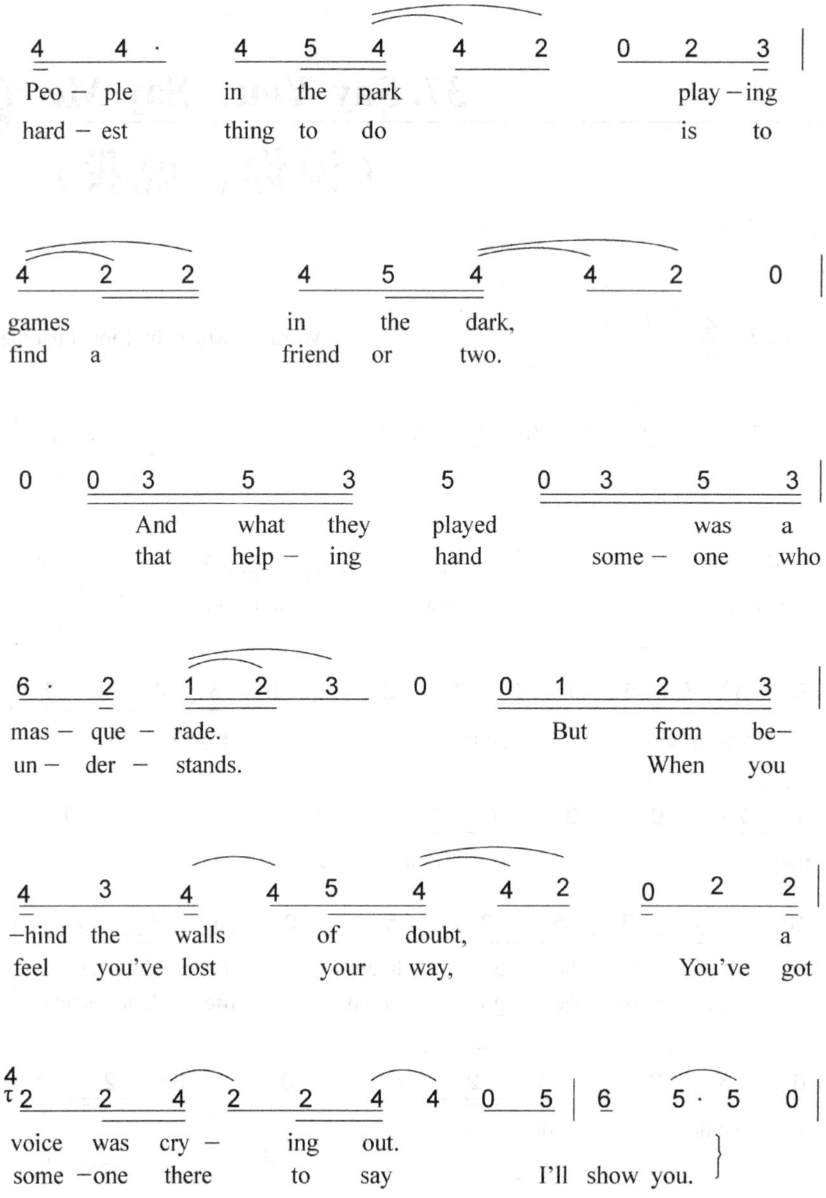
Peo – ple in the park play – ing
hard – est thing to do is to
games in the dark,
find a friend or two.
And what they played was a
that help – ing hand some – one who
mas – que – rade. But from be–
un – der – stands. When you
–hind the walls of doubt, a
feel you've lost your way, You've got
voice was cry – ing out.
some –one there to say I'll show you.

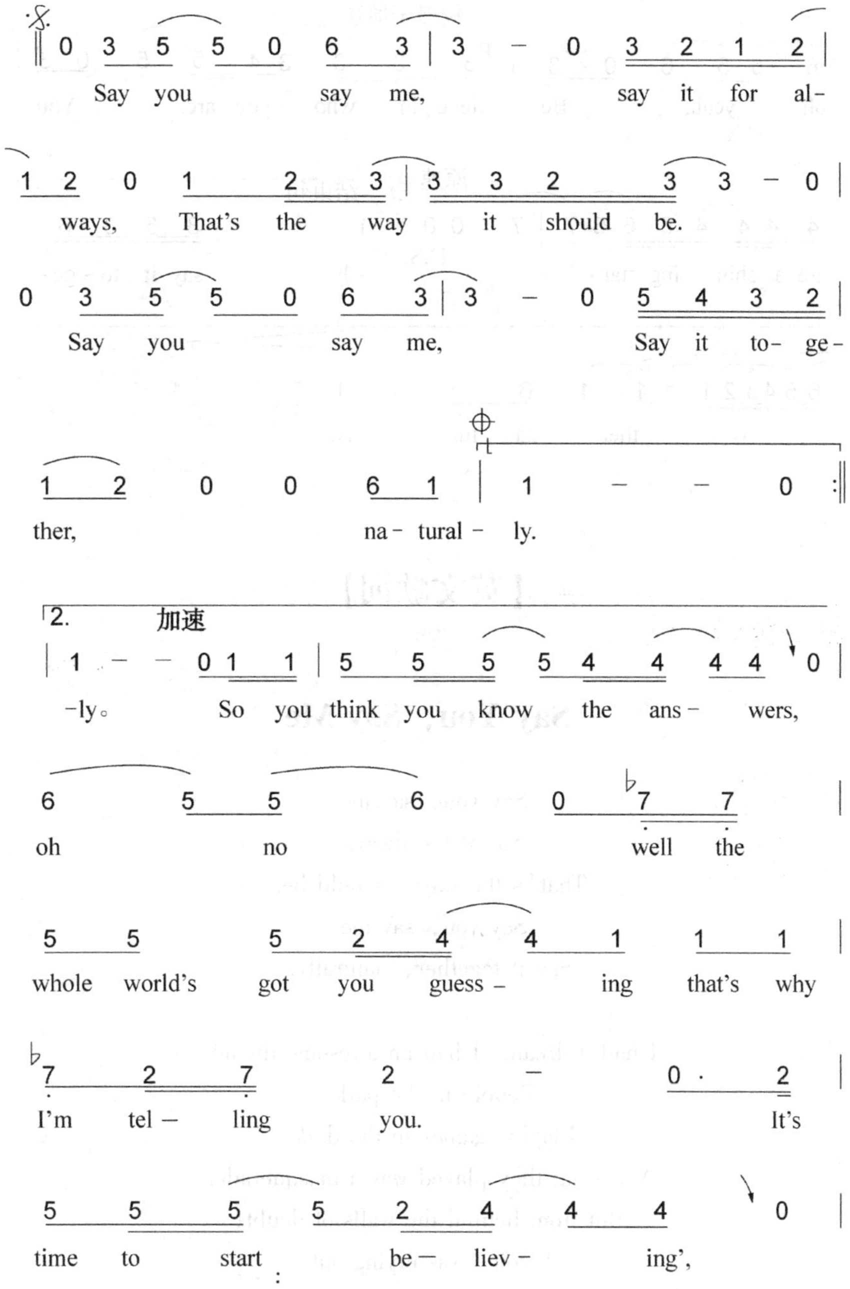
Say you say me, say it for al-
ways, That's the way it should be.
Say you say me, Say it to- ge-
ther, na- tural - ly.
2.
加速
-ly。 So you think you know the ans - wers,
oh no well the
whole world's got you guess - ing that's why
I'm tel - ling you. It's
time to start be - liev - ing',

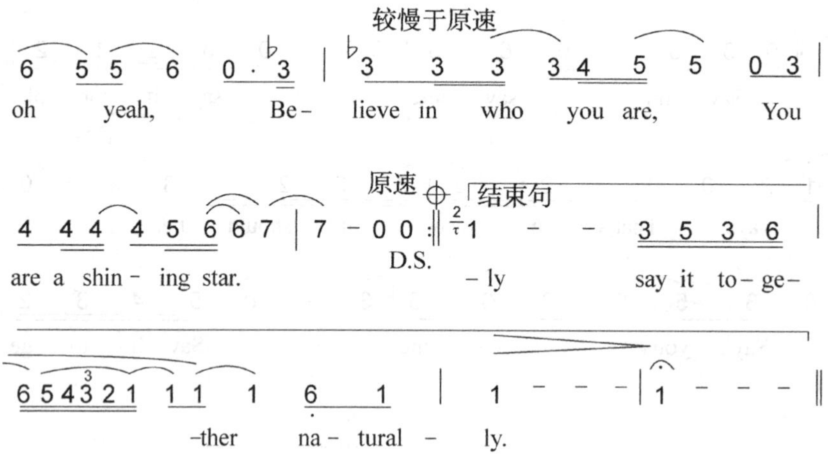

【英文歌词】

Say You, Say Me

Say you, say me.
Say it for always.
That's the way it should be.
Say you, say me.
Say it together, naturally.

I had a dream. I had an awesome dream.
People in the park,
Playing games in the dark.
And what they played was a masquerade.
But from behind the walls of doubt,
A voice was crying out.

Say you, say me.
Say it for always.
That's the way it should be.
Say you, say me.
Say it together, naturally.

As we go down life's lonesome highway.
(It) seems the hardest thing to do is to find a friend or two,
That helping hand, someone who understands.
When you feel you've lost your way,
You've got someone there to say.
I'll show you oo, oo, oo

Say you, say me.
Say it for always.
That's the way it should be
Say you, say me.
Say it together, naturally.

So you think you know the answers.
Oh no!
Well the whole world's got you guessing
That's right I'm telling you.
It's time to start believing
Oh Yes!
Believe in who you are.
You are a shining star...oh.

Say you, say me.
Say it for always.
That's the way it should be.
Say you, say me.
Say it together, naturally.

【参考译文】

说你，说我

说你，说我。
要总是在说，
生活远本应如此。
说你，说我，

一起谈笑，自然又亲密。

我做了一个梦，是个糟糕的梦；
公园里的人们，
在黑暗中做游戏。
他们玩的是一个假面舞会。
但从猜疑的墙后面，
一个声音在大喊。
说你，说我，
要总是在说，
生活原本应如此。
说你，说我。
一起谈笑，自然又亲密。

当我们走上，生活孤独之路，
似乎最难的是，找到一两个朋友，
找个帮忙的手，那人通情又达理。
当你感到，你已迷路时，
你会听见那儿有人说，
我给你指路。

说你，说我，
要总是在说，
生活原本应如此。
说你，说我，
一起谈笑，自然又亲密。

所以你想你已知道了答案。
哦，还没有。
那么整个世界让你迷惑，
是的，我在跟你说，
是时候了，要相信，
哦，是的，
相信你自己。
你是颗闪亮的星。

说你，说我，
要总是在说，
生活原本应如此。

说你，说我，
一起谈笑，自然又亲密。

语言点解析

(1) Say you, say me: Talk about you, talk about me.
(2) Say it for always: 要总是说。
For always 即"always"，不要模仿这一用法。
(3) **awesome**：可怕的
(4) **masquerade**：化妆舞会
(5) **from behind the walls of doubt**：从怀疑之墙后面
from behind：是双介词结构。
例如：
He appeared ***from behind*** the door. 他从门后边出来。
He took a basketball ***from under*** the desk. 他从书桌下拿出一个篮球。
wall of doubt 是一个比喻，指社会上人与人之间互不交流，甚至互相猜疑，似有一堵墙。
(6) Go down life's lonesome highway: 沿生活的孤寂之路
down：沿着
lonesome：lonely
(7) Seems the hardest thing to do is to find a friend or two. = It seems that the most difficult thing to do is to find a friend or two.
The hardest thing: 最困难的事
例如：
To study English is not ***the hardest thing***. 英语并不是最难做的事。
(8) helping hand: a person who is ready to help others
(9) Someone who understands = Someone who is understanding.
understand：在此指通情达理、明白事理
例如：
She is a woman who ***understands***. 她是一个通事理的女人。
(10) lose one's way: 迷路
例如：
He often ***loses his way*** when he is in the town. 他一进城就迷路。
(11) You've got someone there to say. = You have a person who can say.
(12) the world got you guessing: 这世界让你迷惑。
(13) It's time to start believing. 是开始信任别人的时候了。
注意区分 It's time that…与 It's time to do sth. 的含义，在 It's time that…句型中，that 引导的从句用虚拟语气。
例如：

It' *s* (*high*) *time that* you got up. 你早该起床了。

(14) Believe in who you are. =Believe yourself.

注释与赏析

这是美国哥伦比亚影业公司出品的影片《白夜》(White Nights)的插曲，1958年获第58届奥斯卡最佳电影歌曲奖。这首主题歌的词曲均由莱昂内尔·里奇(Lionel Richie)创作并演唱。

莱昂内尔·里奇1950年6月20日出生于美国阿拉巴马的塔斯克吉(Tuskegee)。他中学时学习成绩优异，叔叔送给他一把萨克斯管，祖父教他钢琴，从而开始了他的音乐生涯，也许正是这种萨克斯风情和钢琴的传统规则奠定了里奇软调音乐风格的基础。上大学时，里奇便与一些同学同伴成立了校园演唱组，不仅在学院演唱，而且也走上社会巡回演出，灌制唱片，还荣获过几张金唱片奖和白金唱片奖。后来里奇脱离乐队，开始自己创作音乐和独唱。他的歌曲《说你，说我》在我国流传很广，深受广大音乐爱好者的喜爱。

只要人人都献出一份爱，这世界就会更加美好，可以说这是首歌的主题思想。世界原本该这样；大家说说笑笑，谈论你我他，多多交流，而歌中所唱的现实是：人们戴着假面具生活，在黑暗中玩着游戏，互不吐真情，游戏生活，互不信任，猜疑之墙林立，在这样的墙后，终有人在大声呼吁真诚，歌中还唱道：当我们走上人生的孤寂之路时，似乎人世间最难的是找到朋友，一两个通情达理，乐于为你指路的朋友。所以歌词作者呼唤人间真情，这当然首先要求大家互诉衷肠，既信任别人又信任自己。

世间本是你我他组成，只要说你说我，即大家彼此沟通，互相理解，人与人亲切相待，世间才能变得更可爱。

38. Top of the World
(世界之巅)

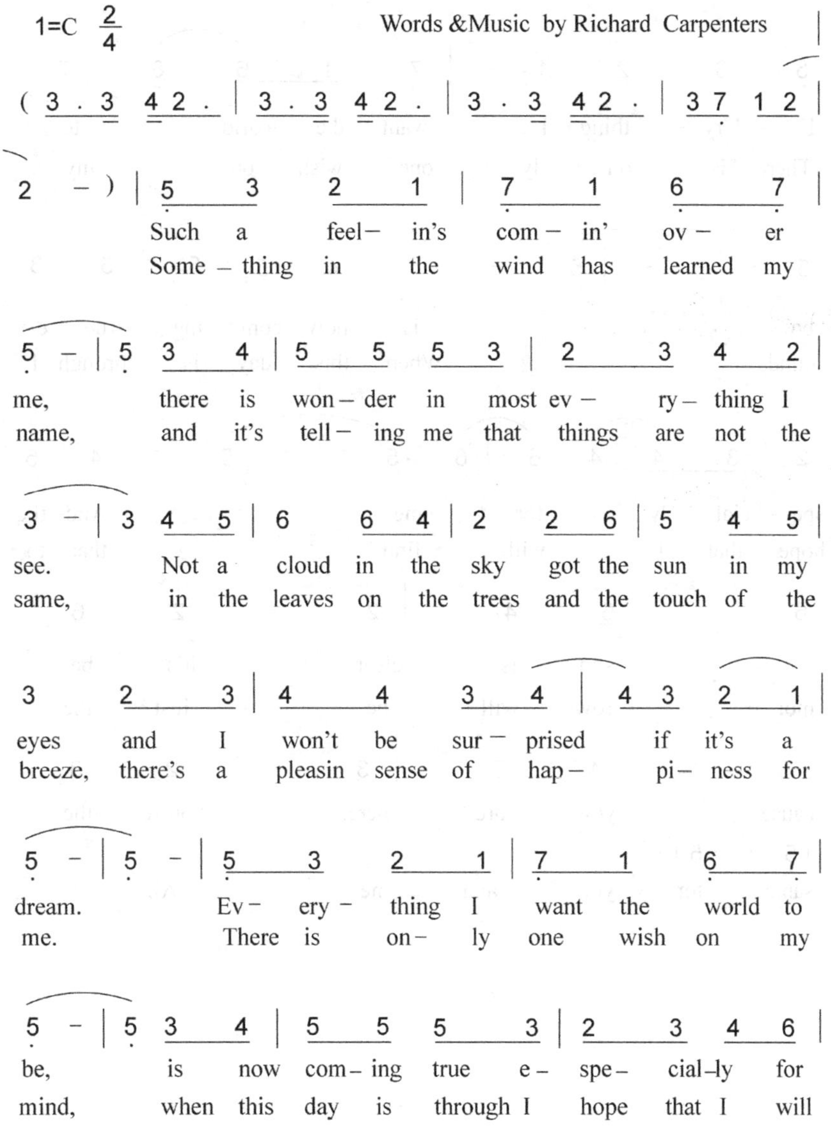

3 – 2 3 | 0 4 4 3 4 |

eyes, And I (4) won't be sur – prised

breeze, There's a pleas – ing sense of hap –

4 3 2 1 5 | 5 – – – | 5 – 0 0 |

if it's a dream.

pi – ness for me.

5 3 2 1· | 7 1 6 6 7 |

Ev – 'ry – thing I want the world to

There is on – ly one wish on my

5 – – – | 5 – 3 4 | 5 5· 5 3 |

be is now com – ing true e –

mind, When this day is through I

2 3 4 4 6 | 6 5 – – | 5 – 4 5 |

spe – cial – ly for me, And the

hope that I will find that to –

6 – 6 4· | 2 – 2 6 |

rea – son is clear it's be –

mor – row will be just the

5 – 4 5· | 3 – 2 3 |

cause you are here. You're the

(5 5)

same for you and me. All I

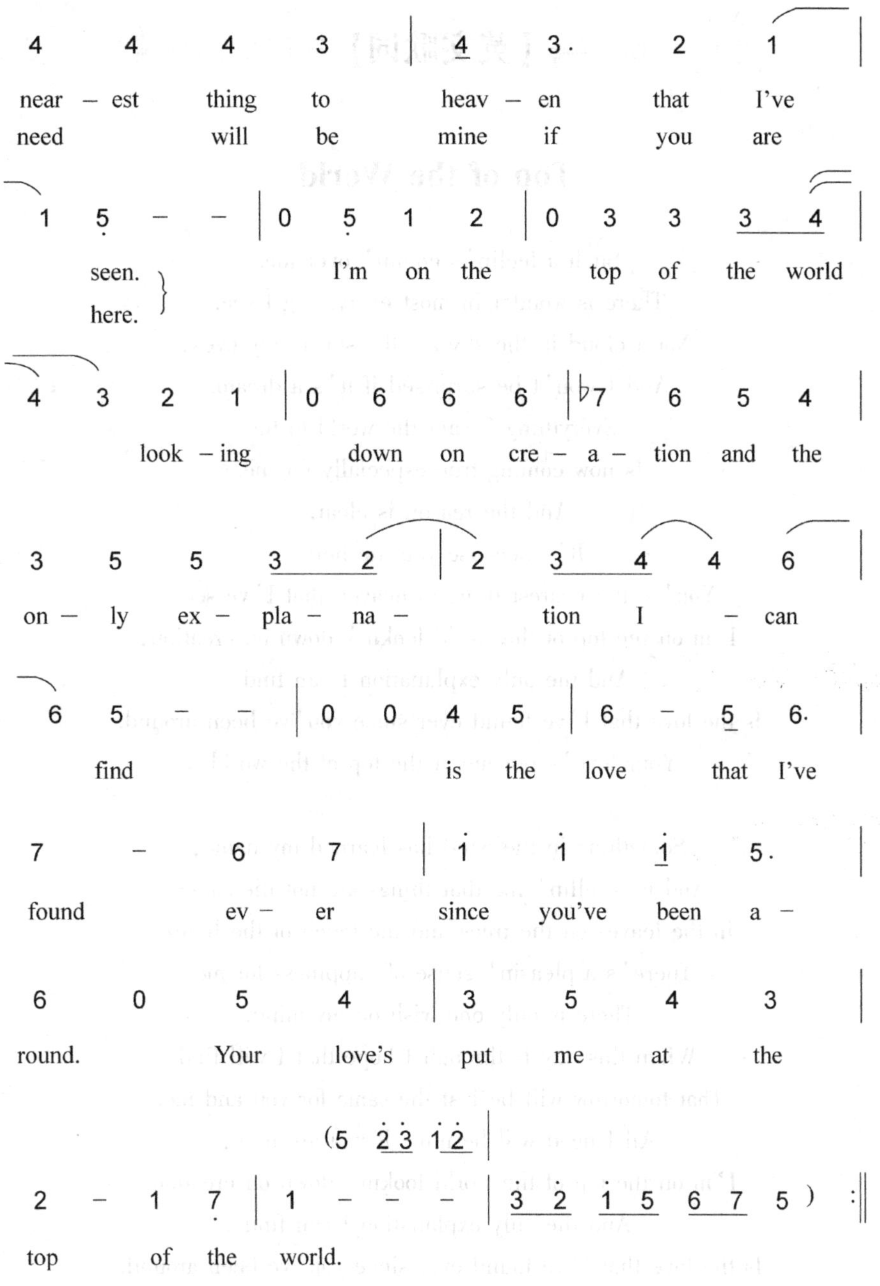
near – est thing to heav – en that I've
need will be mine if you are
seen.
here.
I'm on the top of the world
look – ing down on cre – a – tion and the
on – ly ex – pla – na – tion I – can
find is the love that I've
found ev – er since you've been a –
round. Your love's put me at the
top of the world.

【英文歌词】

Top of the World

Such a feelin's comin' over me.
There is wonder in most everything I see.
Not a cloud in the sky got the sun in my eyes,
And I won't be surprised if it's a dream.
Everything I want the world to be
Is now coming true especially for me.
And the reason is clear.
It's because you are here.
You're the nearest thing to heaven that I've seen.
I'm on the top of the world lookin' down on creation,
And the only explanation I can find
Is the love that I've found ever since you've been around.
Your love's put me at the top of the world.

Something in the wind has learned my name,
And it's tellin' me that things are not the same.
In the leaves on the trees and the touch of the breeze,
There's a pleasin' sense of happiness for me.
There is only one wish on my mind.
When this day is through I hope that I will find
That tomorrow will be just the same for you and me.
All I need will be mine if you are here,
I'm on the top of the world lookin' down on creation.
And the only explanation I can find
Is the love that I've found ever since you've been around.
Your love's put me at the top of the world.

I'm on the top of the world lookin' down on creation.
And the only explanation I can find
Is the love that I've found ever since you've been around.
Your love's put me at the top of the world.

【参考译文】

世界之巅

这样一种感觉涌上我心头；
眼中所见诸多事几乎全是奇迹。
天空中无一片云，太阳在眼中闪动，
若说这是一场梦，
我也不会吃惊。
我愿望的一切都在专为我实现。
原因很明显，因为这里有你，
你是我所见到的最接近天堂的人。
我在世界之巅，俯视地上人间，
我找到的唯一解释
是自你伴随我左右以来我找到了爱。
是你的爱把我放在世界之巅。

风中有一种声音已知道我的姓名。
它在告诉我，事情与过去的已不同。
在树上的叶子里，在微风的轻抚中，
对我来说有一种令人愉悦的感觉。
在我的心里只有一个愿望，
今天结束后我希望
能发现明日将还是一样，为你又为我。
只要有你在，一切都心想事成。
我在世界之巅，俯视地上人间，
我找到的唯一解释
是自你伴随左右以来我找到了爱
是你的爱把我放在世界之巅。

我在世界之巅，俯视地上人间，
我找到的唯一解释
是自你伴我左右以来我找到了爱。
是你的爱把我放在世界之巅。

语言点解析

(1) Such a feeling's coming over me. =Such a feeling is coming over me.

come over: (of a sudden strong feeling) to trouble or annoy

例如：

A feeling of shame *came over* him. 一种羞耻感涌上他心头。

(2) Not a cloud in the sky= The sky was cloudless.

(3) ...got the sun in my eyes= I've got the sun in my eyes. Or I can see the sun shine in the cloudless sky.

(4) **come true**: 实现

例如：

His dream *came true*. 他的梦想实现了。

(5) The reason is clear. = the reason is obvious to be seen.

(6) You are the nearest thing to heaven that I've seen. =You are closest to heaven. 离天堂最近（也就是说离上帝最近）。

(7) I'm on the top of the world lookin´ down on creation…=我站在世界之颠，俯视着世界万物。

look down on: 俯视；轻视

creation: 创造。此处指上帝的创造，即世界。

(8) the only explanation…is：唯一的解释是

例如：

He did not come to see you off. ***The only explanation*** is he was not free. 他没有来为你送行，唯一的解释是他没有时间。

(9) **be around**: be about 在附近

例如：

I'll *be around* by ten tomorrow morning. 我明天上午十点来。

(10) Your love's put me on the top of the world. = Your love has placed me on the top of the world. Or：I'm on the top of the world because of your love.

(11) Something in the wind has learned my name. = Something seems to be calling me in the wind.

(12) **learn** *vt.*: 知道，获悉

例如：

He has *learned* the secret. 这个秘密他已知道。

(13) It's telling me that things are not the same. = It is telling me that the things are different from what they were in the past.

(14) **not the same**: 与以前的不同

例如：

You have changed a lot. You are **not the same**. 你变化很大，已不是从前的那个人了。

(15) In the leaves on the trees and the touch of the breeze, there's a pleasing sense of happiness for me. = There is a pleasing sense of happiness for me in the leaves on the trees and the touch of the breeze.

in the leaves on the trees：在树上的叶子中(指树叶的沙沙声响，这里从听觉着笔)

the touch of the breeze =the gentle touch of the light wind，指微风轻扬时吹在脸上或身上(这里从触觉着笔)

(16) a pleasing sense of happiness = a pleasant feeling of happiness 令人愉快的幸福感

a sense of beauty：美感

a sense of satisfaction：满足感

a sense of responsibility：责任感

a sense of shame：羞耻感

a sense of direction：方向感

(17) **on one's mind**：在心上；有心事；压在心上

例如：

I thought something was **on your mind**. 我想你当时有心事。

Mr. Bennet said, "The matter was ***on her mind***, always." 本奈特先生说："这件事她总是挂在心上。"

(18) (**be**) **through**：(be) over 完了，结束

例如：

Are you ***through*** with your work? 你的工作做完了吗？

I'm ***through*** talking to her. 我已和她说完话。

Is he ***through*** college yet? 他上完大学了吗？

I'll be ***through*** writing soon. 我马上就会写完。

(19). ...that tomorrow will be just the same… = ...that tomorrow will be like today…

(20) All I need will be mine if you are here. = If you are here, everything that I need will be mine.

(21) **all I need** = all that I need; everything that I need

注释与赏析

《世界之巅》由卡伦·卡彭特演唱。卡伦于1983年去世之后，美国曾有人根据她的生平拍成一部《卡伦·卡彭特的故事》。影片里，她是正在唱《世界之巅》这首歌时，因体力不支，身体太虚弱，突然晕倒在舞台上。后被送往医院抢救，终因长时间患"神经性厌食症"，最终未能够挽救她年轻的生命。

《世界之巅》成了卡伦的绝唱。由于有了这段动人的情节，人们在听这首歌时，更加怀恋这位天皇歌星了。

人在什么时候才能感到自己在世界之巅呢？大概是在最幸福的时候。那么，人何时最幸

福？这首歌表达的是：有爱情时，人最幸福；有爱情时，人便产生站在世界最顶端的感觉。世界的顶端是上帝为亚当和夏娃造的乐园。这个乐园和下边的世界都是上帝的创造物。歌中女主人公所咏唱的男子最接近天堂(You are the nearest thing to heaven that I have seen)。毫无疑问，这位给女主人公带来幸福的人就是幸福的源泉。这大概是女主人公所要表达的主要意思。

歌中首先唱道：有一种感觉涌上心头。什么感觉？她所看见的一切都是奇迹：万里晴空、艳阳高照，似梦幻般的美妙。所以女主人公唱道：若说这是梦，我不会感到吃惊。她所希望的一切都变成现实。是什么产生了使梦成真的动力呢？是自己所爱的人！一个最接近天堂的人！这个人便是爱的化身。这里，意象的视野很开阔，女主人公原本是在地上人间，仰望晴空和艳阳，又看见自己所爱之人似在天上，接近天堂。在第二段唱词中，女主人公已不再地上，她已站在世界之巅。她开始俯视人间。从仰望到俯视人间，肯定有一种神奇力量在起作用。女主人公毫不掩饰，她站在世界之巅向人们宣布，对产生这一变化的唯一解释是：自从心爱的人伴她左右以来她便找到了爱。“是你的爱把我放在世界之巅”。

人在幸福时，世界也都欢唱；人在悲哀时，万物也悲伤。此时的女主人公幸福之极，感觉自己声名远扬，风也知道了她叫什么，风也感觉到人身上产生的变化，它在告诉她，一切都变了，爱情使这个世界变得今非昔比(things are not the same)。女主人公何尝不有此感？她感觉：树叶沙沙响，听来欢畅；微风轻拂，感觉这轻轻抚摸令人产生无比的快乐。在如此美妙的爱的世界，女主人公唯有一事压在心上：她希望以后的日子里心情天天如此，明天如同今日，愿幸福感永远继续，愿她希望所要的一切她都能得到。

39. Santa Claus Is Coming to Town
(圣诞老人就要进城)

1=C 4/4

Words by H. Gillespie
Music by J.F. Coots

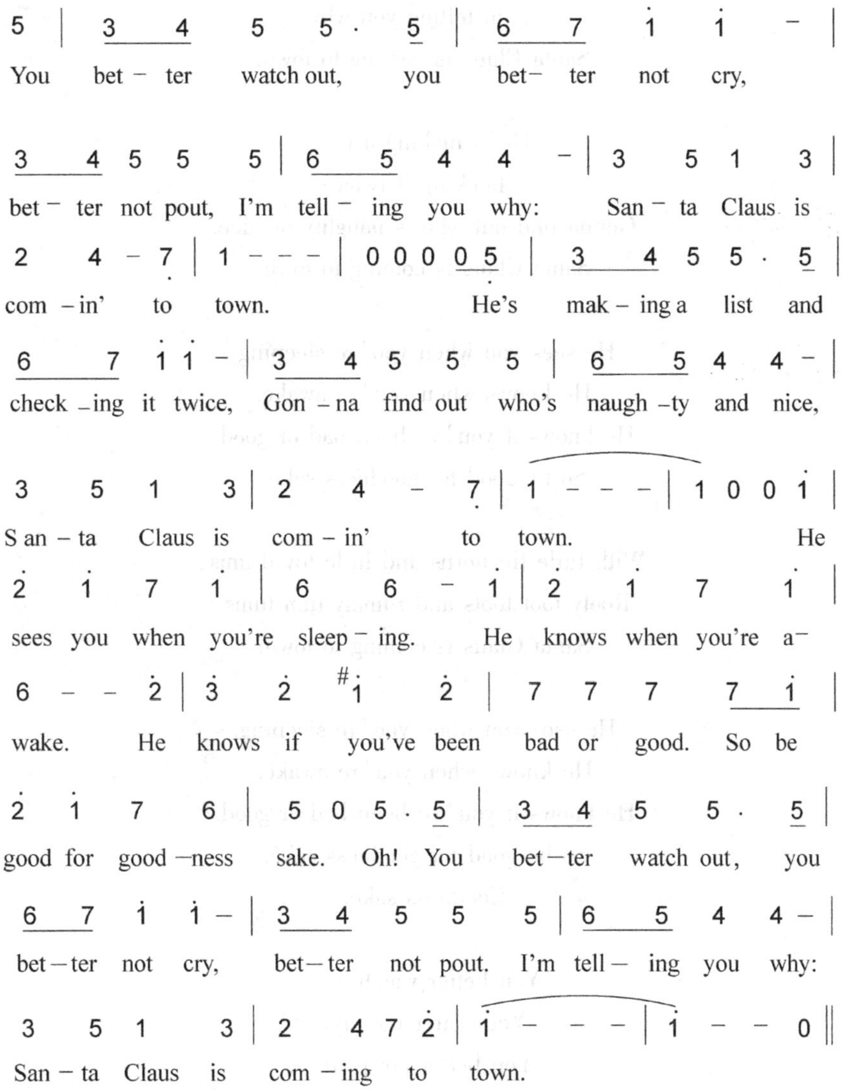

【英文歌词】

Santa Claus Is Coming to Town

You better watch out.
You better not cry.
You better not pout.
I'm telling you why
Santa Claus is coming to town.

He's making a list,
Checking it twice;
Gonna find out who's naughty or nice.
Santa Claus is coming to town.

He sees you when you're sleeping.
He knows when you're awake.
He knows if you've been bad or good.
So be good for goodness sake.

With little tin horns and little toy drums,
Rooty toot toots and rummy tum tums.
Santa Claus is coming to town.

He sees you when you're sleeping.
He knows when you're awake.
He knows if you've been bad or good.
So be good for goodness sake.
Goodness sake.

You better watch out.
You better not cry.
You better not pout.
I'm telling you why.

Santa Claus is coming to town.
Santa Claus is coming to town.
Santa Claus is coming.
Santa Claus is coming.
Santa Claus is coming to town.

【参考译文】

圣诞老人就要进城

你要留神，
你最好别哭，
不要生气，
听我说仔细。
圣诞老人就要进城。

他一一记下，他检查两遍，
要去分清谁听话淘气，
圣诞老人就要进城。
你睡时他会观望，
你醒时他知道，
他知道你是好或坏，
因此你要表现好。

带着小喇叭和玩具小鼓，
喇叭滴滴滴，小鼓嗒嗒嗒，
圣诞老人就要进城。

你睡时他会观望，
你醒时他知道，
他知道你是好或坏，
因此你要表现好。

所以，你要留神，
你最好别哭。
不要生气，

听我说仔细。
圣诞老人就要进城。
圣诞老人就要进城。
圣诞老人就要，
圣诞老人就要进城。

语言点解析

(1) You better = You'd better 你最好
better not = You'd better not 你最好别
(2) **pout**：撅嘴，生气，不高兴。
(3) **make a list**：列表
(4) **gonna** = going to
(5) Who's naughty and nice：谁淘气谁听话
(6) So be good for goodness sake：= So you should be good for goodness sake. 因此看在上帝的面上，你一定要表现好。
(7) Rooty toot toots and rummy tum tums：嘟嘟的喇叭声在响，奇怪的鼓声在嗒嗒地敲。
toot 和 tum 此处既是名词亦是动词。

注释与赏析

这是圣诞前夕，父母唱给孩子们的歌。根据西方习俗，传说中的圣诞老人会在圣诞夜从烟囱爬进屋里，把孩子想要的圣诞礼物放进孩子们头一天就挂在床头的袜子里。当然，只有听话的孩子才会得到他们应得的礼物。听到父母唱着这首“圣诞老人进城来”还有哪个孩子不乖乖地上床睡觉呢？这首歌诙谐有趣，演唱时应显得轻松愉快，富有节奏感。

40. Tie a Yellow Ribbon Round the Old Oak Tree (老橡树上的黄丝带)

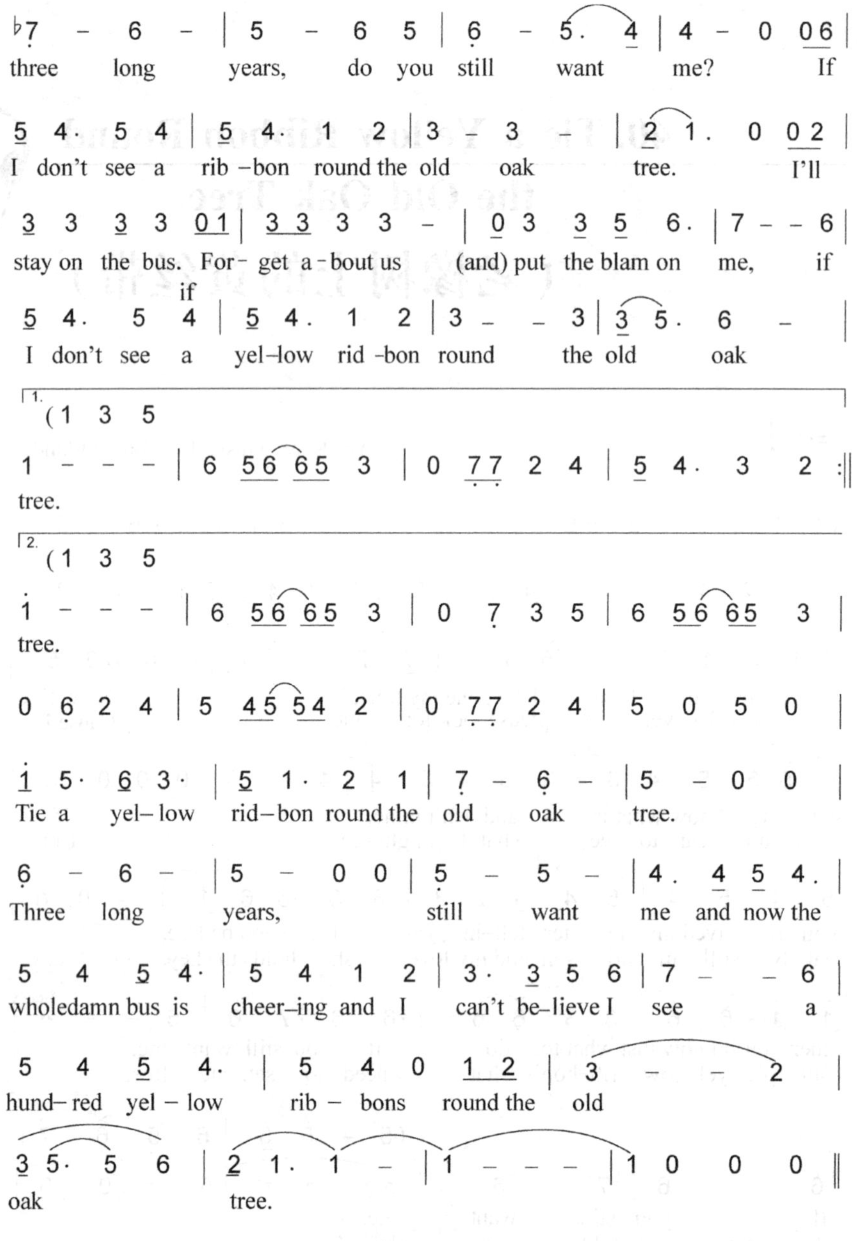
three long years, do you still want me? If
I don't see a rib -bon round the old oak tree. I'll
stay on the bus. For- get a-bout us (and) put the blam on me, if
if
I don't see a yel-low rid -bon round the old oak
tree.
tree.
Tie a yel- low rid-bon round the old oak tree.
Three long years, still want me and now the
wholedamn bus is cheer-ing and I can't be-lieve I see a
hund-red yel - low rib - bons round the old
oak tree.

【英文歌词】

Tie a Yellow Ribbon Round the Old Oak Tree

I'm comin' home; I've done my time.
Now I've got to know what is and isn't mine.
If you received my letter telling you I'd soon be free,
Then you'll know just what to do,
If you still want me; if you still want me,
Whoa, tie a yellow ribbon 'round the old oak tree.
It's been three long years; do you still want me?
If I don't see a ribbon round the old oak tree,
I'll stay on the bus.
Forget about us and put the blame on me,
If I don't see a yellow ribbon round the old oak tree.

Bus driver, please look for me,
Because I couldn't bear to see what I might see.
I'm really still in prison and my love, she holds the key.
A simple yellow ribbon's what I need to set me free.
I wrote and told her please,
Whoa, tie a yellow ribbon round the old oak tree.
It's been three long years (and); do you still whant me?
If I don't see a ribbon round the old oak tree,
I'll stay on the bus.
Forger about us, and put the blame on me,
If I don't see a yellow ribbon round the old oak tree.

Tie a yellow ribbon round the old oak tree.
Three long years, still want me and now
The whole damn bus is cheering.
And I can't believe I see
A hundred yellow ribbons round the old oak tree.

【参考译文】

老橡树上的黄丝带

我服刑已满，我就要回来。
什么属于我现在我才渐明白。
如果你收到我的信知道我将获释，
你会知道怎么做，如果你还把我爱，
如果你还爱我，
在老橡树上系条黄丝带。
我离开三年之久，你是否还把我爱?
如果看不到老橡树上的黄丝带，
我将不下车，
忘掉那过去，过错都归我，
如果我看不到老橡树上的黄丝带。

司机先生，请你帮我看，
因为我无法承受要看到的黄丝带。
我真的仍在狱里，她握着爱的钥匙。
那就是在老橡树上
系一条普通的黄丝带
请在老橡树上系条黄丝带。
我已离开三年之久，你是否还把我爱?
如果我看不到老橡树上的黄丝带，
我将不下车，
忘掉那过去，过错都归我，
如果我看不到老橡树上的黄丝带。

在老橡树上系条黄丝带，
三年了，还爱着我。
现在整个汽车在欢呼，
我真不敢相信
老橡树上系满了黄丝带。

语言点解析

(1) **ribbon**：丝带，缎带

在美国，人们过去常在家乡的树上系上黄丝带，以求远方亲人的平安；现在人们在自己的汽车上系上黄丝带或红丝带，祈求上帝保佑自己平安，成为吉利的象征。

the ribbons on the wreaths：花环上的缎带

the ribbon-cutting ceremony：剪彩仪式

(2) **oak** *n.*：(植)栎属植物；橡树

(3) I've done my time. = I've finished my sentence in prison. 我已刑满了。

本句用了现在完成时，表示到目前所发生的动作或事情已结束。

(4) Now I've got to know what is and isn't mine. =Now I've got to know what belongs to me and what doesn't. 我现在需要知道什么属于我，什么不属于我。

get to know sb. (or sth.)：逐渐了解某人(某物)，这一短语通常表示一个逐渐了解或认识的过程。但在这里 have got to know=have to know.

例如：

We *got to know* each other better with the time passing by. 随着时间的流失我们互相渐渐地更了解了。

He **got to like** her. 他逐渐喜欢起她来了。

(5) If you received my letter telling you I'd soon be free, then you'll know just what to do…=If you've got my letter which told you that I would soon be free from prison, then you'll know what I mean about tying a yellow ribbon round the old oak tree.

(6) **be free**：可以自由，空闲的，有空

例如：

He i *s free* to enter the room. 他得自由出入那个房间。

I' *m free* this afternoon. 我今天下午有空。

what to do 是疑问句+动词不定式构成的短语，在句子中作宾语。

"疑问句+不定式"这一结构在句子中，可以充当名词性从句。

例如：

How to do it is a difficult question. (主语)如何做这件事是一个难题。

The question is ***when to start***. (表语)问题是何时出发。

We had a useful discussion on the question of ***how to repair*** this machine. (介词宾语)我们曾对如何修理这台机器的问题进行了有益的讨论。

(7) It's been three long years. =It's been three long years since I was put in jail. Or: It's been three long years since we parted with each other. 我们分开已有三年之久了。

It's been… =It has been…

(8) Put the blame on me. =Blame it on me. 将过错都归于我。

blame：(名词和动词)过失，责备，归咎

blame sb. for sth. =blame sth. on (upon) sb. 把某事归咎于某人

例如：

Don't **blame it on** (upon) him：Don't blame him for it. 这件事不能怪他。

(9) I'm really still in prison, and my love she holds the key. =Mentally I'm really still in prison, and she holds the key to my love. 我的心仍在监狱中，她握着我爱情的钥匙。

(10) A simple yellow ribbon's what I need to set me free. = What I need is only a simple yellow ribbon round the old oak tree to set me free. 我需要仅是老橡树上的一条黄丝带能让我获自由。

set sb. free：释放某人，使获得自由。

例如：

They **set** the war prisoners ***free***. 他们释放战俘。

The slaves were **set free**. 奴隶被释放了。

(11) Now the whole damn bus is cheering and I can't believe I see a hundred yellow ribbons round the old oak tree. =Now all the people in the bus are crying and shouting and I can't believe what I see a hundred yellow ribbons round the old oak tree. 现在公共汽车上所有的人都在欢呼，而我真不敢相信我看到老橡树上系有上百条的黄丝带。

cheer v. t. & n.：使高兴，鼓舞，欢呼。

例如：

The good news ***cheered*** (up) everybody who heard it. 喜讯使每一个听到的人感到高兴。

We ***cheered*** victory. 我们为胜利而欢呼。

cheer-leader：啦啦队队长

cheer oneself hoarse：欢呼时喊哑嗓子

注释与赏析

这首歌曲的原型来自于一个广为流传的民间爱情故事，该故事于1971年10月14日在“New York Post”杂志上进行了登载。后来，美国一位新闻记者Pete Hamill把这个故事进行了整理创作。故事的名字叫《回家》(Going Home)。主人公叫文戈(Vingo)。故事中，作者描写的老橡树上系的是黄手帕(Yellow Handkerchiefs)。在股市开始之前，作者这样写到：“几年前，在纽约格林威治村，我碰到一个姑娘，从她那里第一次听到了这个故事，这故事很可能每隔几年就会重新出现，成为一个带有不少新说法被再次讲述一遍的神秘的民间传说。然而，我仍相信这个故事确实曾发生在某个地方某个时间。”这个故事刊出不久，被改编成音乐作品，而且还被改编成电影，由电影明星高仓健和千惠子主演的日本影片《幸福的黄手帕》也同样以这个故事为蓝本。黄手帕也好，黄丝带也好，都是爱情的信物和象征。

从洛德代尔堡上车的几个年青人，在公共汽车驶到新泽西时，他们注意到了一个穿着一套不合身便装的人，坐在那里一动不动，看不出年龄，表情冷淡，沉默寡言，他就是文戈。当公共汽车驶进华盛顿郊外的一家餐馆时，文戈却生根似地仍坐在车上，年轻人觉得诧异，试图了解猜测他可能是远航商船的船长，抛妻离家的人或者或者是解甲归田的老兵。一位女孩主动与他接触，说他们要到美丽的弗罗里达州去度假。可是文戈只是轻声附和，心不在焉。女孩的热情使文戈终于说出了自己的身世。他在纽约坐了三年牢，现在要回家，坐牢初曾写信给妻子说她要是受不了，孩子们老问这问那的使她太伤心，就干脆忘掉他，另嫁别人。文戈拿出妻子和孩子的照片给年轻人们看，从照片上可看出他妻子具有一种朴实的美，是个了不起的好女人。三年多来他们未再通过信，文戈现在获释不知道妻子是否改嫁，是否还能接受他。他出狱前写信给妻子说如果她没有别的男人，还想让他回家，就在家门口的老橡树上系一个黄手帕。

当公共汽车越来越接近文戈家布伦斯威克时，年轻人们坐在靠窗户的位上往外看，盼望着布伦斯威克快点到来，只有文戈不敢张望，他正鼓足勇气准备迎接失望。突然间，全车的人都沸腾起来，站起来又喊又叫又跳。文戈却坐在那望着老橡树惊呆了，树上系满了黄手帕，二十条、三十条，或许几百条，这些黄手帕像欢迎的旗帜迎风飘扬，这时文戈站起身来，向家走去……

这个故事刊出不久，汤尼·奥兰多(Tony Orland)便根据故事内容创作了歌曲《老橡树上的黄丝带》(“Tie A Yellow Ribbon Round The Ole Oak Tree”)，伴着歌声这个故事也传遍了全世界。黄丝带也成了美国"欢迎被囚禁的人重获自由"的标志。这首风格迥异热情朴实、乡情村味的《老橡树上的黄丝带》，多少年来一直流行于广大青年之中，创造了爱的奇迹。黎明乐队最初于1973年演唱了这首名曲，到1979年这首歌已被灌片出版达1000次以上，并在世界各地广为流传。

41. Rainy Days and Mondays

（雨天和周一）

Words & Music by
Paul Williams & Roger Nichols

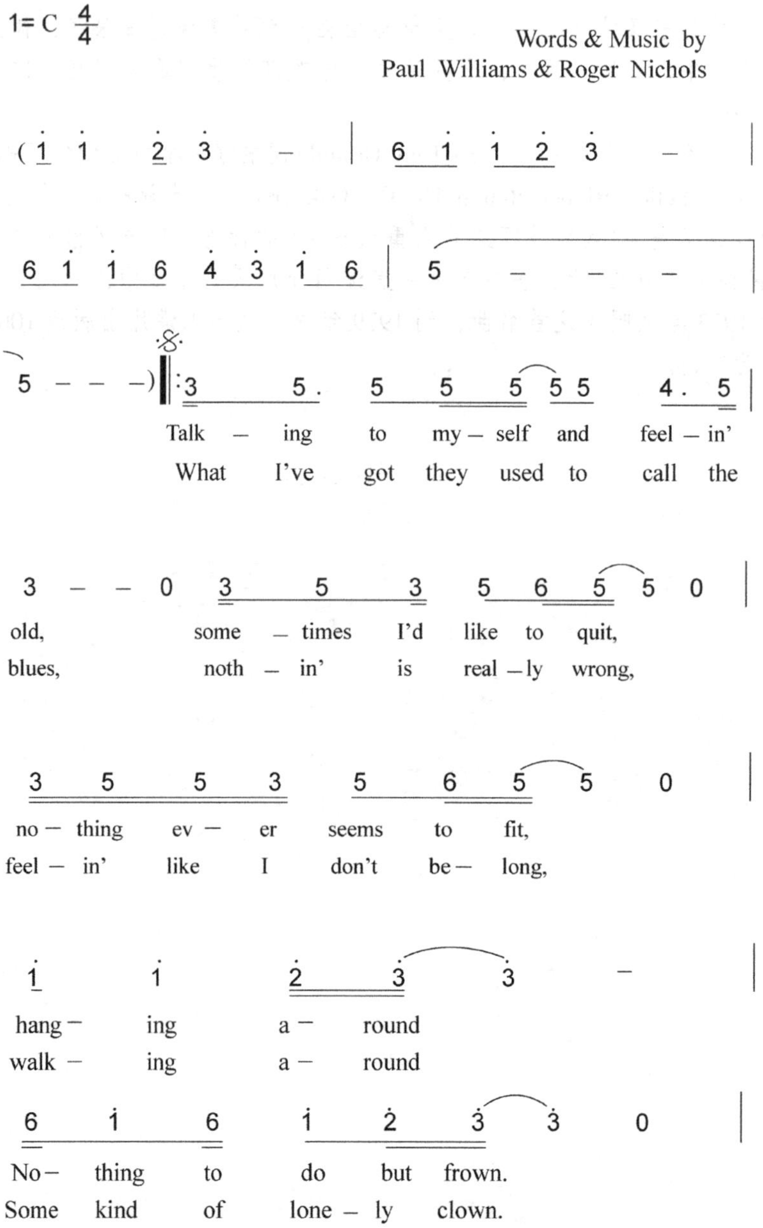

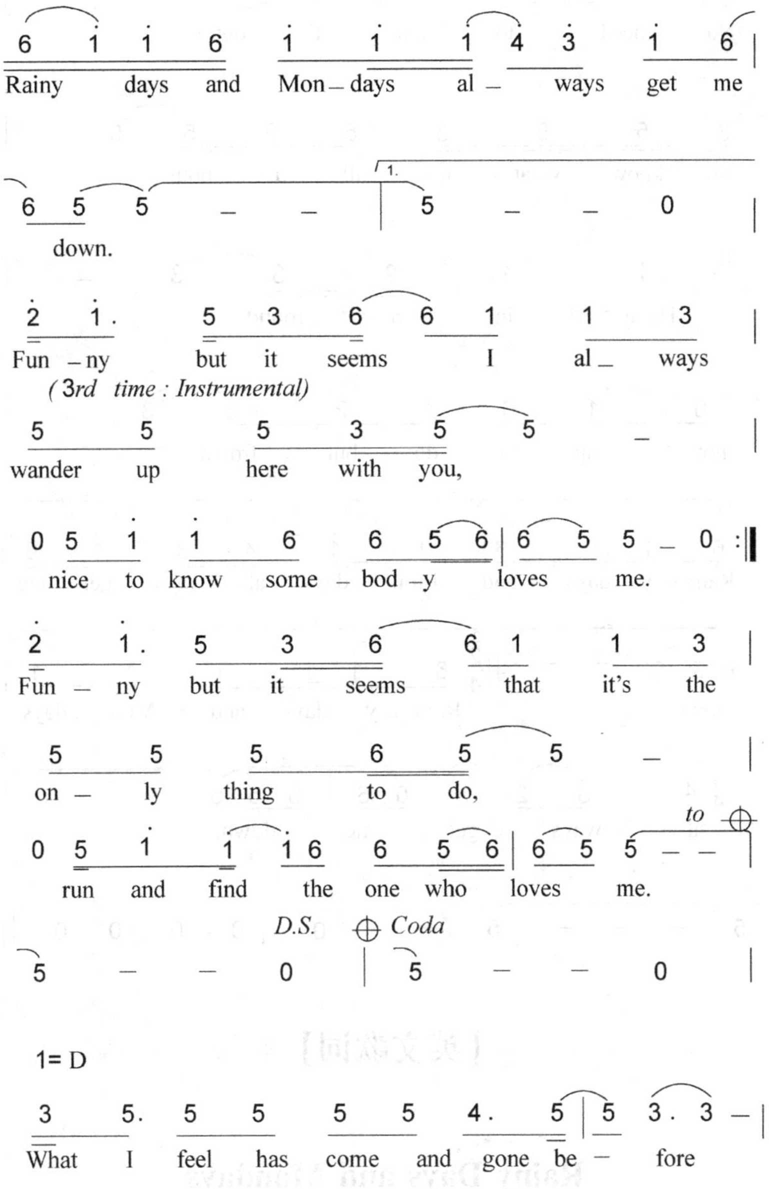
Rainy days and Mon – days al – ways get me
down.
Fun – ny but it seems I al – ways
(3rd time : Instrumental)
wander up here with you,
nice to know some – bod – y loves me.
Fun – ny but it seems that it's the
on – ly thing to do,
to
run and find the one who loves me.
D.S.
Coda
1= D
What I feel has come and gone be – fore

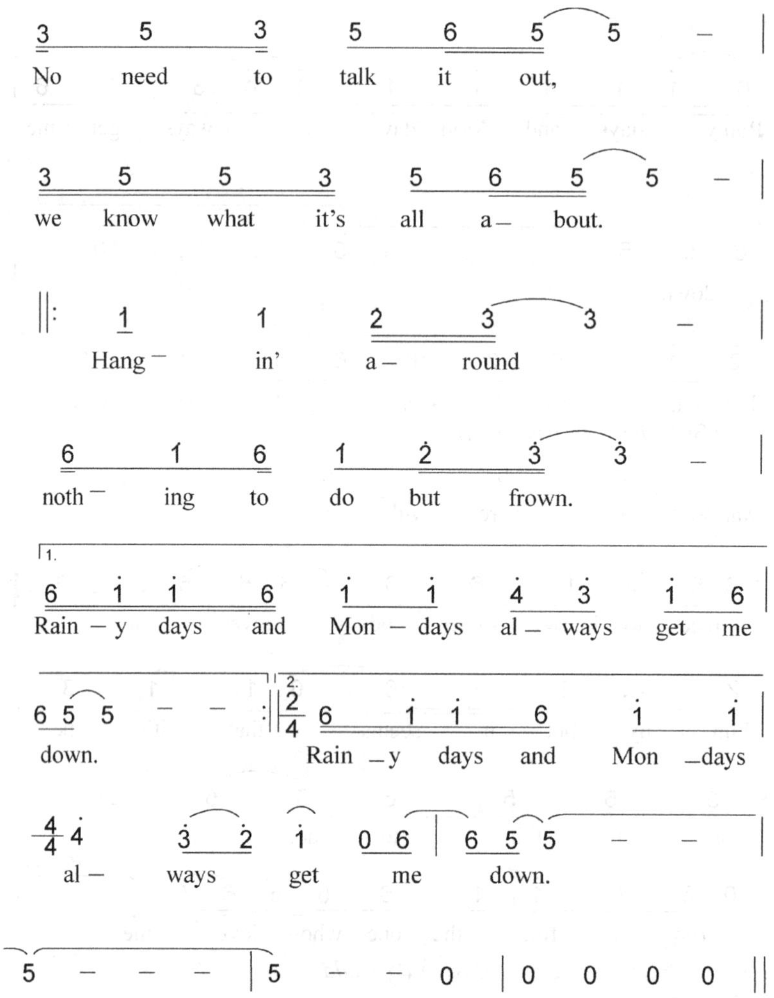

【英文歌词】

Rainy Days and Mondays

Talking to myself and feeling old,
Sometimes I'd like to quit.
Nothing ever seems to fit.
Hangin' around, nothing to do but frown,
Rainy days and Mondays always get me down.

What I've got they used to call the blues,

Nothing is really wrong,
Feeling like I don´t belong.
Walking around some kind of lonely clown,
Rainy days and Mondays always get me down.

Funny but it seems I always wind up here with you,
Nice to know somebody loves me.
Funny but it seems that it´s the only thing to do,
Run and find the one who loves me.
What I feel has come and gone before.
No need to talk it out,
We know what its all about.
Hanging around nothing to do but frown.
Rainy days and Mondays always get me down.

Funny but it seems that it's the only thing to do,
Run and find the one who loves me.
What I feel has come and gone before.
No need to talk it out,
We know what it's all about.
Hanging around nothing to do but frown.
Rainy days and Mondays always get me down.
Hanging around nothing to do but frown.
Rainy days and Mondays always get me down.

【参考译文】

雨天和周一

我对自己说我已老,
我有时想抛弃一切,
什么都是让我心烦。
无所事事,四处闲逛。
周一和雨天总让我沮丧。

人们说我患了忧郁症。
一切都没变糟,
只是我无所适从,形影相吊。

周一和雨天总让我沮丧。

常与你闲逛却使我觉得很有趣，
得知有人爱我真欢喜！
只有与你闲逛才使我觉得很有趣。
去找一位钟爱我的人。

往事如烟已随风飘去，
记忆虽犹新，
再说已无益，
无所事事，四处闲逛。
周一和雨天总让我沮丧。

只有与你闲逛才是我觉得很有趣，
去找一位钟爱我的人。
往事如烟已随风飘去。
记忆虽犹新，
再说已无益。
无所事事，四处闲逛。
周一和雨天总让我沮丧。
无所事事，四处闲逛。
周一和雨天总让我沮丧。

语言点解析

(1) **talk to oneself**：自言自语
例如：
He has a habit of **talking to himself**. 他有自言自语的习惯。

(2) I'd like to：我想，我希望
would(should) like to do：想……，希望……
例如：
I ***would like to*** go there. 我想去那里。

(3) **quit**：离开(人，地方)，放弃
例如：
She ***quit*** the room in anger. 她生气地离开房间。
Quit worrying about me, please. 请不用为我担心。

(4) Nothing ever seems to fit = I feel that there is nothing to fit me around 似乎没有一件适合我做

的事情。

(5) Hangin' =hanging around

hang around sb.：聚在……附近

例如：

The students ***hung around*** the veteran worker. 学生们聚在老工人身旁。

(6) Nothing to do but frown：无所事事，愁眉不展。

nothing but：不过是，只是，只能

例如：

He did ***nothing but*** complain. 他只能发发牢骚而已。

(7) **get sb down**：使我情绪低落

down *adj.*：(在情绪、健康等方面)处于低落状态。

例如：

He is badly ***down***, we'd better have a heart-to- heart talk with him. 他情绪很不好，我们最好能跟他谈谈心。

What I've got they used to call the blues. =They used to call what I've got the blues. 人们说我患了忧郁症。

(8) **used to**：过去常常，向来，通常

例如：

He ***used to*** visit his uncle on holidays. 他在休假日子常去拜访他叔叔。

(9) **call sth. sth.**：认为……是……，把……说成是……

例如：

I don't ***call Russian a hard language***. 我认为俄语不难。

I ***call that a shame***. 我把那看成是耻辱。

(10) **the blues**：忧郁，烦闷，沮丧。

例如：

He was in ***the blues***. =He had the blues. 他闷闷不乐。

(11) Feeling like I don't belong = It seems that I feel I don't belong to the world like. 似乎感到自己无所适从。

like 是介词，表示"像"。注意不要与 feel like 弄混。

feel like：想要

例如：

I ***feel like*** taking a walk. 我想要散步。

(12) So kind of lonely clown：很有点像孤独的小丑

so：很，非常，极

例如：

We ***so*** want to see the performance again. 我们真想再看一次这场表演。

I'm ***so*** glad that you've come. 你来了，我真太高兴了。

(13) **kind of**：有点儿，有几分

例如：

I *kind of* thought he would come. 我似乎感到他会来。

I' m feeling *kind of* tired. 我感到有点累。

(14) Funny but it seems I always wander up here with you. =But it seems funny that I always wander up here with you. 常与你在这儿闲逛却使我觉得很有趣。

(15) **funny**：有趣的，滑稽的

例如：

It' sa *funny* story. 那是一个很滑稽的故事。

(16) Nice to know somebody loves me. 知道有人爱我使我心欢喜。

(17) It' s the only thing to do. 这是唯一要做的事。

It 指上面提到的"wander up here with you".

(18) Run and find. = go and seek for.

run：赶紧，赶快，赶去

例如：

We *ran* to his aid. 我们赶去帮助他。

(19) No need to talk it out. = There is no need to talk it out. 没有必要把它说出去。

注释与赏析

《雨天和周一》("Rainy Days and Mondays")这首歌曲由卡伦·卡彭特(Karen Carpenter)演唱。卡伦·卡彭特是70年代美国红影星。70年代初，她与她的哥哥查理·卡彭特组成兄妹演唱组，因一首歌《靠近你》而名声大振，开始走红。前总统尼克松称他们为"最出色的美国青年"。1983年卡伦·卡彭特因神经性厌食症在洛杉矶去世，年仅32岁。卡彭特兄妹在13年演唱生涯中，灌制过无数张唱片。其中，曾13次获得金唱片奖，3次最佳演唱奖，2次获得"格莱美"大奖。

这是一首非常抒情的歌曲。当一个人痛失所爱，当往事如烟，不堪回首，当令人心碎的阴郁的雨天和令人心烦的新的一周到来的时刻，烦恼与不幸就会悄悄袭上心头，你就会如歌中所唱的那样"无所事事，四处闲逛""无所适从，形影相吊"，无名的烦恼和惆怅，无法抑制的忧郁和沮丧就会与你相伴，如泣如诉的歌声就会脱口而出，如烟如缕。

42. I Just Called to Say I Love You
（电话诉衷情）

Words & Music by Stevie Wonder

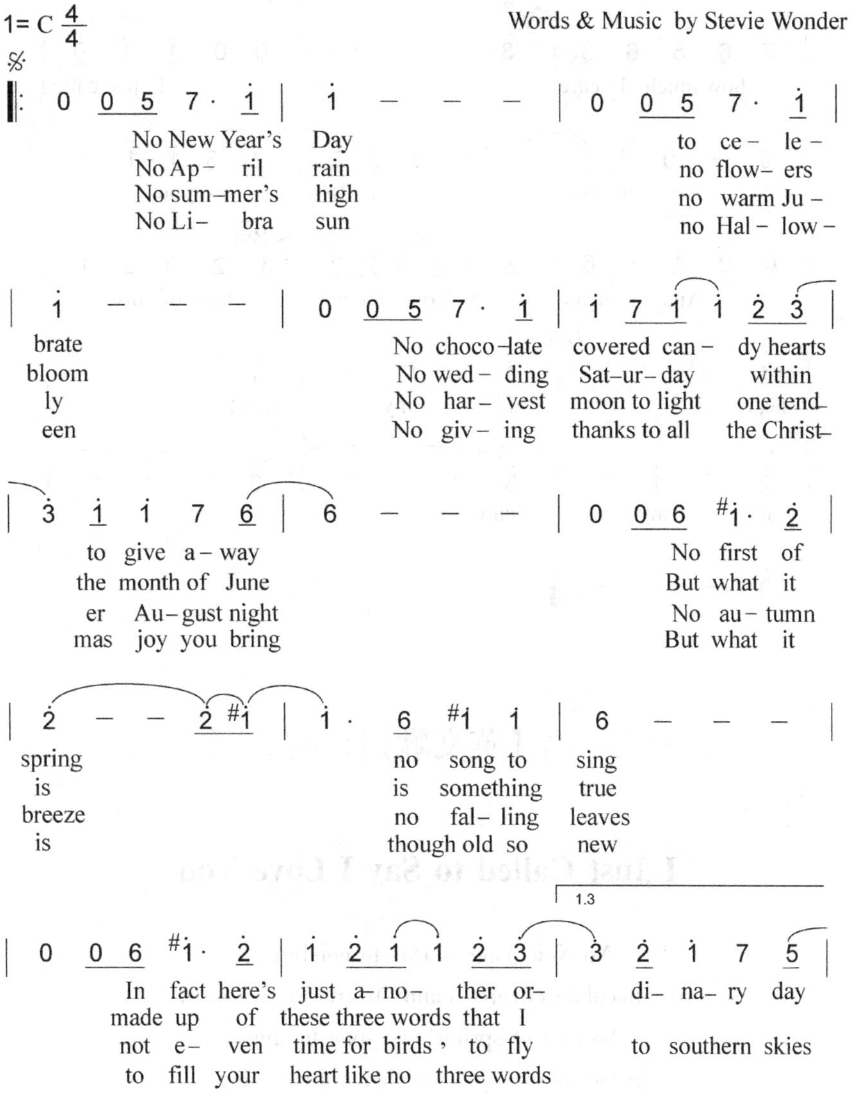

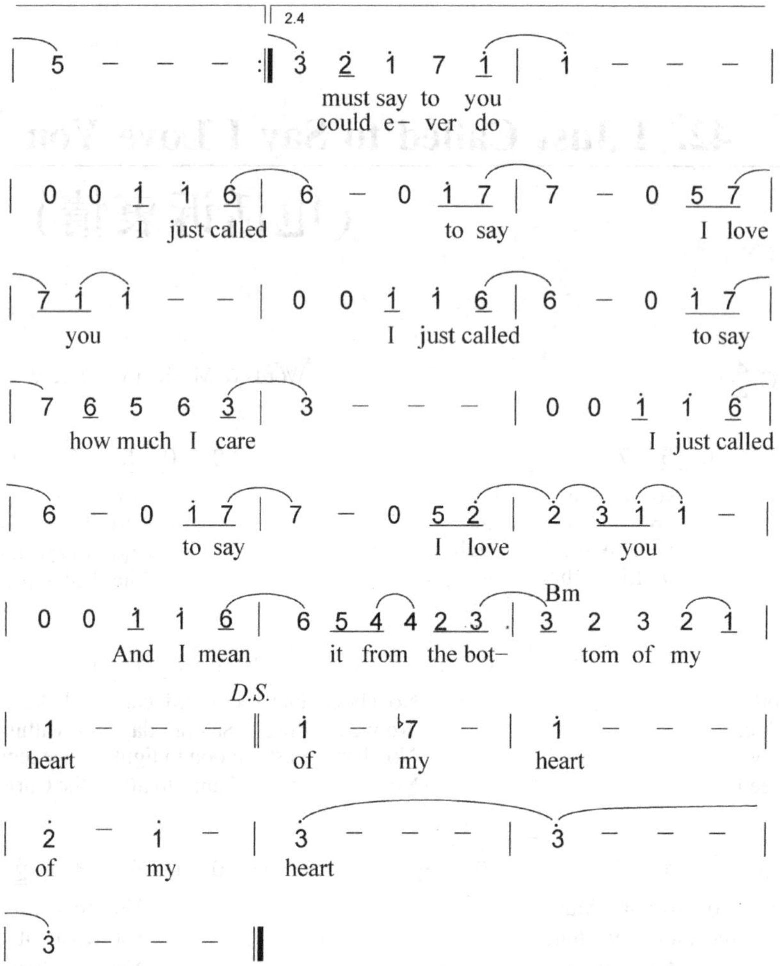

【英文歌词】

I Just Called to Say I Love You

No New Year's Day to celebrate,
No chocolate covered candy hearts to give away,
No first of spring, no song to sing,
In fact here's just another ordinary day.

No April rain no flowers bloom,
No wedding Saturday within the month of June,

But what it is.... . is something true.
Made up of these three words that I must say to you,

I just called to say I love you.
I just called to say how much I care,
I just called to say I love you,
And I mean it from the bottom of my heart.

No summer's high, no warm July,
No harvest moon to light one tender August night,
No autumn breeze, no falling leaves,
No even time for birds to fly to southern sky.

No liberal sun, no Halloween,
No giving thanks to all the Christmas joy you bring,
But what it is though old so new
To fill your heart like no three words could ever do.

I just called to say I love you,
I just called to say how much I care.
I just called to say I love you,
And I mean it from the bottom of my heart.

【参考译文】

电话诉衷情

不为庆祝新年元旦，
不为赠送夹心巧克力糖果，
不为初春，不为歌唱，
实际上这只是另一个平淡的时刻。

不为四月的雨，不为五月的花，
不为六月周末的婚礼，
但为什么……为真情实感。
由三个字组成，我要对你说，

我打电话只为说我爱你。
我打电话只为说我多么喜欢你，
我打电话只为说我爱你，
这话出自我的心底。

不为盛夏，不为七月炎热，
不为满月照耀八月温柔的夜，
不为秋日的微风，也不为飘零的落叶，
甚至也不为大雁南飞的季节。

不为慷慨的太阳，不为万圣节前夜，
不为致谢你带来圣诞快乐，
但为了什么，虽旧犹新
这三个字永远充满你的心间。

我打电话只为说我爱你，
我打电话只为说我多么喜欢你，
我打电话只为说我爱你，
这话出自我的心底，
出自我的心底，出自我的心底……

语言点解析

(1) No New Year's Day to celebrate. 不为庆祝新年元旦。
celebrate *vt*.：庆祝，祝贺
例如：
They ***celedrated*** his birthday. 他们庆祝他的生日。

(2) No chocolate covered candy hearts to give away. 不为赠送夹心巧克力糖果。
give away：赠送，分发（奖品），放弃（机会），泄露（机密）等
例如：
She has ***given away*** all her money to someone who needs it best. 她把自己所有的钱都给了最需要的人。

(3) In fact here's just another ordinary day. = As a matter of fact it is just another ordinary day here. 实际上，这不过是另一个普普通通的日子。
in fact：as a matter of fact 实际上，事实上
例如：
He is, ***in fact***, a hard worker. 他嘛，实际上是个很勤劳的人。

(4) No wedding Saturday within the month of June. 不为婚礼在六月举行。
注：在美国六月是举行婚礼的最佳月份。所以，许多年轻人把自己的婚礼安排在六月举行。

(5) And I mean it from the bottom of my heart. = What I said came from the bottom of my heart. 我说这话出自我的心底。

(6) No harvest moon to light one tender August night. = It is not a full moon to give light to one tender August night. 不为满月照耀八月温柔的夜。

(7) No autumn breeze no falling leaves. =It is not autumn breeze nor falling leaves. 不为秋日的微风，也不为秋日的落叶。

(8) No liberal sun no Halloween. 不为慷慨的太阳，也不为万圣节前夕。
Halloween *n.*：(西方国家的风俗)万圣节前夕，(指十月三十一日，这夜儿童可以纵情玩闹，他们戴奇怪的面具，穿奇怪的服装，尽兴玩耍，直到深夜。)
Hallowmas：万圣节(十一月一日)。

(9) No giving thanks to all the Christmas joy you bring. = It is not giving thanks to you for all the Christmas joy you bring. 不为你带来圣诞快乐致谢。
Christmas n. (基督教)圣诞节，(12 月 25 日)耶稣的诞生日，是基督教最大的一个节日。

(10) But what it is though old so new to fill your heart like no three words could ever do. = It is the very three words though old so new that could ever do to fill your heart and that could never express my heart. 正是这三个虽老犹新的字永在你的心间，但却表达不完我对你的爱。

注释与赏析

斯蒂维·旺德在我国已经成为众多歌迷所熟悉的一位双目失明的黑人歌星，《电话诉衷情》是他为 1984 年美国影片《红衣女郎》(The Woman In Red)所配的插曲。此歌一经推出便获巨大成功，立即风靡欧美各地，它虽是电影插曲，却比影片本身更富生命力，获得了第 57 届奥斯卡最佳歌曲奖，登上了欧美几乎所有国家的流行歌曲排行榜，成为旺德形象的新象征。

斯蒂维·旺德于 1950 年 5 月出生在密执安州的萨吉诺(Saginaw)，曾十几次荣获葛莱美音乐大奖及奥斯卡最佳电影歌曲奖。作为盲人歌星，他付出了比常人更多的心血，靠自己不懈的努力取得了伟大的成就。他的名声日贯中天，是美国音乐界一个多才多艺的国宝。他最具代表的作品是 1996 年 8 月 4 日晚在美国亚特兰大奥运会闭幕式上，用极富于感情色彩的歌声把闭幕式推向高潮。

旺德在音乐风格上的独具特色来自他的黑人音乐的天赋。他把黑人音乐的节奏融入白人的音乐旋律，获得了混合的灵歌特性。他的词融洽了民族感情，拉近了种族距离，并在自己音乐的艺术风格中汇入了多重特色，因而得到了黑人和白人的共同青睐。实际上这首歌曲表达的意思并不复杂，没有冲突的悲伤，也没有离别的惆怅，一句话“打电话只为说我爱你”。我爱你也就像自然界的一切事物那样自然，那样不可抗拒。

43. Careless Whisper

(无心快语)

Words &Music by George Michael and Andrew Ridgeley

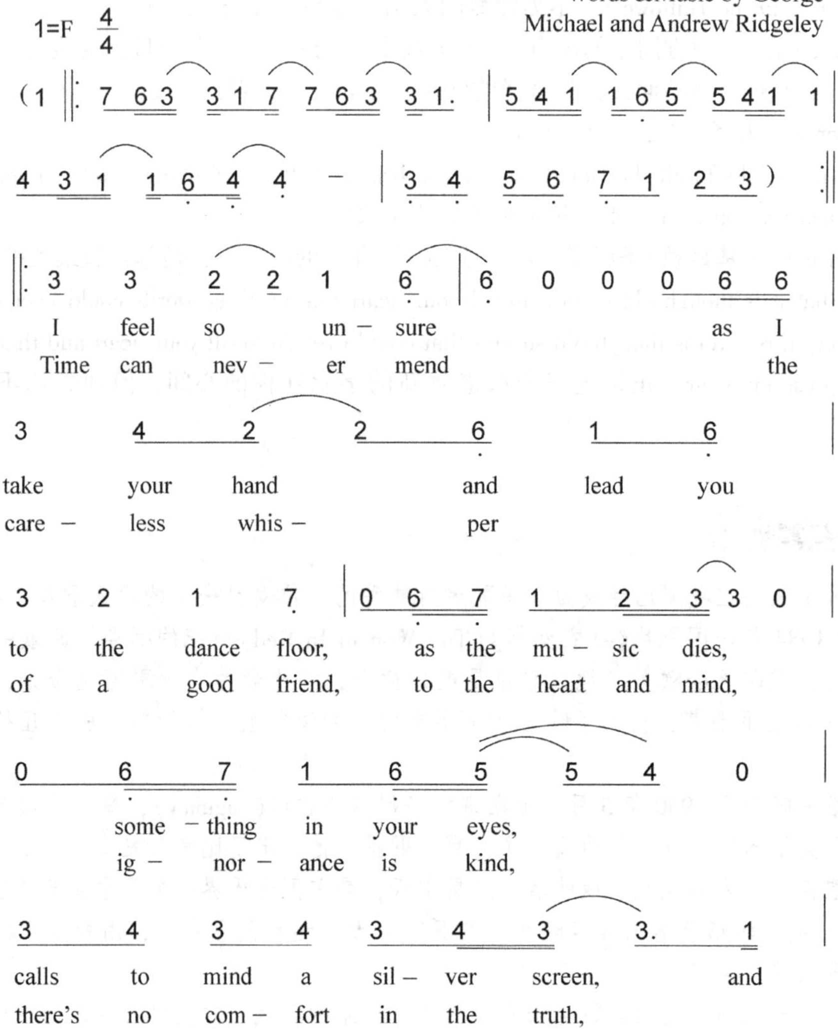

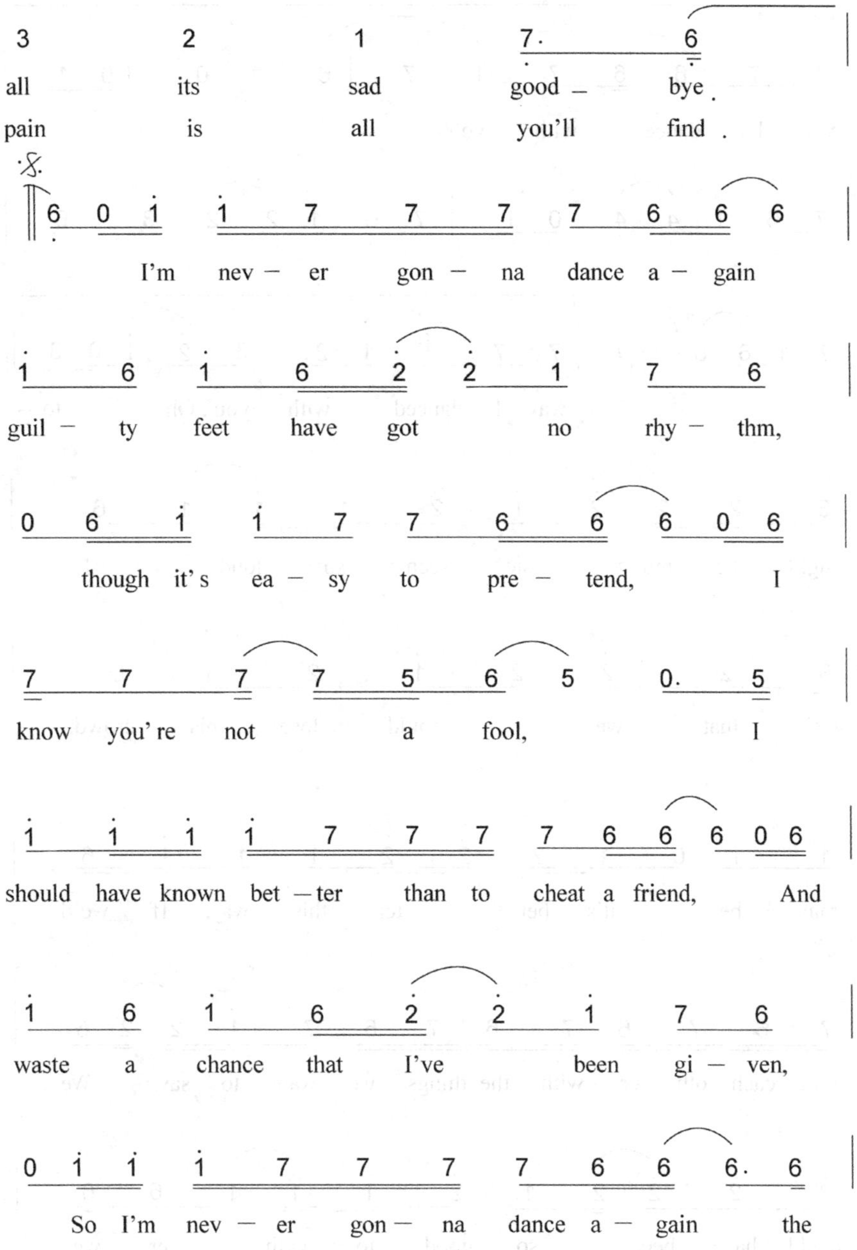
all its sad good – bye.
pain is all you'll find.
I'm nev – er gon – na dance a – gain
guil – ty feet have got no rhy – thm,
though it's ea – sy to pre – tend, I
know you're not a fool, I
should have known bet – ter than to cheat a friend, And
waste a chance that I've been gi – ven,
So I'm nev – er gon – na dance a – gain the

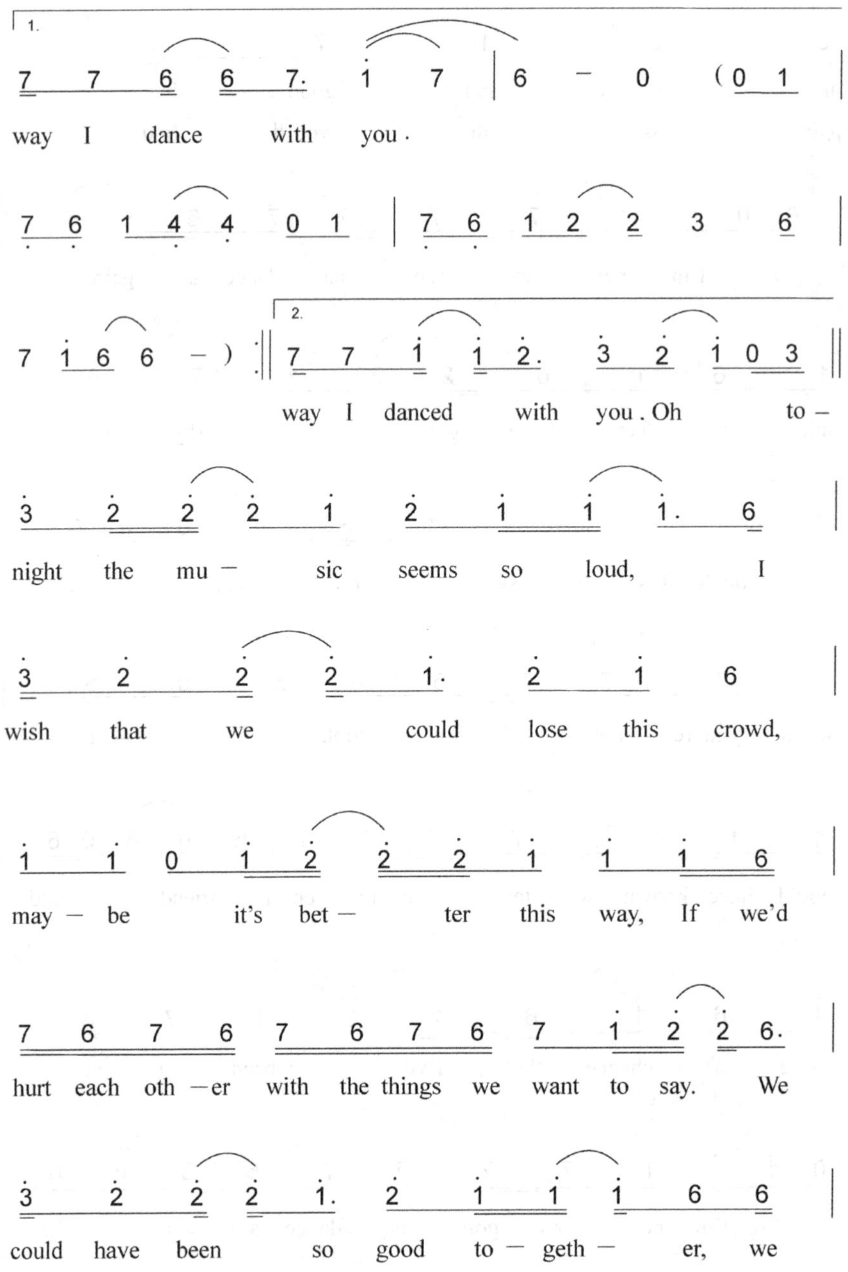
way I dance with you.
way I danced with you. Oh to –
night the mu – sic seems so loud, I
wish that we could lose this crowd,
may – be it's bet – ter this way, If we'd
hurt each oth – er with the things we want to say. We
could have been so good to – geth – er, we

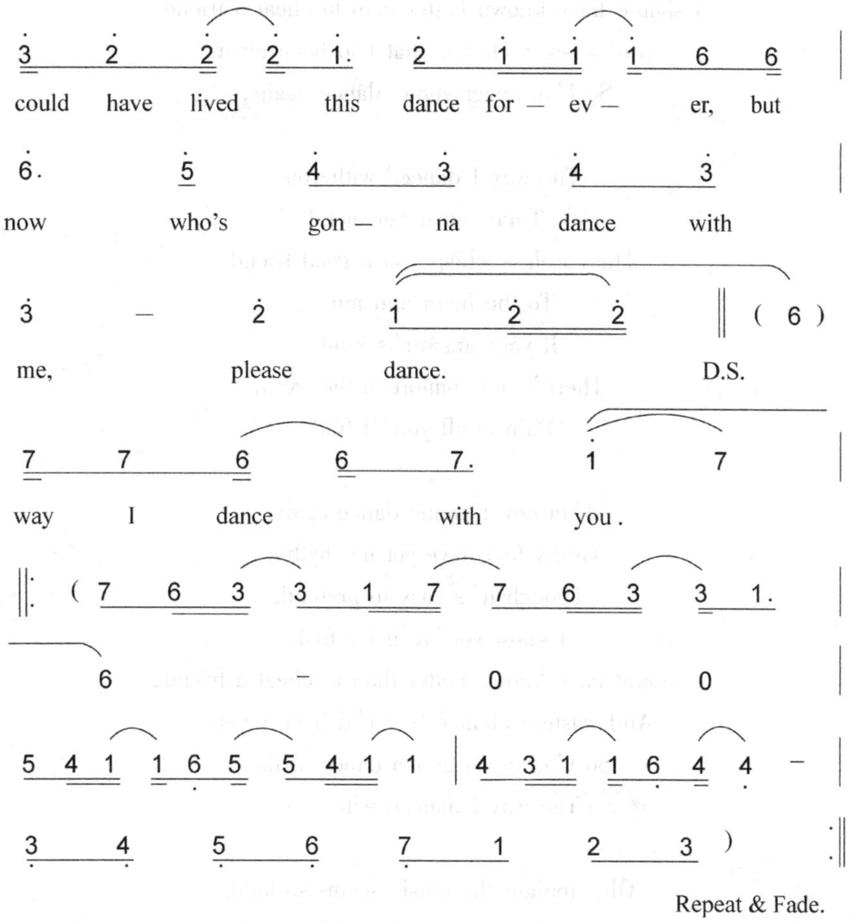

【英文歌词】

Careless Whisper

I feel so unsure,
As I take your hand and lead you to the dance floor.
As the music dies, something in your eyes.
Calls to mind a silver screen, and all its sad goodbyes.
I' m never gonna dance again.
Guilty feet have got no rhythm.
Though it' s easy to pretend.
I know you' re not a fool.

I should have known better than to cheat a friend,
And waste a chance that I'd been given.
So I'm never gonna dance again,

The way I danced with you.
Time can never mend
The careless whisper of a good friend,
To the heart and mind,
If your answer's kind...
There's no comfort in the truth.
Pain is all you'll find.

I'm never gonna dance again.
Guilty feet have got no rhythm,
Though it's easy to pretend.
I know you're not a fool.
I should have known better than to cheat a friend,
And waste a chance that I'd been given.
So I'm never gonna dance again,
The way I danced with you.

Oh, tonight the music seems so loud.
I wish that we could lose this crowd.
Maybe it's better this way,
If we'd hurt each other with the things we want to say.
We could have been so good together.
We could have lived this dance forever,
But now, who's gonna dance with me?
Please dance.

I'm never gonna dance again.
Guilty feet have got no rhythm,
Though it's easy to pretend.
I know you're not a fool.
I should have known better than to cheat a friend,
And waste a chance that I'd been given
So I'm never gonna dance again,
The way I danced with you.

【参考译文】

无心快语

噢，我感到是那样信心不足，
当我牵着你手步入舞厅，
一曲奏完时我看到你眼里含有雾层，
那是伤悲的离别之情。

我再不能跳下去了。
内疚的脚步跟不上节奏。
尽管易于伪装，
可我知道你不蠢，
你更清楚不该欺骗朋友。
给我的机会已丢尽，
所以我再也无法与你像以前那样跳下去。

就这样和你跳舞，时间也无法改正，
一位朋友的无心快语，
对心灵来说不知也是善待，
真理不会安慰，知道便是痛苦。

我再不能跳下去了，
内疚的脚步跟不上节奏。
尽管易于伪装，可我知道你不蠢，
我本应更清楚不该欺骗朋友，
给我的机会已失去，
所以我再也无法与你像以前那样跳下去了。

今晚觉得音乐那么吵闹，
希望我们能离开这喧嚣之所，
也许这样感觉会更好。
我们想说的话会把我们伤害，
我们可以很好地在一起，
我们本可以永远地共舞下去，
现在有谁会来与我共舞？
请留步。

我再不能跳下去了，
内疚的脚步跟不上节奏。
尽管易装知道你不蠢，
你更清楚不该欺骗朋友，
给我的机会已失去，
所以我再也无法与你像以前那样跳下去了。

语言点解析

(1) I feel so unsure as I take your hand and lead you to the dance floor. =I feel so uncertain when I take your hand and guide you to the dancing hall. 当我牵着你的手步入舞厅时，我感到那么信心不足。

lead：(常用作动词)带领、引导、指导、通达、导致

例如：

The road will ***lead*** you to the parking pot. 这条路将把你带到停车场。

(2) Guilt feet have got no rhythm. 内疚的脚步踏不住节奏。

(3) You should have known better than to cheat a friend.

know better than to do sth. 不会笨得做某事

例如：

He ***knows better than to go*** there alone. 他不会笨得一个人去那里。

(4) Waste a chance that I'd been given. 我失去了所给予的好机会。

waste v. t.：浪费，充分利用、使消瘦

例如：

Don't ***waste*** money on trash. 不要浪费钱去买无用的东西。

towaste efforts 徒劳

towaste a good opportunity 失去良机

towaste *n.* & *adj.*：浪费、废品的、无用的

例如：

His idle talk is just ***waste*** of time. 他的空谈简直是浪费时间。

a ***waste*** product 废品

waste water 废水

(5) So I never gonna dance again the way I danced with you. 我决不会再用以前和你一起跳舞的方式跳舞了。

the way：后面常常跟从句，构成做某事的方式(方法、样子)。

例如：

I'm interested in ***the way*** foreigners talk and laugh. 我对外国人谈笑的举止很感兴趣。

(6) Time can never mend the careless whisper of a good friend: Time can not improve what the friend: Time can not improve what that the friend whispers carelessly at all. 时间无法弥补好朋友的无心快语。

mend *vt.*：修补、修理、改正、康复

例如：

He ***mended*** all the broken toys. 他把坏玩具都修好了。

(7) To the heart and mind ignorance is kind. = Ignorance is kind to the heart and mind. "不知"倒是一种快乐。(此处为倒装句，为了诗与歌脚韵的一致)

be kind to：(后面跟名词或名词性词组)对……亲切、善待

(8) We could have lived this dance forever. = If only we could get along like this dance forever. 我们要是能永远像跳舞一样友好相处就好了。此处 **could** 加上完成时态是虚拟语气的用法，所述之事与事实相反，仅为一种意愿。

注释与赏析

《无心快语》是威猛乐队(Wham)荣登流行排行的冠军歌曲。威猛乐队是80年代驰名世界的美国摇滚乐组，其两位核心人物乔治·迈克尔和安德鲁·里奇利都出生于1963年，里奇利比迈克尔仅大了几个月。两人在童年时均酷爱音乐。迈克尔5岁时开始学习音乐，练习作曲；里奇利因为音乐与母亲多次发生争执，对流行音乐几乎到了痴迷的程度。他俩在高中时就已相识，从此开始了两人的友谊与合作。威猛乐队也是由于两人联合推出了第一张单曲《威猛包装》而成为后来乐队的名称。后由于经营问题，1986年乐队宣布解散，里奇利停止了音乐生涯，但迈克尔却孜孜不倦地追求音乐事业，不断地推出音乐新作，终于在音乐界树立起自己崇高的形象和低位。

这首歌曲描写的是一对恋人产生矛盾与误解的过程，这是生活中常见的事，也许每一个读者都遇见过，该如何解决、对待呢？也许"不知"倒是一种快乐，听到似成一种妨碍。但是一个人能够理性地去正确处理这类事情，而不是"一点就着"的火爆脾气，该会好些。虽然这首歌已广为熟悉，但它的词意却十分不易搞清楚，尤其是它的背景有不同的解释。听众应多掌握哲学、文学等理论知识，扩大知识面，培养出理智的情感与高尚的品德。唯有如此，才可以超脱常人为人处事的德行，表现出超群的品行素质，达到真善美的境界。

44. Hotel California

(加州旅馆)

Words by DonHenley& Clenn Frey
Music by Don Felder & Joe Walsh

1=D 4/4

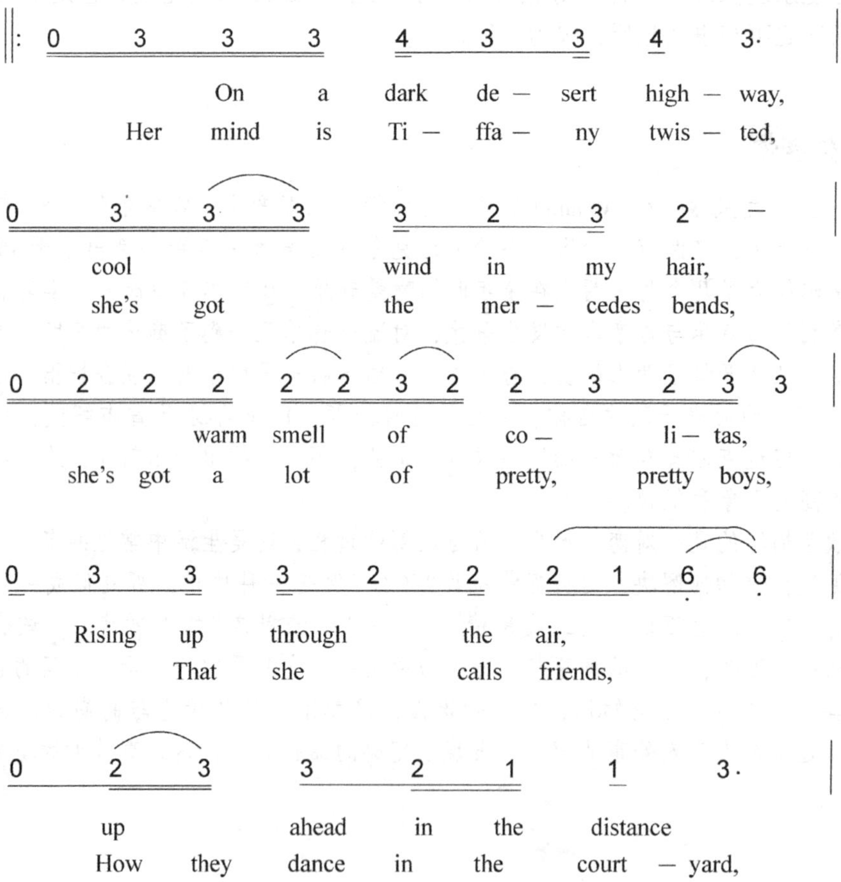

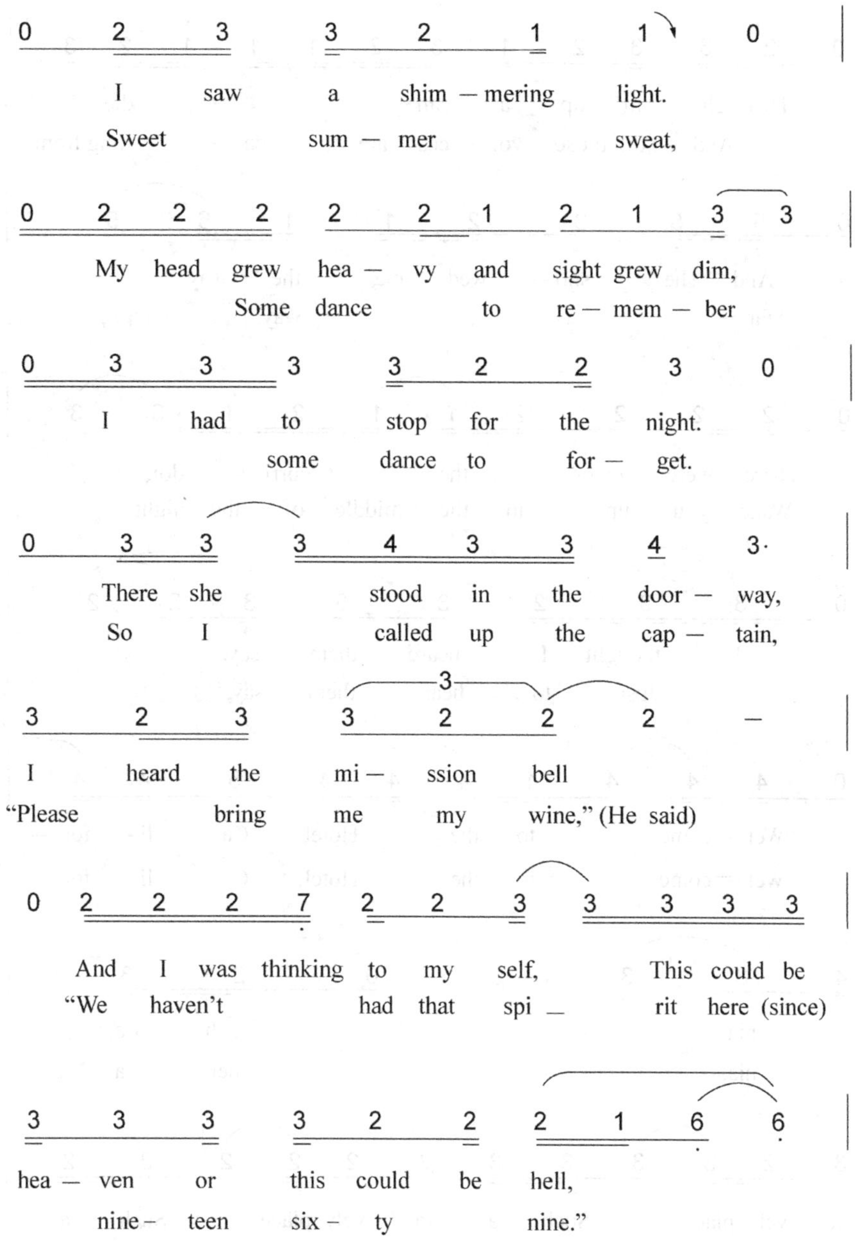
0 2 3 3 2 1 1 0
I saw a shim — mering light.
Sweet sum — mer sweat,
0 2 2 2 2 2 1 2 1 3 3
My head grew hea — vy and sight grew dim,
Some dance to re — mem — ber
0 3 3 3 3 2 2 3 0
I had to stop for the night.
some dance to for — get.
0 3 3 3 4 3 3 4 3·
There she stood in the door — way,
So I called up the cap — tain,
3
3 2 3 3 2 2 2 —
I heard the mi — ssion bell
"Please bring me my wine," (He said)
0 2 2 2 7 2 2 3 3 3 3 3
And I was thinking to my self, This could be
"We haven't had that spi — rit here (since)
3 3 3 3 2 2 2 1 6 6
hea — ven or this could be hell,
nine — teen six — ty nine."

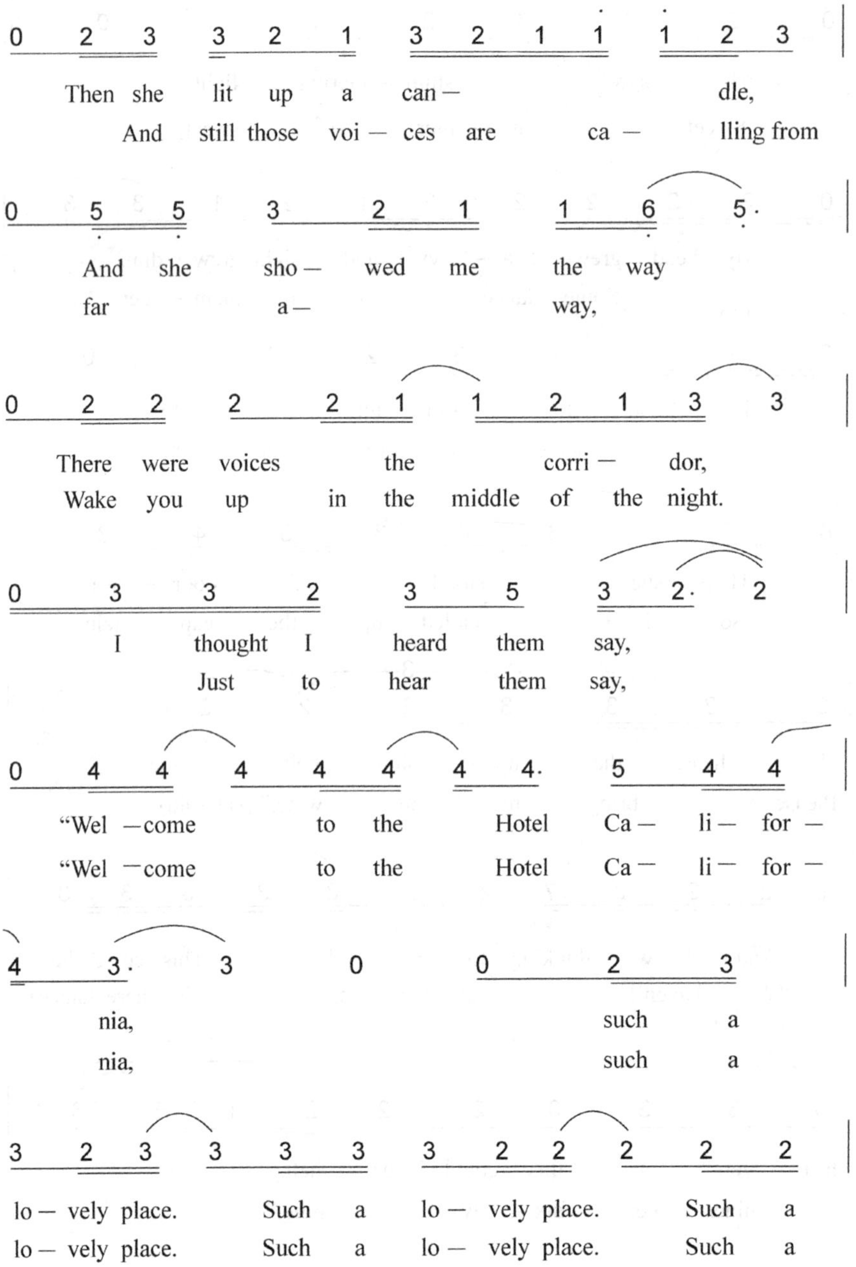
Then she lit up a can— dle,
And still those voi— ces are ca— lling from
And she sho— wed me the way
far a— way,
There were voices the corri— dor,
Wake you up in the middle of the night.
I thought I heard them say,
Just to hear them say,
"Wel—come to the Hotel Ca— li— for—
"Wel—come to the Hotel Ca— li— for—
nia, such a
nia, such a
lo— vely place. Such a lo— vely place. Such a
lo— vely place. Such a lo— vely place. Such a

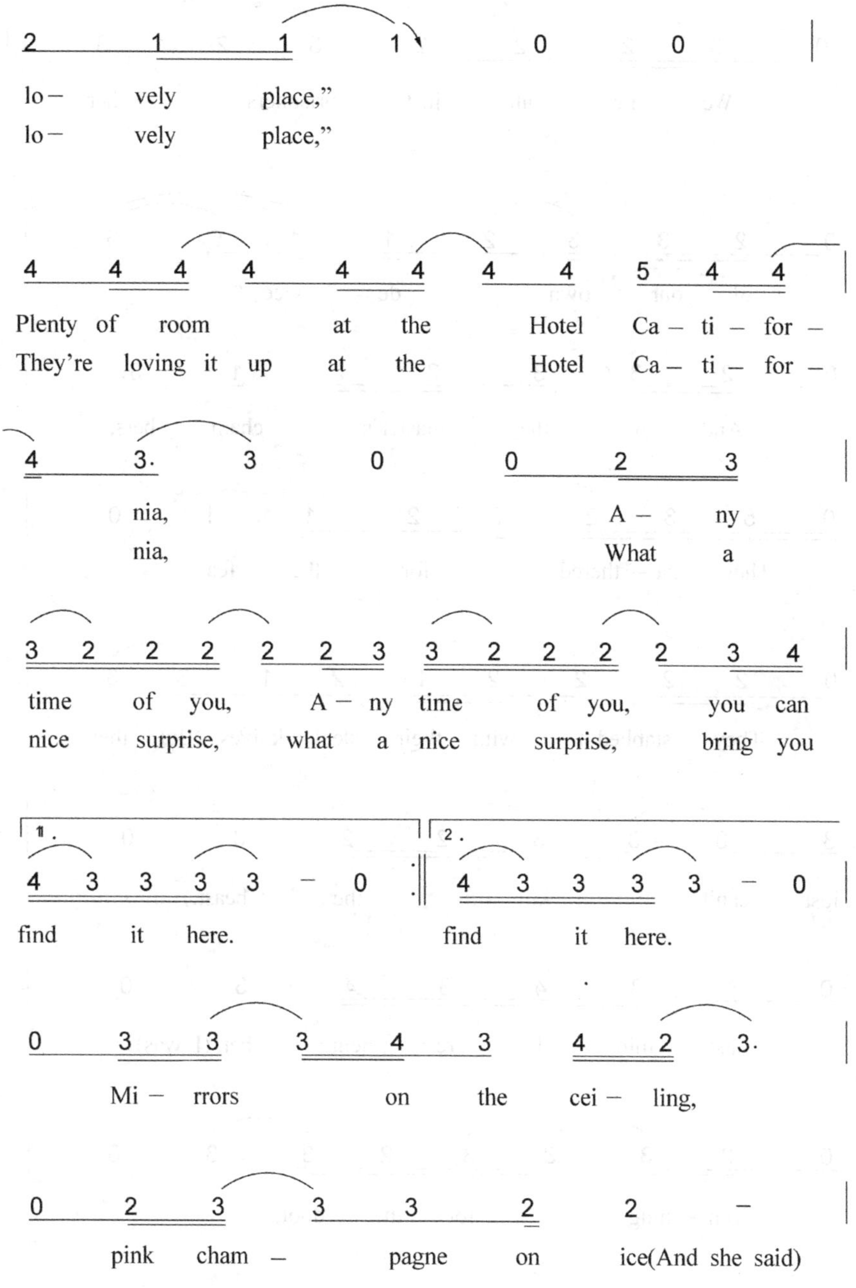
lo – vely place,"
lo – vely place,"
Plenty of room at the Hotel Ca – ti – for –
They're loving it up at the Hotel Ca – ti – for –
nia, A – ny
nia, What a
time of you, A – ny time of you, you can
nice surprise, what a nice surprise, bring you
1.
2.
find it here.
find it here.
Mi – rrors on the cei – ling,
pink cham – pagne on ice(And she said)

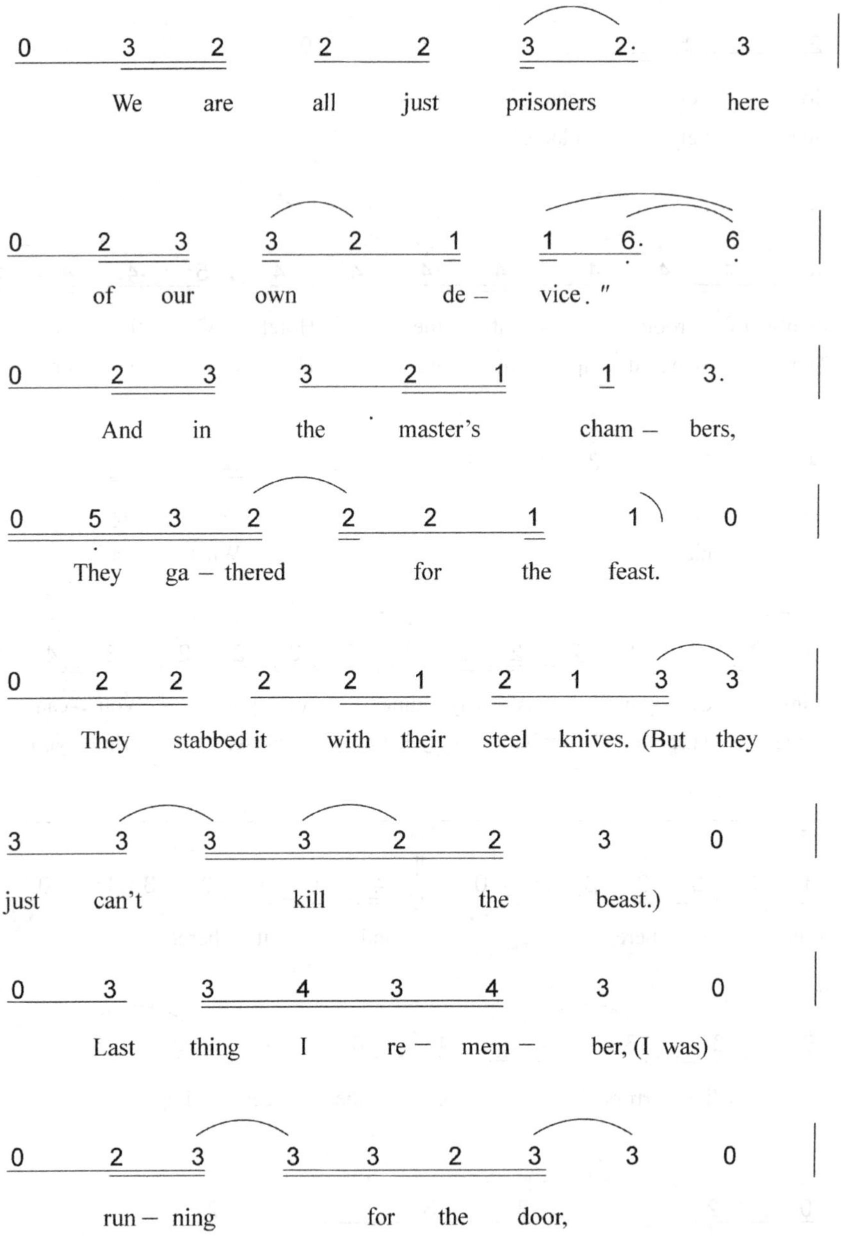
We are all just prisoners here
of our own de – vice. "
And in the master's cham – bers,
They ga – thered for the feast.
They stabbed it with their steel knives. (But they
just can't kill the beast.)
Last thing I re – mem – ber, (I was)
run – ning for the door,

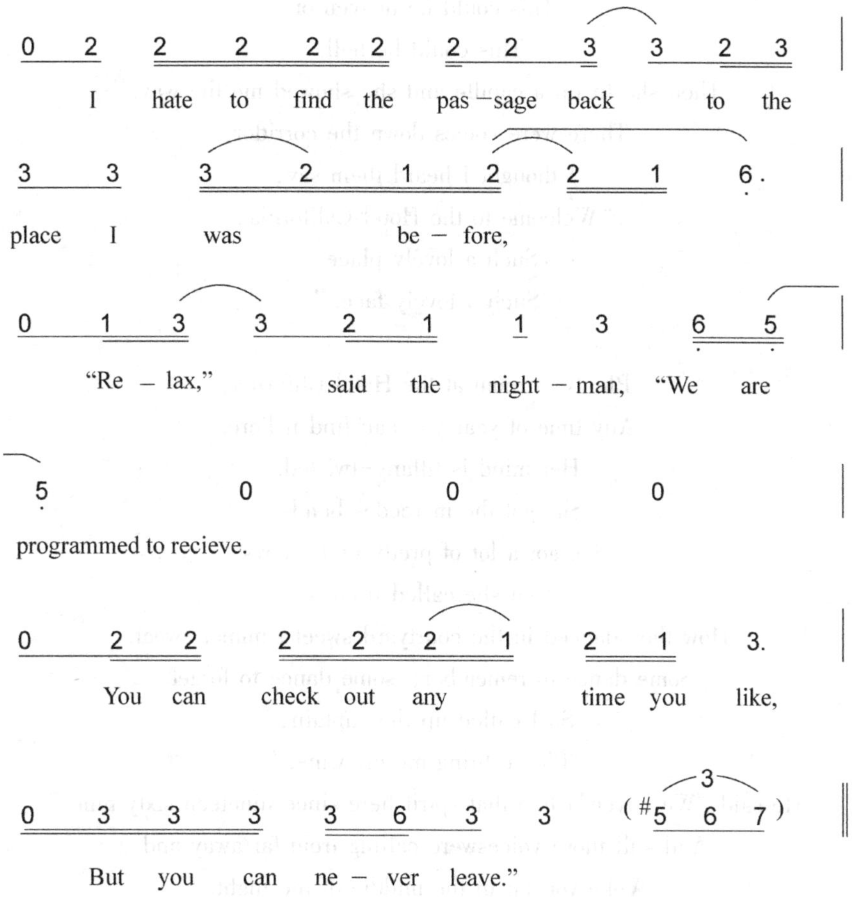

【英文歌词】

Hotel California

On a dark desert highway cool wind in my hair,
Warm smell of colitas rising up through the air,
Up ahead in the distance I saw a shimmering light.
My head grew heavy and my sight grew dim.
I had to stop for the night.
There she stood in the doorway.
I heard the mission bell
And I was thinking to myself,

This could be heaven or
This could be hell
Then she lit up a candle and she showed me the way.
There were voices down the corridor.
I thought I heard them say,
“Welcome to the Hotel California,
Such a lovely place.
Such a lovely face. ”

Plenty of room at the Hotel Clifornia,
Any time of year you can find it here.
Her mind is tiffany-twisted.
She got the mercedes bends.
She got a lot of pretty pretty boys
That she called friends.
How they danced in the courtyard sweet summer sweat.
Some dance to remember, some dance to forget.
So I called up the captain,
″Please bring me my wine. ″
He said,″We haven't had that spirit here since nineteen sixty nine. ″
And still those voiceswere calling from far away and
Woke you up in the middle of the night.
Just to hear them say,
″Welcome to the Hotel California,
Such a lovely place.
Such a lovely face. ″

Theywere livin' it up at the Hotel California.
What a nice surprise bring your alibis.
Mirrors on the ceiling.
The pink champagne on ice.
And she said,″We are all just prisoners here of our own device. ″
And in the master's chambers
They gathered for the feast.
They stabbed it with their steely knives,
But they just could kill the beast.
Last thing I remember I wasrunning for the door.
I had to find the passage back,

To the place I was before.
"Relax," said the night man,
"We are programmed to receive."
You can check out any time you like.
But you can never leave!"

【参考译文】

加州旅馆

在黑暗的沙漠公路上，
清风吹拂我的头发，
空气中充满桉树宜人的芳香。
我看见远处夜空灯光闪亮，
我感到头重视线也朦胧，
我只好驻足投宿。
她就站在前边的门廊旁，
我听到使命般的钟声。
我心里在暗暗揣想：
这是地狱还是天堂。
她点亮了蜡烛为我引路，
忽听到有声音来自走廊尽头，
似乎听见他们在说：
“欢迎到加州旅馆来。
多么可爱的地方，
多么可爱的面庞。”

加州旅馆有足够的客房，
一年中任何时间，你都能在此逗留。
她心里只想贵重的东西，
她有豪华的奔驰轿车，
她结识许多男孩子做朋友。
他们在院子里纵情跳舞，
美好的夏季多么甜蜜。
记住了这些舞友，忘掉了那些舞伴，
因此我唤侍者，
“请拿酒来”。

(他说)“(自从)1969年到现在我们没有那兴致”。
这时从远处又传来那声音,
半夜把你唤醒。
似乎听见他们在说:
“加州旅馆欢迎您,
多么可爱的地方,
多么可爱的面庞。”

他们在加州旅馆纵情欢乐。
多么令人惊喜,
你有来此的理由。
玻璃天花板锃亮,
冰块冰镇的粉红香槟。
(她说)“我们愿意做这儿的囚犯。”
他们聚集在豪华的房间,
盛宴款待,纵情欢乐。
钢制的餐刀刺向兽肉,
却不能杀死自己心中的兽性。
我只记得最后快步奔到门口,
我必须找到回去的路。
值夜的服务员说:
“别紧张,我们将接受您再来”。
您想说明时间付账都可以,
但这经历却会令您难忘。”

语言点解析

(1) On a dark desert highway cool wind in my hair: On a dark desert highway, cool wind was blowing in my hair. 在黑暗的沙漠公路上,清风吹拂着我的头发。

desert 一词重音不同,有不同的词性和含义

① [ˈdezət] *n.* & *.adj.*: 沙漠、不毛之地;沙漠的,荒芜的,无人居住的

② [diˈzət] *vt.*: 丢弃,舍弃

③ [ˈdezət] *n.*: 功过;[常用复数]应得的赏罚;美德。

(2) Warm smell of calyptus rising up through the air. =The air is filled with the fresh and warm smell of calyptus. 空气中充满了新鲜、温馨的大麻香。

(3) Up ahead in the distance I saw a shimmering light. =I saw a shimmering light in the distance above the night sky. 我看见远处夜空灯光闪亮。

(4) There she stood in the doorway. =She stood there in the doorway. 她站在前边的门廊口。
there 或 here 这两个词放在句首时，表示强调。例如：
There they come. 他们来了。
Here(there) comes a bus. 公共汽车来了。
注意：当 there 和 here 出现在句首，主语是代词时，用正常语序；如果主语是名词时，主谓必须倒装，如上面例子。

(5) I was thinking to myself , this could be heaven or this could be hell. 我心里暗暗揣想：这会是地狱还是天堂。

(6) think to oneself：暗想。如：say to oneself 自言自语。

(7) Welcome to the Hotel California：欢迎到加州旅馆来。
welcome *adj.* & *n.*：受欢迎的；欢迎
例如：
Welcome to our school 欢迎到我们学校来参观。
A warm ***welcome*** to Prof. Michael Smith. 热烈欢迎迈克尔·史密斯教授！

(8) Her mind was tiffany twisted.
tiffany *n*：上浆亚麻薄布；[美国]昂贵的珠宝店。
twisted *adj*：扭曲的、歪曲的。此处引申为昂贵的、贵重的。
例如：
She thinks about the ***twisted*** things in jewelry stores. 她心里只想着珠宝店里贵重的东西。
注：这句话说明在当时"反主流文化"一代人放纵的一种表现，只注意到物质的东西，而思想变得畸形。

(9) So I called up the captain , "Please bring me my wine". =So I asked the service man to get me my wine. 我叫侍者给我拿酒来。
captain *n.*：此处不指船长、上校；而是指旅馆服务员的领班。

(10) They were livin' it up at the Hotel California. = They had more than a good time at Hotel California. 他们在加州旅馆纵情欢乐。
live it up [俚语] 意为：狂欢一场；(反常的)纵欲欢乐。

(11) Bring you alibis. =Hotel California gave you a good feeling, which you have your reason to come. 在加州旅馆尽兴成为你来的理由。
Alibi [ˈæləbaɪ] *n*：[法律]不在犯罪现场；[口语]借口、托辞
例如：
What's your ***alibi*** for being late this time, Jones? 琼斯，你这次迟到的借口是什么？

(12) We are all just prisoners here of our own device：We become guests of the Hotel California willingly. 我们都自愿成为加州旅馆的囚犯。
device *n*：计划，设计，方法，心愿
one's own device 是词组，意为：某 人自己的计划，方法或意愿；自便。
注：由于加州旅馆如此吸引人，我们大家都计划或自愿做加州旅馆的囚犯。Prisoners 此处仅是虚指。

(13) And in the master's chambers: And they are in the best room of the Hotel California. 他们住在加州旅馆最豪华的房间。

注释与赏析

二战后，美国经济迅速发展，进入空前的繁荣阶段。但在这表面辉煌的背后也滋生出各种社会问题。60年代至70年代间，在美国出现了被称为“反主流文化”(Counter Culture)的一代人。这部分人大都以青年人为主，反对越南战争，反对父辈的传统文化和价值观念，不满于当时社会上存在的一些诸如人权、自由等社会问题；他们崇尚个性，追求自由，欲争取更多的社会权利，却又找不到出路，因此，他们逐渐自我放纵，寻欢作乐：酗酒、吸毒、纵欲、留长发、穿奇装异服、癖好摇滚、参加一些反传统的活动。这首《加州旅馆》正是这一背景时代的作品，它在讽刺美国社会，鞭笞时弊的同时，也描绘出当时美国青年颓废的一面。

《加州旅馆》是当时把乡村摇滚、民谣音乐珠联璧合的鹰乐队的代表作品，也是他们艺术生涯中的旷世之作，受到了全球众多歌迷的喜爱，曾获得全美排行榜第一名和1977年美国的葛莱美大奖。

加州旅馆是比喻和象征，作者把加州比拟为整个美国，描写美国人的心理，反映出美国的写实状态：一个在沙漠艰难旅行的人，停下来住进加州旅馆(即美国)，前面有(上帝的)钟声在召唤，又有蜡烛引路。“是天堂还是地狱”，是任何一个做美国梦的人常常发出的疑问。美国欢迎你来，那么到底美国是一个什么样的地方呢？虽然在歌中叙说的是在加州旅馆发生的事情，但却是美国社会的一个缩影。美国有足够的空间迎接你，可向你提供一切，甚至有人会出卖灵魂和肉体。接着歌中叙述了旅馆的夜生活：杂乱无章、纵欲作乐和虚度时光。但又欲罢不能，找不到出路。

45. The Last Waltz
（最后的华尔兹）

1=D $\frac{3}{4}$

Words and Music:Gorden Mills

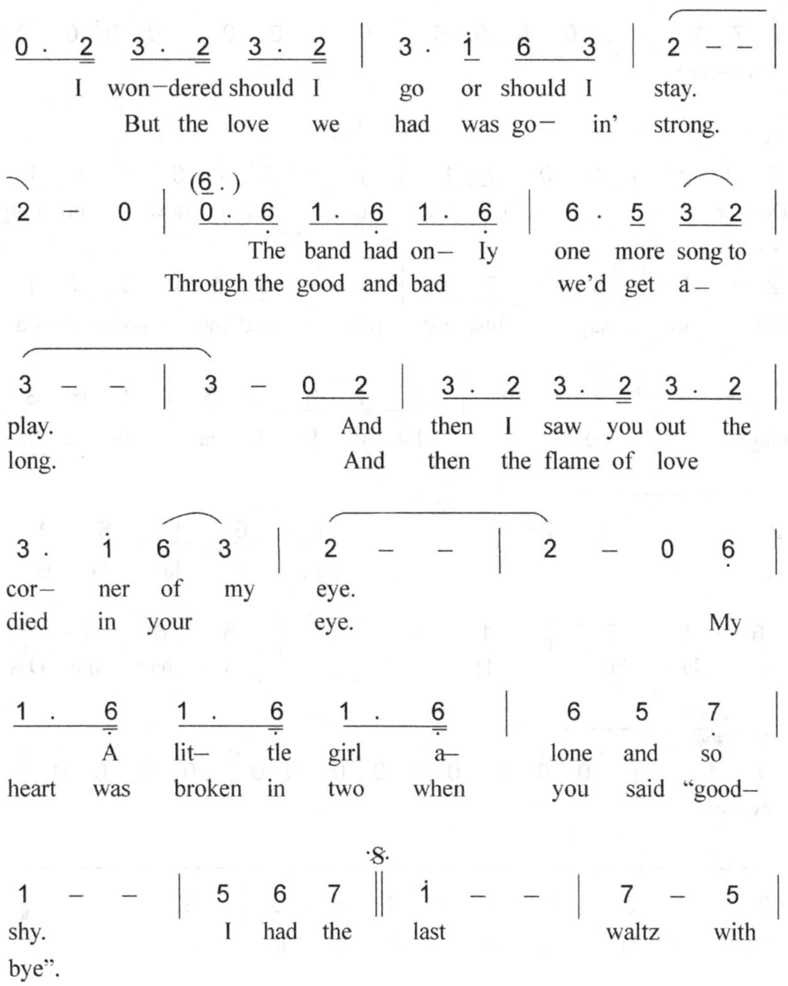

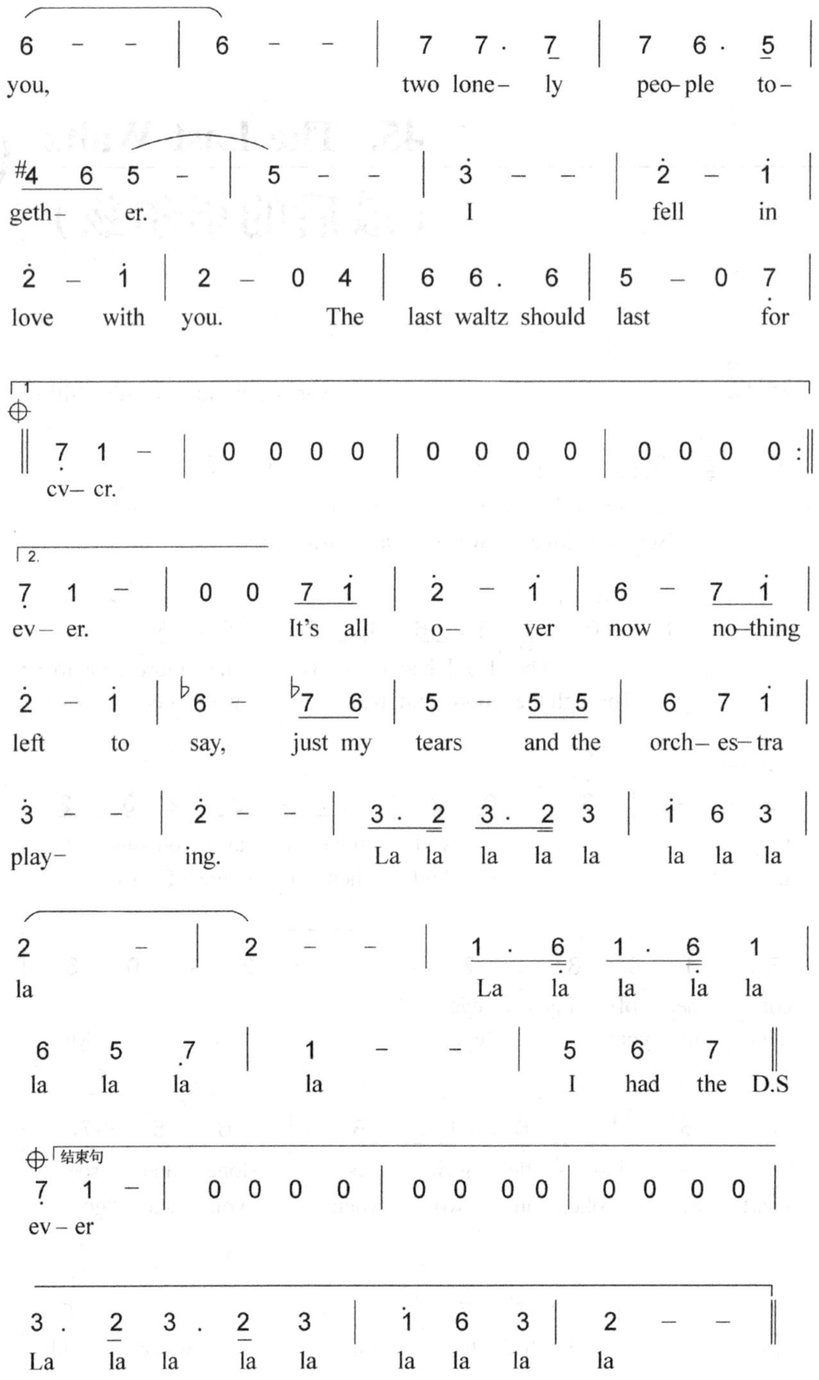
you, two lone- ly peo- ple to-
geth- er. I fell in
love with you. The last waltz should last for
1.
ev- er.
2.
ev- er. It's all o- ver now no-thing
left to say, just my tears and the orch- es- tra
play- ing. La la la la la la la la
la La la la la la
la la la la I had the D.S
结束句
ev - er
La la la la la la la la la

【英文歌词】

The Last Waltz

I wondered should I go or should I stay.
The band had only one more song to play.
And then I saw you out the corner of my eye.
A little girl alone and so shy.
I had the last waltz with you.
Two lonely people together.
I fell in love with you.
The last waltz should last forever.

But the love we had was going strong
Through the good and bad we get along.
And then the flame of love died in your eye.
My heart was broke in two when you said goodbye.
I had the last waltz with you.
Two lonely people together.
I fell in love with you.
The last waltz should last forever.

It's all over now, nothing left to say,
Just my tears and the orchestra playing.
La la la la la la la la la.
La la la la la la la la la
I had the last waltz with you.
Two lonely people together.
I fell in love with you.
The last waltz should last forever.
La la la la la la la la la.

【参考译文】

最后的华尔兹

我不知该走，还是该留；
乐队只剩下，一首歌要演奏。
这时我从眼角余光看见你，
一个小姑娘孤单又害羞。
我与你跳了最后这一曲，
两个孤寂的人在一起。
我爱上了你。
这最后一曲应永远继续。

自认为我们的爱
越来越强烈，
不管好与坏
我们共度时光。
后来爱的火焰
在你眼里消失。
当你说“再见”时，
我的心碎成两片。

我与你跳了最后这一曲，
两个孤寂的人在一起。
我爱上了你，
这最后一曲应永远继续。
现在全完了，
再没什么可说了。
我的泪在流，
乐队仍在伴奏。
啦，啦，啦……

语言点解析

(1) I wondered should I go or should I stay. =I wondered whether I should go or stay.
(2) The band had only one more song to play. = The band would play the last song.

play 在此是“演奏”的意思；

song 在此是“舞曲”的意思。

(3) **out the corner of one's eye**：从眼角余光。

例如：

She said her boss doesn't like her and often looks at her ***out the corner of his eye***. 他说她的老板不喜欢她，经常斜眼看她。

(4) A little girl alone and so shy. = A little girl without companion and not bold enough to invite others to dance.

(5) I had the last waltz with you：I danced with you to the last piece of music of waltz.

(6) Two lonely people together：you and I were both lonely.

(7) I fell in love with you. 我爱上了你。

(8) The last waltz should last forever：The last waltz should go on and on.

这一句中的第二个 ***last*** 是“持续”“继续”的意思。

例如：

The film ***lasted*** two hours. 那部电影演了两小时。

(9) But the love we had was going strong：We were falling in deeper and deeper love with each other.

go strong：变得越来越强烈。

(10) **get along**：相处；过活

例如：

We ***got along*** very well with each other. 我们彼此间相处得很好。

(11) **the flame of love**：爱的火焰

the flame of hatred：恨的火焰

the flame of jealosy：妒火

(12) died in your eye：disappeared from your eyes

(13) My heart was broken in two. = my heart was broken into two

(14) Just my tears and the orchestra playing. = What is left is only my tears flowing and the orchestra playing.

注释与赏析

此歌曲的原唱是恩格尔伯特·哈泼丁克(Engelbert Humperdinck)。他于1936年5月2日出生于印度马得拉斯(Madars)省，父母均是英国人。10岁时随父亲回到英国。他利用余暇时间学习萨克斯风长达六年之久。21岁时，英国正处在The Beatles的狂热中，他的音乐没有遇到知音，根本没有出路。后来，他的音乐被小有名气的经纪人Gorden Mills听到了。Engelbert听从了Gorden的建议，将他的艺名从Gerry Dorsey改成了Engelbert Humperdinck，这是德国一个著名作曲家的名字。此后，他与Decca唱片公司签约，出了几张不好不坏的唱片。

转机发生在1966年，Mills因故赴美洽公，在美国听了一首不怎么红的乡村歌曲“*Release Me*”，突发灵感，将它带回英国改写，交给Engelbert唱。不料这首歌一在电视台播出，电视台的Call in电话立刻满线，观众都在询问这位歌手是谁，这张唱片哪里可以买到。1967年1月13日，Engelbert的这张单曲唱片在伦敦上市，隔日就将The Beatles的“Penny Lane”挤下来，成为流行排行榜第一名，并且气势如虹连贯六周榜首。从此Engelbert一飞冲天，紧接着“There Goes My Everything”与“The Last Waltz”均获得佳绩，其中“The Last Waltz”更蝉联七周冠军，一上市便成为金唱片。Engelbert还创下一项记录：一日之内于英美两国销售唱片八万张，这是一项令人咋舌的佳绩。从此，他时来运转，声誉鹊起，进入了当代大牌歌手的行列。1968年Engelbert受邀在白金汉宫为女王伊丽莎白二世伉俪演唱，并获女王召见，当时英国乐坛仅有The Beatles能获此殊荣。

Engelbert的唱片至今已卖出1亿3000万张，获四次格莱美大奖提名，成为全球金奖得主以及在好莱坞星光大道上拥有一颗星。其实Engelbert最吸引人的不只是他独特的嗓音，而是他本人，他的幽默与谦虚，他的慷慨与爱心。至今为止，他的慈善捐款已达上百万美元，他支持白血病研究基金会，他还致力于儿童AIDS的防治。目前Engelbert定居在名人荟萃的比佛利山庄，享受天伦之乐。

套用一句评论：“这些音乐乍听之下并不花俏也不绚丽，像一桶酿制了很久的老酒。你得让它在嘴里细细地漱、慢慢地咽，并且得有一定的阅历，才能慢慢体会这些音符背后暗藏的静静流淌的历史的大河，和它之所以能用如此单纯的乐器交叠出这样丰厚深沉的力量的惊人才华。”

这首歌尤其适合在酒吧演奏，夜色晦暗，孤独的男人和害羞的女孩共舞最后一曲华尔兹，Engelbert那独特的带有迷人魔力的浪漫嗓音将一个美丽的爱情娓娓道来。那是只有两个人的舞池，没有拥挤，没有狂热，只有安静的旋转，悠扬的音乐。一曲舞毕，男人爱上了姑娘。是因为那种气氛还是对同样孤单的人的惺惺相惜，我们不得而知，但可以肯定的是，姑娘最后回到了现实，男人却深陷其中，无法自拔。姑娘最后留下的，只是那一句Goodbye，一曲终了，满心破碎。

只有跳舞的人才能领略那舞中情。这首歌唱的是两颗孤寂的心灵因共舞生情，又因分别而伤感，讲述了一个舞场上产生的“爱情”故事。这段情是短暂的，给主人公的愉悦是临时的，但这一短暂美好的幸福，使人在幻想中又把更大的幸福渴望。

参 考 文 献

[1] 严继华，李东风．美国流行歌曲 101 首[M]. 上海翻译出版社，1987.
[2] 李正栓．英文金曲赏析(1-2)[M] 开明文教出版社，1998.
[3] 金木．英文金曲赏析(3)[M]. 开明文教出版社，1998.
[4] 徐学谦．英文金曲赏析(4)[M]. 开明文教出版社，1998.
[5] 陈观亚，宁建新．英文金曲赏析(5-6)[M]. 开明文教出版社，1998.
[6] 陈观亚，陈小军．英文金曲赏析(7)[M]. 开明文教出版社，1998.
[7] 徐学谦，王海燕．英文金曲赏析(8)[M]. 开明文教出版社，1998.